THEATRE
THROUGH THE AGES

In the middle of a square
erect a pole decorated with flowers,
gather the people round it
and you have a feast.
Better still:
present the spectators as the show,
make them actors themselves,
make each one see himself
and love himself in all the rest,
so that their oneness grows.

J J Rousseau—*Lettre à d'Alembert*

THEATRE
THROUGH THE AGES

Cesare Molinari
Translated by Colin Hamer

McGraw-Hill Book Company
New York   St. Louis   San Francisco
Toronto

Library of Congress Cataloging in Publication Data

Molinari, Cesare, date
    Theatre through the ages.

    Translation of Teatro
    Bibliography: p.
    1. Theater—History. I. Title
PN2105.M613   792'.09   74-1165
ISBN 0-07-042665-1

Printed in Italy by A. Mondadori Editore Verona

Designer: Giuliana Nannicini
Jacket and art work: Fiorenzo Giorgi
Editor: Mariella De Battisti
Coordinating Secretary: Margherita Forestan

Opposite: Marco Marcola, *A commedia dell'arte* in the Arena at
Verona, 1772. Chicago Art Institute.
Frontispiece: Anonymous engraving showing an actor dressed as
King Lear, taken from the collection *Galarie dramatique* published
in Paris in 1930. It was probably made for Jean François Ducis'
1769 production of this Shakespearian tragedy.

CONTENTS

Introduction

Many histories of dramatic art have been written
in recent years, some of them longer than others,
some of them more generously illustrated, more lavish at times
with factual information, or in their attention to critical problems.
Almost invariably they are well received because
even today 'the cultivated public'
(as a nineteenth-century Italian actor might have said)
manifests a keen interest in the theatre at the very moment when
this form of communication, this art
(call it as you like it)
seems inevitably eclipsed by the spread
of other powerful means of communication
which rely on the same essential ingredients as theatre
(movement, gesture and speech)
but surpass it in flexibility and effectiveness.

Challenged by cinema and television
theatre had no alternative than to vanish overnight
or find itself once more, no longer a way of using words,
but much more a social service.
How it provided this service in days gone by
could not emerge from any history of theatre
that was primarily concerned with
drama production.
Accordingly, and also because in most instances
histories of theatre limit themselves to a study
of dramatic literature,
the horizons of this book
are the performance itself, the movement into action.

We shall think about theatre from this point of view especially
in its official, institutionalised forms of expression
but conscious all the time of the existence of an alternative theatre,
more free, more directly in touch
with the need for frankness in cultural expression:
a theatre that has not left much behind,
but which may be the most authentic approach.

The spectator can make himself the main character:
So there are so many things to see:
That is why in some cases we have decided
to provide a complete account of one production
instead of an incomplete one of productions which are quite different.

Chapter 1

THEATRE AMONG PRIMITIVE PEOPLES

By devoting the first chapter of a history of the theatre to 'primitive' peoples we might be taken to consider this history, along with that of culture and civilization in general, as having followed a single line of development from its putative 'origins' to its makeshift culmination on the contemporary landscape. This idea implies on the one hand that such development coincides with technical progress, with the growth of man's capacity to dominate and exploit the forces of nature, and on the other hand that every single step in man's evolution recapitulates all the preceding stages, just as a cross-section through the trunk of a tree presents a complete picture of its growth. In other words, the 'primitives' living today have no history of their own, but represent the first rung on that ladder whose summit is Western civilization. This way of measuring and evaluating human progress is as allowable as countless others that have been proposed, but it is equally arbitrary and one-sided. In particular it prevents our seeing how even those societies whose external structure is only slightly susceptible to change, can renew themselves either on the basis of their own inner resources or by means of mutual contact. Thus the black Bantu and the white explorer are both portrayed in the mimes of the pygmies, but are clearly extraneous to the original themes proper to their culture. A more serious defect of this standpoint is that it closes our eyes to human and cultural heritages different from our own, but no less deserving of acceptance and esteem. Any attempt to stem the tide of progress in our own culture would be absurd, but to enrich its waters with the living streams of other worlds of value has been the signal merit of certain strong movements within our culture. As we shall see, avant-garde theatre is not the least of these influences, but pre-eminent among them is the new ethnological school that sees Jean-Jacques Rousseau as its great precursor. He knew what he was doing when he suggested that the theatre needed to move out of the restricted confines of particular buildings in order to become one great community celebration, as is the case among many so-called 'primitive' societies.

Therefore, in turning to consider the theatre among primitive peoples we are not attempting to make contact with the origins of the theatre as we know it, but to become acquainted with quite different theatrical forms. Such knowledge is a priority for anyone conditioned to sitting in a darkened auditorium and watching professional actors give an interpretation of an already existing script. He needs to realise which are the key-elements of the problematic notion conjured up by the word 'theatre'. The different forms theatre can take are as rich as they are varied, and cannot be fully dealt with in a single chapter, nor even in an extensive survey, granted our present state of knowledge. To leave anyone with a different impression would be quite misleading.

The concept of theatre embraces social and organisational factors as well as elements which concern culture, language and self-expression. So to understand the place of theatre within any particular

Chad (Equatorial Africa). Tribal dance of the Sarakaba farmers

13

human group, it is necessary to specify the different moments of its emergence. For instance, among many peoples, especially those with an agricultural economy, theatrical occasions, involving the entire community, are linked with the recurring cycle of the seasons. In a specific instance this connection may assume some definite ritual meaning of atonement. The performance aims both to celebrate and promote the renewal of that cycle whose regularity is crucial for the community's own survival.

The Nahuatl, a Central American people, celebrated the return of summer with a show to represent and render propitious a renewal of fertility. A pole about fifty feet high was set up in the centre of the village, with a brightly coloured image of the fertility god on top of it and, on a platform underneath, two boys attached at the waist to the ends of a long rope wrapped round the pole. In the clearing below, seventy men, half of them dressed as women, engaged in a frenzied dance. This would be abruptly interrupted and the two boys would throw themselves off the platform and climb down to the ground with a slowness that called for great acrobatic skill, following the coils of the rope round and round the pole. The dance was then joyfully resumed – fertility had been restored to the fields.

The ritual meaning of such periodic spectacles is not always equally obvious. At times it has dwindled away to vanishing-point and at others there has never been anything more than a chronological link. In any case, agricultural communities are not alone in connecting their principal theatrical shows with the returning seasons. A few hunting peoples, especially those in the Arctic regions, do the same, not to herald the harvest, but to celebrate the end of the long Polar night. Thus the Eskimos living in the Copper River delta have a rather complex drama to represent both the theft and the subsequent liberation of the sources of light. This involves a narrator, male miming actors and a chorus of women.

The timing of theatrical festivals can coincide with regular cycles of activity other than those in nature or may be determined quite independently. The Yahgan, a peaceful people living in the poorest and most inhospitable corner of the globe, Tierra del Fuego, have been methodically and brutally exterminated by white men. They were scattered fishermen living in small family units. For this reason the shows they staged during festivals to initiate young people into the tribe were very infrequent and almost haphazard. On the other hand, the Bambute pygmies in the Upper Ituri river valley meet for theatrical games almost every day. The little men of the primeval forest give this expression to their highly civilized

pleasure in being together and living without any chiefs or authority-figures.

Theatrical activity is also often associated with the events of group-life rather than being assigned to set periods. Birth and death, which we look upon as strictly personal in character, are for many peoples events that concern the entire social group, and they give rise to collective manifestations. Many of these are of a theatrical nature. To celebrate a funeral the Yahgan staged a mock-battle in which each side accused the other of having been, directly or otherwise, the cause of the death of the deceased. The moral significance of this collective acceptance of responsibility to the individual quite transcended their desire for purification. By contrast, the pygmies of Gabon evoke the memory of the deceased by reproducing in mime the main features of his life. They are not so much commemorating as renewing the presence of something that might seem gone beyond recall.

Moreover, many peoples find in theatre a powerful means of integrating the various stages of life and use it to blur the distinction between past, present and future in favour of a single global experience that transcends the individual and embraces the group's entire history and destiny. In this way the Aranda of central Australia paint their bodies, don head-dresses which are highly abstract in design, and then participate in an equally stylized mime in which there is very little movement. They are identifying themselves with the heroes of 'Dream Time', mythical beings who established their tribal customs and culture in a very remote past, which is, nevertheless, always present – this, of course, is the dream. The Gabon and Kivu pygmies are quite different. In a mime of life-like accuracy, with minute and even fastidious attention to detail, they anticipate the elephant- or big-game-hunt that will take place in precisely the same way and with exactly the same results some days later.

This is not a question of magic, which is a much more restricted and closely defined notion. And even if in both cases one could invoke that idea of 'participation' with which the old ethnologists loved to explain the peculiar mentality of primitives, the horizons disclosed by the two experiences are radically different. The Aranda use theatre because they want to establish contact with the elusive, spiritual double of life, the ever-present dimension of dream. However, when the pygmies perform in all its detail an action without any existing objective, their mime pre-ordains the concrete action which is its exact double. In speaking of 'the theatre and its double' Antonin Artaud is probably thinking uncon-

Ivory Coast (West Africa). Characters with fantastic animal-head masks in procession during an initiation-rite

Ivory Coast (West Africa). Baulé Dancers. The raffia costumes cover the body completely

Central African Republic. A native in head-dress depicting a bird.
This is a totemic bird embodied in the native who is, therefore,
shown pecking (*right*)

Ivory Coast (West Africa). A dancer from the Man region wearing
a mask with exaggerated human features

sciously of both these possibilities. Obviously the
Australian aborigines need a profound understanding of their own mythological culture. A land without
mythical associations could not be their home-land,
since myth plays a rôle of extreme importance in their
way of life. The pygmy has to concentrate instead on
a detailed and concrete appreciation of the natural,
surrounding world of animals, plants and other
phenomena. Indeed, so intimate is his knowledge
that he can reproduce it by embodying it within
himself without even externalising it. The pygmies
are all past masters at imitating the sounds and
movements of animals, and this is often the central
theme in their theatre. Theirs is perhaps the most
complete sort of knowledge that exists, at least as far
as concrete realities are concerned.

It is easy to understand why the concrete expressions of these two contrasting ways of looking at
things should be so different. In contrast with the
pygmies' realistic mimes and their accompanying
carefully measured rhythms, we find the geometrical
abstraction of the aborigines' costumes, masks and
gestures. This seems less easily explained when we
remember that the mythical hero they evoke, is held
to be identical with that totemic ancestor of whose
'flesh' they claim to be made. However, the key to
the problem may reside precisely in this ambiguity.
The totemic ancestors of certain tribal clans in
Black Africa are leopards or civets, with whom the
natives identify directly, reproducing the appearance
and movements of these animals in their rites. But
the totemic ancestors of the Australian aborigines
are not mere animals; they are men, heroes who were
transformed into animals at some point in history.
Perhaps this explains the marked differences between
the structural relationships of the various elements in
these two theatrical forms. The pygmies emphasise
mime, which *says* much more than any words, but
the mythical story-telling practically exhausts the
meaning of Aranda theatre.

It is, in fact, among the chief functions of aborigi-
nal theatre to transmit to those being initiated both
that mythological-cultural heritage without which
their social life would disintegrate and guidance for
their moral conduct. During the initiation ceremonies of the Kulin, a people in the southern half of
the continent, didactic dramas are frequently performed to show the aspirants what they can and
cannot do now that they have become men.

For that matter the transmitting of their mythical-
cultural heritage in representational terms is a
regular feature of theatre among all peoples and is
possibly the main reason underlying its frequent
connection with initiation rites. Such rites may be

limited to a very short ceremony or form part of a cycle extending over several years. As a rule, three phases are essential: the aspirants are subjected to tests of their physical or mental powers of endurance; the spirits reveal themselves to the initiates through the medium of masks or mere sounds, and it is explained to them that human beings are impersonating the spirits who are, nevertheless, real. Different degrees of severity in segregation on the basis of caste or sex restrict the uninitiated's appreciation of the human realities hidden behind the spirit-masks and determine the lay-out of the theatrical setting, as well as the nature of the relationship between the actors and their audience. When the drama is unrelated to initiation rites, it is performed in the centre of the village or some other convenient place. Everyone in the audience has a place in the chorus and anyone who wants to show off or make his voice heard is free to act in the show. Sometimes there is no audience at all. A minimum number of actors is needed to represent the paddling of a canoe or a struggle between a shark and a sword-fish, impersonated by two lines of men, but there is no maximum limit. Everyone is actively involved. On the other hand, when the performance has some secret meaning, the audience must be segregated from the actors or, at the very least, each must keep to his pre-determined rôle.

The *Kina* of the Yahgan, the large hut that serves as a shelter for the actors, stands about fifty yards from the village. The men, covered with abstract designs, emerge from the hut with slow, repetitive movements, like sea-spirits coming up out of the waters. The women look on from the village. In other cases, they hide their heads under a mat so as not to see the men standing above them and making a devilish din to make them believe the place has been taken over by spirits.

Instead of this, the Kamilaroi aborigines use a series of puppets to mark out a space for the spirits of their ancestors. This is remote from the village and only initiates and novices are allowed in. Other performances take place indoors, a good example being those in the chief's house among the Kwakiult of British Colombia. By continuously changing various tight-fitting masks of soft material, he impersonates the different spirits all by himself and re-enacts their mighty deeds. The most striking impersonation is that of the Sun, represented as a shining male figure, surrounded with rays and walking round endlessly in a circle. The other characters appear only at irregular intervals. There are other instances where only the shaman is permitted to act the part of the gods. Whether or not he uses a mask, he attempts total self-identification with the divinity, often by going into a state of trance. This sometimes appears to involve a real splitting of his personality, as the relationship between the actor and his rôle is pushed to the extreme.

From a consideration of the location of the theatrical performance, we have been brought face to face, in this way, with the problem of what is nowadays called stage-management. The pygmies do not use masks: theatre among them is confined to mime and vocal mimicry and their themes are limited to the representation of human and animal life. Similar representational forms can be found among many other peoples. Thus the Bushmen in Angola have a markedly rhythmic dance to represent a struggle between an ostrich and an elephant. Scenes representative of marine life are very common with the Yahgan. It is when such representational forms as these are linked with or replaced by the other sorts that we have mentioned, and are integrated into religious ceremonies, and especially into rites of initiation, that the mask becomes an almost invariable stage-prop. Anyone at all can take part in theatre among the pygmies, even if the entire tribe often prefers to form a circle round a particularly interesting old man and listen to the stories he acts out, but not everyone can own a mask. Indeed, many may not, and some undoubtedly do not realize that masks are being used. Only very rarely are women allowed to own or make use of masks. The almost universally held belief that in times gone by they alone could own and use them to imitate spirits and to terrorize the men, brings out very clearly the mask's almost invariable character as an instrument of power. Naturally such power is exercised in a variety of ways and at different levels. There is an enormous difference between a particular group of individuals possessing a secret that identifies them with the gods, and their having the exclusive right to act in a religious festival with the arrangement and real nature of which everyone else is quite familiar, though its powers of evocation are not in doubt.

Two examples to illustrate this are provided by peoples geographically remote from each other: the Kono in former French Guinea, and the Elema in New Guinea.

The function and number of the Kono masks is strictly controlled. There are fifteen of them. Some of these are divinities with magical powers. They enter into village life both on the occasion of initiation rites, and whenever an individual begs them to solve some private problem in exchange for a suitable offering. Ritual sacrifice is made to these masks. A group if initiates is in their service and accompanies

Ivory Coast (West Africa), Boutlé region. Zauli dancer in his raffia costume

Ivory Coast (West Africa), Boutlé region. Zauli dancer executing a war-dance

them whenever they are brought out. Then there are the spirits who promote public order and hygiene and may accordingly be said to serve the community. Finally there are the purely comic masks that take part in the festivities, but are never allowed to mingle with the other ones. Masks of the first type are handed down from generation to generation as the special heritage of priests and warriors, each mask being kept in great secrecy and its owner taking care not to be identified when it is brought out. The other sorts of masks are entrusted by the elders to suitably qualified persons and their possession is not hereditary. Each mask has definite metaphysical characteristics. It also has its own psychological individuality. The face on the masks is a human one, distorted to a greater or less degree to convey a sense of the sacred and to heighten the general effect. Only the warriors' mask resembles a particular animal – the goat. Anyone wearing a mask also puts on a costume, comprising a long, billowing raffia skirt and a sort of shawl that covers the whole body. The human being vanishes inside the divinity and the uninitiated do not

realise there is a priest underneath the semblance of the god.

The Elema, whose villages are concentrated above the Gulf of Papua in the coastal region of New Guinea, make only three types of mask: Kovave, Eharo and Hevehé. The meaning and efficacy of all three is identical. They are spirits of the woods or the sea that visit the villages, and have a general aura of benevolence. They differ only in external appearance and in the timing of their appearance. The Kovave are rather like ironic, high-crested, shining birds: the mask covers the head completely and rests on a short, round, raffia tunic which encases the arms and the trunk, but leaves the legs free. When the wearer raises his arms as he runs along, the raffia takes on the appearance of flimsy wings and the character as a whole resembles a strange sort of ostrich. The Kovave is, in fact, a swift mover, responding cheerfully to the teasing of the children, whom he then chases and hits in a playful way. The Eharo are equally jovial. Their grotesque appearance has undisguised totemistic undertones, but their chief

Senegal. Kaukouran dance, a ritual mime. The woman's presence
indicates that this is a fertility rite

function is to ease the tension of the ceremonial cycle whenever it takes a dramatic turn. This cycle takes its name, Hevehé, from the spirit-masks who are its protagonists. It may last for years. The Hevehé begins when the uninitiated villagers hear a loud and uneven, but not a threatening sound coming towards them from the sea. They run to their huts for shelter. The spirit of Ma-hevehé, the mother of Hevehé, is on her way. This noisy spirit is made up of a group of men who come into the deserted village and enter a large building, rather like an avant-garde architect's impression of a Gothic cathedral, where they deposit a few pieces of wood. These are her daughters and the building is the *eravo* or men's house. Inside it there begins, at this point, the construction of the large Hevehé masks. On the crowning day of the cycle the women invoke them with shouting. They then emerge on the terrace of the *eravo* and go down into the village to dance. When they go back, the feast is over and both the masks and the building are abandoned.

As many as one hundred and twenty-two Hevehé masks have been counted. This practically means one for every adult male in the village. The lower part of these huge, egg-shaped masks is level with the wearer's face and is painted with elements reminiscent of his nose, eyes and mouth, while the upper part, extending for at least six feet upwards, carries abstract decorations symbolising both the owner's clan and his individual spirit. Anyone may have his own Hevehé or invent one. Whoever chances to meet a friendly spirit in a dream or in a vision when out hunting, sets out to make a corresponding mask. Among the Elema there is no official mediator between men and their spirits, just as there is no chief, although the old are always treated with respect. The man-spirit relationship is immediate and festivities and shows belong to everyone. The spirits' presence in the village is real, but everyone knows the wearers of the masks that come down and make such close contact with the uninitiated among the population.

Rites of propitiation proper, such as gestures of prayer, invocation and sacrifice, cannot be included in the idea of theatre, unless this notion is used very loosely. Hence, I cannot say I have come across any theatrical form to which the representational element is foreign, although the character represented can be a canoe, an elephant, a god. Dance, too, is mainly representational, but it is often hard to determine at what point the use of disguise passes the limits of an ornamental transformation of the dancer's own body to become the full assumption of a different ritual personality. This applies to a Bororo dance described by Lévi-Strauss in the following terms: 'The dancers were covered with leaves from head to toe and, since it was impossible to see their faces, one imagined they were higher up and level with the feathered crowns which surmounted their costume. In this way the characters were unthinkingly credited with a height disproportionately great. In their hands they held bundles of straw or sticks decorated with leaves. ... Initially the male dancers displayed themselves alone, dividing into two groups facing one another from either end of the arena. With shouts of "oh! oh!" they ran towards each other, and then wheeled round so as to maintain their original positions. At a later stage in the proceedings a few women mingled with the male dancers and there ensued an endless farandole in which the forward movement consisted of hops. This was directed by nude coryphaei walking backwards and shaking rattles in the dancers' faces, while another group of men chanted from a squatting position.'

However, we must remember that the original meaning of a traditional dance has often been forgotten or has changed as far as the actors are concerned, not only because its origin belongs to a long lost time, but also on account of constant im-improvisations and individual improvements. In any case, there do exist dances where the actors impersonate no one except themselves. This is particularly true of erotic dances. The most common pattern is that of a row of men facing a row of women. Among the pygmies the girls leave their row one by one, approach a young man, and make him an invitation by thrusting their genitals violently forward. However, among Negro tribes the two rows approach each other with tiny, measured steps, their bodies convulsed by violent spasms, their faces serious and intent, and they come so close that the girls' lips brush against those of the men.

An originally identical formula embraces two different concepts of theatre, corresponding to two different concepts of love.

Chapter 2

Polion the painter. Chorus of lyre-playing Satyrs. Vase no 25.78.66. Greek Art, New York, Metropolitan Museum of Art, Fletcher Fund, 1935

THE ORIGINS OF GREEK TRAGEDY AND THE SATYRIC DRAMA

Granted that the origins of theatre cannot be traced to the drama of so-called 'primitive' peoples, we can recognise the historical foundations of our Western theatrical tradition in the fully developed Greek tragedies and comedies, staged in Athens during the fifth century BC.

This begs the question of the earlier emergence of Greek theatre, an answer to which is crucial for our interpretation of subsequent developments.

Single passages in Aristotle's *Poetics* and the *Histories* of Herodotus indicate a link between tragedy and a lyrical, choral chant known as the 'dithyramb'. We find this connection fascinating, because the dithyramb was sung to the accompaniment of dancing. In other words, it was a form of theatre, not merely a literary genre.

Unfortunately, both references are of doubtful interpretation. Thus Aristotle states that tragedy derived from the *exarchontes*, who initiated or provided the musical setting for the dithyramb. His use of the plural has led scholars to think of two separate choruses, one comprising the satyrs, animal-like characters depicting the ancient spirits of nature, who subsequently formed part of the retinue of Dionysus, the god of ecstasy. However, the *exarchontes* might well have been no other than the chorus, which sang the entire dithyramb. Alternatively, leaving aside his use of the plural, the reference could be to the coryphaeus, or possibly to the author of the dithyramb, who conducted the chorus and took the solo parts himself. For since, with the

passage of time, the dithyramb was reduced to the repeated chanting of a chorus during the procession, the coryphaeus (*exarchon*) may very well have been expected to fill in the long pauses by improvising a lyrical narration and singing it solo. The author would afterwards set down this monody in writing. In this way Aristotle's remark would be literally true, because tragedy would derive not from the dithyramb itself, but from this narration of the *exarchontes*, a more or less improvised account of the deeds of a mythical hero, interspersed with dances and choral singing. In other words, as time went on, the *exarchon* separated from the chorus, became an independent performer and began to impersonate his hero instead of merely reciting his deeds. In this way a new dramatic form was born.

To turn to Herodotus. He relates how, during a war against the Argives, Cleisthenes, tyrant of Sicyon, abolished the cult of the Argive hero Adrastus, transferring the sacrifices to Melanippus, but assigning the related *tragikoi choroi* ('tragic' choruses) to the god Dionysus. The interpretation of this passage is of interest both as regards the Dionysiac origin of tragedy and in connection with the meaning of the term 'tragedy' itself.

Now, it is possible that Herodotus's actual word, *apedoke*, does not mean simply 'transferred' or 'assigned', but 'restored'. Furthermore, Adrastus may have been the Argive equivalent of Dionysus. The reference would, therefore, support the thesis of tragedy's having a Dionysiac, and so a sacred and ritual origin. On the other hand, if Cleisthenes' gesture really was an innovation in favour of the cult of Dionysus and the *tragikoi choroi* were older than this cult, the ritual and religious significance of tragedy would be diluted considerably and even, at least in reference to Dionysus, eliminated in practice. This would entail the construction of alternative theories to account for the appearance of tragedy. In other words, it would become necessary to question the generally admitted ritual grandeur of the genre. After all, some scholars claim it was purely by chance that, throughout the fifth and fourth centuries, the staging of tragedies coincided with the Dionysiac festivities. Thespis, the legendary 'inventor' of tragedy, was allowed to put on his shows in the pit of the theatre of Dionysus because that was the only suitable place, and this purely practical motive was the beginning of the link between tragedy and the Great Dionysia.

However, to get back to Herodotus, what did the great historian mean when he mentioned the tragic choruses? Was he referring to the dithyramb enriched by the *exarchon*'s improvisation, or to choruses of goats (*tragoi*)? If the latter, 'tragedy' probably means precisely the 'song of the goats' (*tragon oide*), in other words, the chanting of a chorus in animal costume, this being no other than the second chorus added to the official one for the dithyramb and the fruitful, original seed from which sprang the tragic genre. The first hypothesis implies a merely extrinsic link between tragedy and the *tragos* (goat), perhaps simply that a goat was the prize won by the best dithyrambic chorus. There is also a third hypothesis, denying the connection between tragedy and the *tragos* and tracing the etymology of the word to an Indo-European term connected with the idea of force and might. Tragedy, therefore, would be the song of the hero, he who, straight after the early narrative phase of the dithyramb, was impersonated by the *exarchon* of the dithyrambic chorus, who recounted or represented his mighty deeds and, more particularly, his sufferings. Such an interpretation would skirt round the thorny problem of the transition from the licentious displays of the satyrs to the majestic gravity of classical tragedy. Yet the truth of the matter is that there exists an abundance of visual evidence in favour of a close link between goats, satyrs and tragedy. The more recent as well as the earliest vase-paintings of choruses in animal-costume both indicate the link between the satyric dances and the themes of heroic saga and also show how the mythic heroes were able to rise above the grotesque horse-play of the satyrs.

Tragic plays were staged during the annual festival in honour of Dionysus, the Great Dionysia, held in March. Each author presented a 'tetralogy' or group of four plays, three being tragedies, while the fourth was grotesque in character and had a chorus of satyrs (half-men, half-horses), hence the name 'satyric drama'. Because the satyric drama represents not a fossilized stage in the development of tragedy, but a form emerging out of the latter's consolidation as a classical genre, it seems likely that both sorts of theatre spring from a common source, and in this choruses of satyrs or goat-men will have played some part.

Let us consider in more detail the forms that may have been taken by the satyric dances and by satyric drama in general. It needs to be noted right away that almost all paintings in which satyrs are represented provide valuable evidence about the history of the theatre, if only because they depict masked characters—not mythological beings, but those who impersonated them on special occasions. This evidence shows that the satyrs' part may have been simply choreographic, or may have included dramatic, representational acting. A safe opinion is that in some instances their part was limited to a rather decorative function, separate from the dramatic performance proper. The so-called 'Pandora Krater' may favour this view. Its upper section shows gods carrying gifts to Pandora, while, underneath, a group of satyrs sways to the sound of a flute. Their stylized dance-steps are wide but clear-cut and their movements seem frozen in geometrical patterns.

In other instances the chorus of satyrs provides the sole motif for the vase-paintings, and these illustrate the wide range of treatment permitted in the choreography of this sort of theatre. Thus the satyric dance might be a wild, frenzied rush, a symbol of the forces of nature breaking out in the characters. The kalpis in the Boston Museum illustrates this. On the other hand, it might be a slow, stately procession, with deliberately exaggerated movements, a sort of skit on other, more serious performances. The chorus of lyre-playing satyrs painted by an artist called Polion affords a good example. His vase illustrates different nuances in the attitudes of the chorus. The leader is showing off rather pompously, while the straggler at the end is pretending to be embarrassed, as he smothers his desire to leap into the air and concentrates on trying to get a sweet sound out of his instrument.

There are also definite cases, and these are possibly more numerous, in which the action of the satyrs passes beyond choreography to real acting and involves the divinely heroic personages of the

Chorus of dancing Satyrs. Kalpis. Boston, Museum of Fine Arts.
'Satyr' is a generic term for animal-like characters. Choruses of
Satyrs are made up more often than not of half-human, half-
horselike creatures with horses' tails and goat-men wearing
sheepskin girdles

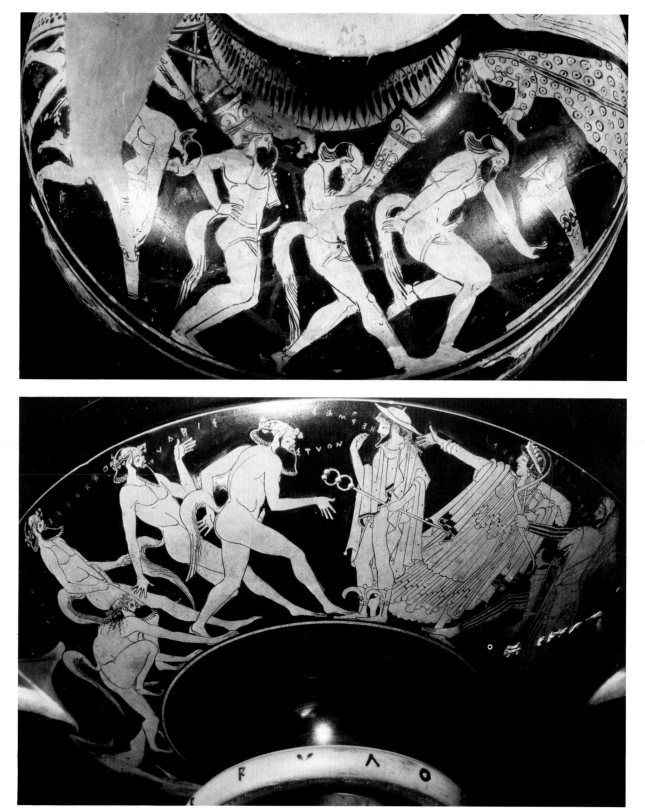

The Byrgos Painter. Satyrs attacking Hera and Iris, protected by
Hermes. Kylix. London, British Museum

Satyrs dancing round Prometheus. Krater. Gotha, Schlossmuseum

Olympian world in its horseplay. Such was the satyric drama in literature, a genre crystallised by an early fifth century author, Pratinas, of whose works only a few fragments remain. A very interesting illustration of this representational sort of satyric drama is on a *kylix* decorated with red figures, dating from between 500 and 480 BC, the very time when the tragedies of Aeschylus were being given their first performance. It is the work of the 'Byrgos Painter', an artist who worked regularly for Byrgos the potter. The importance of this vase is enhanced by the fact that the action takes place round an altar which can be readily identified as the *thymele* erected in the centre of the pit in Greek theatres. The action of the satyrs is depicted in two contrasting situations. On one side we see them trying to rape Iris, grabbing her by the arms in long, determined and violent movements, descriptive of the sudden eruption of their savage lust. These movements are artistically resolved in the close concentration of the lines, and these are repeated spread out vividly across the surface enclosing the person of the terrified goddess, so that she is ineluctably caught up in the awesome motif. On the other side, by contrast, the satyrs are trying to take Hera by surprise, but their plot is foiled by the intervention of Hermes and Herakles. The satyrs are terrified, their movements are abruptly broken off and freeze into poised immobility, as if their

wild nature has been locked in at its very point of explosion. The presence of the god and the hero has brought the satyrs to a halt, but dignified or solemn poses are not involved – Hermes' gesture is even vulgar and commonplace, 'What are you up to? What do you think you're trying to do?' It is the inhibited gesture of someone lacking courage, but trying to make other people afraid.

Similarly, on a famous vase preserved in Richmond, while Ulysses' companions try to blind Polyphemus a few satyrs provide a counterbalance to the action with gestures of exaggerated tension, and these are reflected in the otherwise serious action of the heroes.

To say that in this form of satyric drama the chorus of half-animals had a definite representational and 'dramatic' rôle does not mean they neglected their primary choreographic function, although this often merged into and blended with the acting. This can be seen in a krater thought to refer to a lost satyric drama of Aeschylus, *Prometheus the Fire-bearer*. The satyrs' pose suggests the typical steps of the *sikinnis*, the Greek name for the characteristic dance of the satyric drama (the *emmeleia* and *kordax* belonged to tragedy and comedy respectively). These steps consisted in the main of abrupt, rapid movements, and these were often frozen in poses accentuating the angularity of the body as much as possible. The result

Gods bringing gifts to Pandora (*upper frieze*). Satyrs dancing (*lower frieze*). Krater. London, British Museum. This illustrates the juxtaposition, albeit on different levels, of Olympian gods and a chorus of half-animals

29

Actors and the satyric chorus. 'Pronomos Vase' (called after the flautist—*bottom centre*). Naples, Museo Nazionale. Besides Dionysus and Ariadne, not depicted as actors, the recognisable characters in the upper part comprise Herakles, King Laomedon of Troy, and his daughter Hesione. Details of this vase are shown on pp 30–1 and 33

exarchon or someone named by him, who impersonated with all traditional seriousness the god or hero whose mighty deeds he was singing about or even re-enacting. With which of these forms are we to identify the famous 'Pronomos Vase', undoubtedly among the more significant pieces of evidence for our understanding of Greek theatre? The subject of the decorations on one side of this large vase is a group of actors and not an actual performance, while the other side presents a totally unrelated satyric fantasy. The vase is important because of its definite and immediate reference to theatrical usage. This is evidenced by the masks that the satyrs of the chorus as well as the other actors are holding in their hands; only one member of the chorus has put his mask on already. We can, therefore, unhesitatingly classify the costumes of both satyrs and actors as theatrical and see in the incipient dance-step of the only masked member of the chorus a characteristic pose in the *sikinnis*. In this respect the painting on the Pronomos Vase merely confirms conclusions based on other sources of evidence.

Now, the personages to either side of the divine couple, Dionysus and Ariadne, depicted in the centre of the vase, are wearing long chitons with sleeves, and these tunics are adorned with multi-coloured figures and patterns of archaic design. A passage in the *Choephori* of Aeschylus confirms this. In speaking of his tunic, Orestes describes it as being decorated with hunting scenes. These were rich and dignified costumes, quite different from those in everyday use, though in no sense ostentatious and certainly not grotesque. The features on the masks in the actors' hands are only slightly exaggerated and, in the male face, express carefully controlled emotion. Herakles is wearing a short costume, which may have been considered customary, and the actor beside him is probably Silenus, who was part of the chorus. It seems possible to conclude from all this that characters such as these would hardly have been directly mixed up in the horseplay of the satyric chorus. Admittedly there are good reasons for dating this vase from about 410 BC, but this does not rule out its portraying a much older theatrical situation, especially if those scholars are correct who regard it as a copy from an older votive painting.

The following is a summary of the conclusions to be drawn from an examination of the Pronomos Vase: (1) When we find costumes in other paintings similar to those worn in this one by actors with tragic masks it is fair to suppose some link with theatre; (2) It is hard to think of tragedy as originating in horseplay, and in some cases, reflecting the more ancient usage, the acting of the satyric chorus

was a continuous series, so that the dance never degenerated into an ornamental leap from pose to pose, but always carried a precise representational meaning, the *phora* (to use the Greek technical terms) evoking the *schema*, the movement the corresponding expression, or, in other words, the attitude that rendered the movement significant, so that nothing detracted from the instinctive violence of the acting.

Therefore, although it is true that in the satyric drama, as Pratinas enshrined it in literature at the beginning of the fifth century, myth was frequently brought down to the level of horseplay on the part of the satyrs, we can suppose there was a time in which the development of the satyric chorus was quite separate from the acting of the protagonist, the

must have been kept separate from that of the actors; (3) Although tragic costume was multi-coloured and ornamental, with a different cut from that in everyday use, it was light and simple and never designed with the idea of making its wearer seem bigger or more important; (4) The masks were 'realistic' in character, although their features and expressions were slightly exaggerated; (5) The *cothurni* were merely finely made boots and did not increase the actor's height nor obstruct his movements, as they did in the later Alexandrian and Roman periods.

These remarks already refer to tragic plays proper, and they are the subject of our next chapter.

Chapter 3

Iphigenia in Tauris. Vase. Naples, Museo Nazionale. Although the lay-out of the *skene* is quite plain, the characters are not wearing theatrical costume. Orestes and Pylades are nude. Iphigenia (*right*) has on an ordinary dress. The figure on the left is wearing oriental attire

GREEK TRAGEDY IN THE FIFTH CENTURY BC

Before considering the stage-productions of the great Athenian tragic poets of the age of Pericles—Aeschylus, Sophocles and Euripides—it will be as well to pause for a moment and see how theatres and stages were built. These general remarks have special reference to the theatre of Dionysus Eleuthereus at Athens, in which the great tragedies had their *premières* during the Great Dionysia.

In Sophocles' day the range of steps for the spectators, the *cavea*, was still more oblong than semi-circular, so that the lay-out of the theatre kept close to the pristine design. Cretan and Mycenaean palaces with similarly shaped courtyards have been excavated and it seems likely that spectators used these.

Even more fascinating is the question of the space used for the actual performance. Scholars adhering to the older tradition believe that this probably took place on two distinct levels by the time the tragedies of Thespis were first staged and certainly by the time of Aeschylus (around the turn of the 6th century BC). The gyrations of the chorus took place in the pit, while one and, at a later date, two or three actors performed on a raised platform at the back of the pit. This pit or orchestra (from *orcheomai*, the Greek verb 'to dance') was initially oblong and later circular in shape, and was surrounded by the steps for the spectators. The platform for the actors rested on a wooden dressing-room, the *skene*, which was also used to provide a backdrop. The platform itself was the equivalent of our modern stage.

Other scholars, however, claim that both chorus and actors performed in the pit. The division into two levels came much later, in the Alexandrian period, when the *skene* grew into a roomy, two-storey building with a first-floor roof serving as a stage. In the fifth century, when the works of Aeschylus, Sophocles, Euripides and Aristophanes were being performed, the actors never had a proper stage. Indeed, even the *skene* was unknown to the earlier tragic playwrights, Thespis and Pratinas, and did not exist when Aeschylus put on his first works. The pit was then surrounded by a narrow paving, either at or only slightly above ground-level, and it was on this that the chorus and actors made their entrance, approaching by means of a gang-way which stood out against the open landscape—the *parodos*, named after the chorus's entrance hymn. The acting occupied the pit itself. The *skene* was a later development designed as a dressing-room for the actors, each of whom had to play more than one part. It was only by chance that it served as a neutral backdrop for the dramatic action. The tradition goes that it was Aeschylus who had the *skene* decorated with paintings and architectural motifs. Later still, the central door was occasionally dignified by an elaborate portico. Then, probably about 450 BC, two small, jutting wings, the *paraskenia*, were added on, with doors or, possibly, decorative columns.

Acceptance of either of these theories in preference to the other leads to a radically different view of the Greeks' notion of theatre. In the first hypothesis, the actors would have performed in a clearly defined space, as they do nowadays, although, despite an unavoidable division between the singing of the chorus and the main action, this latter would have had additional breathing-space since they could overflow into the pit. However, the second hypothesis makes the chorus a dramatic character in its own right, closely involved in the transactions of the other actors. The unbroken expanse of the pit allowed complete freedom of movement, distances were magnified and the choral dances could go on without interruption, even when all the other actors made a collective exit.

Once the *skene* was introduced, the backdrop it formed became the focus of the action, though the chorus still used the *parodos* for their entrance. As the addition of the *paraskenia* extended the *skene* into the pit, it was inevitable that the whole of the latter should appear to be an enlargement of the space supposedly marked off by the *paraskenia* themselves. The actors' performance was possibly centred on this smaller area, but was never shut up in it. The enlarged space cannot have seemed in any way restrictive, since its only limit was the fixed circle of spectators.

Modern scholars generally prefer this second theory. This, then, was the architectural and theatrical setting for the original performances of the great tragedies, produced by the playwrights themselves. It was a unique and momentous experience in the annals of the theatre. In the course of the next hundred years, the architectural lay-out became definitive. The pit was made circular and the steps were adjusted accordingly, but this made no great difference to the functional relationships established in the more oblong sort of theatre.

Now, in attempting to re-construct in broad outline the original performances of the ancient tragedies, we can avail ourselves of the rather meagre indications in the texts themselves. These usually refer to what happens on the stage without saying how it happened. However, we can also consult a few vase-paintings, although the evidence they yield is less certain and direct by far than that of the vases depicting the satyric drama. Besides this, we can draw upon scattered references in later literature— Aristotle, for instance, or the grammatical writings of Julius Pollux. Living in the second century AD, he left exhaustive notes regarding the colouring, the hair-style, the thickness of the beard and the set of the eye-brows in the different masks. He also described the composition of the chorus. It is impossible to say how applicable his remarks are to tragedy in the classical era.

Classical tragedy, whatever its origins and development, consisted of a dialogue between two or three actors, who were continually changing their costumes and masks as they impersonated a variety of characters. Their exchanges were sometimes with one another and sometimes with a chorus of fifteen, whose spokesman was the coryphaeus. Such dialogues made up the different episodes or, to use the modern word, acts in the tragedy, and were interlaced with *stasima*, lyrics sung by the full chorus, whose entrance hymn was given a different name, the *parodos*. No actor was ever present during the singing of the *stasima*, but one and even two actors might enter into the singing and occasionally the dancing of the chorus at some moment when the dramatic tension had reached its height. This lamentation was the *kommos*. How, then, did the chorus and actors use voice and gesture to gain their effect?

Julius Pollux, whose statement is supported by Aristotle, says the chorus made its entrance in three rows of five, and that this arrangement was maintained throughout.

However, what little evidence can be extracted from the extant tragedies flatly contradicts this. There is, too, in Boston, a late fifth-century Attic pyx showing Nausicaa playing ball with her handmaidens. Since her costume is definitely theatrical, the reference may be to a production of one of the lost plays of Sophocles, of whom, in this very connexion, tradition has it that he was himself a skilful dancer. The handmaidens, who most likely made up the chorus, are depicted in the most varied of poses. In any case, it would seem impossible to play ball within the limits of the stage as described by Pollux.

We shall consider this question in more detail in the light of examples drawn from the tragedies of the three great fifth-century playwrights: Aeschylus (525–456), Sophocles (496–405), and Euripides (480–406).

The clearest evidence from the seven extant tragedies of Aeschylus is in the *Eumenides*, as we shall see. However, in the *Seven against Thebes*, when his city lay under seige from a Greek coalition favouring the restoration of his brother, Polyneices, to the Theban throne, where would be the dramatic meaning of the clash between the noble rage of proud King Eteocles and the womanish fears of the chorus of Theban virgins, if one had to rule out any possibility of their terror and confusion being expressed, not merely by them wringing their hands, but also by their running across the pit, throwing themselves to the ground and clinging to the altar? The evidence in the text is, in any case, clear enough,

Epidaurus, the theatre—the only remaining theatre definitely built in the 4th century BC with its structure basically intact: a circular pit with a separate *skene*. Other theatres were modified in Roman times to integrate the pit into the seating-area

since Eteocles reproves the chorus for 'throwing yourselves in this way onto the statues of the guardian gods', and for their 'frantic shouting, while clinging to the statues of the gods'.'

Again, *The Suppliant Women* is essentially a choral tragedy, telling the story of the Danaids seeking asylum in Athens from the attentions of their cousins, who wanted to marry them. Very little would be left in the performance unless the dialogues (for I am not speaking of the *stasima*) were 'acted out' by their choral protagonists, unless, at the very least, an opening and closing of the lines of the chorus accompanied the alternations of fear and hope, of certainly regarding the justice of their cause and dismay about the opposing claims of violence. It is quite out of the question that no more than a striking contrast in the colour of their clothes expressed the clash between the white-clad Egyptians and the Danaids. Whether a full second chorus was used, or merely a group of extras, some explicitly violent mime must have been performed.

This is not to say that the chorus lost the sense of its own identity. It always acted as one body, but was quite free to move about or to re-arrange the relative positions of its members. There is a story about the pit being often marked out with white guide-lines to facilitate the gyrations of the chorus, and its internal arrangement was endlessly adaptable. The chorus, especially in the tragedies of Aeschylus, was a character in its own right, expressing feelings and emotions by its motion and configuration. Schlegel's definition of the chorus as an 'ideal spectator' is as wrong-headed as it is famous.

This mobility of the chorus was a single ingredient in a very rich and complex sort of theatre. Other factors were the actors' multi-coloured costumes, the deployment of groups of extras and various decorative accessories, the latter being especially used in those tragedies Aristotle dubbed 'theatrical'. One of his examples is Aeschylus' *Prometheus Bound*. Zeus has had the hero chained to a rock to punish him for giving fire to mortals. Ocean and a chorus of

39

nymphs hear his lamentations and arrive on the scene in gilded chariots. At the end of the play the earth trembles and 'the voice of thunder resounds darkly'.

The *Eumenides* provides the clearest evidence of the chorus' participation in the action proper. Clytemnestra, wife of Agamemnon, King of Argos, whom she has murdered, is killed in her turn by her own son, Orestes. As the play opens, probably within the confines of the *paraskenia*, the chorus of Furies is roused from sleep by her ghost. The chorus then leaves the pit, which is unusual, but only to return in disarray in search of Orestes. Subsequently they dance around him in a frenzy, expressive of his own remorse and madness, and they toss their black veils in a most terrifying way. In all likelihood it was the theatrical performance of these fearsome females that allowed Aeschylus to translate into the language of the stage that nightmarish atmosphere which pervades his trilogy, the *Oresteia*.

This trilogy is the only one in the whole of Greek theatre to have been preserved in its entirety, although the satyric drama is missing. It tells of Agamemnon's return from the Trojan war and his murder at the hands of his wife (*Agamemnon*); of Orestes' matricide to avenge his father (*The Choephori*); of the sufferings inflicted on Orestes by the guardian-gods of the house of Atreus and his being pardoned in an Athenian court convoked by Athena (*Eumenides*). The whole trilogy must have been staged with tremendous pageantry, with an abundance of scenic and choreographic innovations. This may have been the first occasion on which the *skene* was allotted a definite rôle. It offered scope for novel uses of space, in conjunction with the *paraskenia*. Some authorities think they were used, in the *Eumenides* at least, to represent two different places, Apollo's temple at Delphi and that of Athena in Athens. Aeschylus's formula thus resembled the medieval idea of presenting different scenes simultan-

40

eously.

Unfortunately, we can only imagine how a work of this grandeur was actually staged. A tetralogy was customarily performed in the course of a single day, so that the *Agamemnon* would be staged at early dawn. Even so, it is hard to say whether the sombre, gloomy atmosphere with which it begins was communicated to the audience merely by the watchman's speech and an appropriate mime, or whether the successive kindling of beacons bringing news of the fall of Troy from Asia to the royal palace of Argos was suitably represented by the unexpected twinkling of fires being lit in the morning twilight. This is more than likely, if one recalls that the last scene of the *Eumenides* which closes the whole trilogy includes a highly theatrical, sumptuous, torchlight procession, as 'the grand, tragic pathos of Aeschylus merges into the deep, delicate harmony of the typically Hellenic sense of symmetry'.

There is another scene, particularly rich in dramatic possibilities, which we can reconstruct with more confidence, at least in·outline. It was among the highlights of the trilogy—the entrance of Agamemnon and Cassandra in a chariot coming from a great distance (indicated by the use of the left-hand *parodos*). As they were followed by a large retinue of soldiers returning from Troy, the chorus must have taken up a position to the right and in front of the *paraskenium*. The gilded chariot would draw up in the middle in front of the *skene* and at some distance from it, closer perhaps to the altar erected in the centre of the pit than to the *skene* itself. A long crimson carpet was then laid by Clytemnestra from the chariot to the main doors of the *skene*. The architecture of the theatre and the evidence in the text favour this theory and, if it is true, it is easy to picture these great, sweeping movements being executed with parade-ground precision along lines precisely laid down beforehand. The chorus too, in serried ranks that imparted to their welcome a touch of reserve, were associated with this polished, external display of ceremony, loaded with deep, underlying tension. There was no joy about this hero's home-coming. The magnificence of the weapons and hangings was overshadowed by the envy of the gods and their avenging Justice.

The theme of a tragic conflict between two opposing claims to justice runs right through the works of Aeschylus. It is implicit in the *Agamemnon* and made explicit in the *Choephori*. In this play both the dramatic action and the collision inside the actors' minds between opposed but interwoven feelings, advance with an unhurried rhythm towards their inevitable crescendo. Any study of the text makes it extremely unlikely that this tragedy was ever performed with that poker-faced intonation and woodenness of gesture which authorities have undiscriminatingly attributed to ancient classical theatre. The pictorial art of the times does reveal a preference for broad, sweeping gestures, but there are instances of a reserved and modest expression of emotion. Thus quite a wide range of stage-gestures were there for the actors to use, without any need of stilted pomposity or bombastic self-indulgence. The tragic actors' costume, it will be remembered, usually consisted of the long *chiton* with sleeves and the *himation*. This sufficed to evoke the archaic atmosphere of myth and to suspend one's everyday feelings, but it did not obstruct the fully human presence of the characters.

In any case it was probably only in his later tragedies that Aeschylus envisaged such an elaborate production. The earlier ones presumably were set against the neutral backdrop of the *skene*, or even the open landscape. In the *Persians* the ghost of King Darius comes to tell his wife Atossa why their son Xerxes was defeated at Salamis. One can imagine how striking such an apparition would be in this setting. At all events, it was Aeschylus who established the general lines and many of the details of Greek theatrical usage in the fifth century—costumes, masks, choreography and stage-settings.

Nevertheless, the concrete form and meaning of the stage-productions of the tragedies of Sophocles were probably quite different.

As well as being the poet of the great character with a single, uncontrollable, ruling passion, Sophocles is the master of speech and dialogue, developing his plot along lines which may take an unexpected turn, but are always inevitable. In his plays the rapid parry and thrust of single lines and half-phrases, the *stichomythia*, is developed into overpoweringly dramatic action. Clearly, this was reflected in the actual performance.

Sophocles' characters on stage must have seemed grander than the elusive, complex creations of Aeschylus. They were also more capable of action, more mobile, more dynamic. The meaning of the clashes between the formidable antagonists in his dramas—Antigone and Creon, Electra and Clytemnestra, Philoctetes and Ulysses—could be clearly seen on the stage and was not merely heard.

In producing his plays, Sophocles probably made use of a large number of skilfully deployed extras in conjunction with his main characters. Several references in the texts suggest this. On occasion the activities of these extras were of decisive significance in the interpretation of his play. In *Antigone*, for

example, the heroine has been found guilty of burying the corpse of her brother Polyneices despite King Creon's prohibition. The procession that leads her to her death would resemble just as much a nupital ceremony as a funeral rite. It was this identification, within the sorrowful figure of the girl, of marriage and death that expressed the identity of triumph and defeat. State law was broken in the name of complete self-sacrifice to honour the unwritten law. This myth offers the first example of the moral duty of civil disobedience.

The function of the chorus was different, and with Sophocles it lost the pre-eminence Aeschylus had given it. This does not mean it was confined to the lyrical *stasima* between acts, but the coryphaeus and the chorus as a character in its own right are rarely to the fore. In *Philoctetes* and *Ajax* the choral action is obviously dramatic, but the chorus is no longer a protagonist, nor even the second lead. Its action is subordinated to that of the hero. When, in *Ajax*, he has already committed suicide because of his affront in being denied the use of Achilles' weapons and the chorus makes a scattered return to the pit in search of him, their action is merely an episode and has no follow-up. The arrangement of the chorus into ranks

and files may very well stem from the theatre of Sophocles. On the other hand, his very last tragedy, *Oedipus at Colonus*, assigns a much larger and continuous rôle to the chorus, almost a last homage to the already dead tradition of the great plays of Aeschylus.

The varied structure and the changing distribution of the chorus in the tragedies of Euripides suggest rather similar considerations. Even compared with Sophocles the literary importance of the chorus decreases in the plays of Euripides. Nevertheless, many of his tragedies indicate his keen interest in experimenting with the positioning of his chorus. In *Rhesus* he uses the chorus not precisely as a leading character, but to create the atmosphere and suggest the setting for the drama. The chorus mingles with the extras, or replaces them to represent the confused, indiscriminate intermingling of watchmen and soldiers inside the Trojan camp at dead of night.

The Greeks called the producer the *choregus*, or choir-master, and it is not hard to see why. It was with Euripides that his function was distinguished from that of the author and actor and given to someone else. However, like most writers for the stage, Euripides envisaged a model performance and made this explicit in his stage directions. These give us some idea of how, in the conditions existing at the time, his plays may have been staged.

The figurative arts also reflect the great success enjoyed by Euripides immediately after his death. Fairly closely contemporary pictorial evidence which refers to performances of his works, allows us to draw certain general conclusions about Greek theatre in the years immediately following 400 BC.

The sparse and crude design of one vase from Magna Graecia precludes its telling us much about costumes or acting, but it definitely confirms the lay-out of the *paraskenia*, the doors of which provided entrances from the different localities sometimes represented by it. Indeed the painting suggests that the *skene* itself had no longer any dramatic function and was merely a neutral backdrop. Other vase-paintings allow us to study the actors' attitudes. It is very interesting to compare two vases depicting the *Andromeda*, a lost play, possible by Euripides. The costumes are the same as those of the 'Pronomos Vase', but the two painters were thinking of very different productions. The first shows the heroine tied to a rock, the outlines of which are lightly traced in ivy. On a second vase she is bound to two columns, part of the *paraskenium* or else of the portico in front of the central door. Stage usage rather than realism dictated this way of depicting the rock in the myth. In classical Greek theatre scene-painting, more

or less in perspective, played only a very small part, and in any case that part was purely decorative.

Both vases, however, show the heroine supremely calm and serene. Perhaps the artists wished to reproduce that gentle sadness with which Euripides' heroines faced their final moment. Most vase-paintings of this period, in fact, that refer to tragic themes, represent the gestures of the various characters as quiet and restrained.

This cannot have been a hard and fast rule. A different vase from southern Italy depicts scenes from the *Medea*, another well-known tragedy by Euripides, or a play based on this. It is in a violently moving and tense mime that the actors interpret the overwhelming pathos of the blackest tragedy in antiquity, and yet they never fall into that rhetorical, emotional hyperbole which characterised theatre in Roman and Alexandrian times.

Before concluding this chapter on tragedy, it seems well to recall Aristotle's highly detailed examination of the structure of fifth century tragedy in his short treatise, the *Poetics*. He wrote about 330 BC, many years later, but this does not lessen the fascination of this short work, which was to provide the basis for all the French and Italian treatises on theatre.

There is valuable information in it about the history of theatre, and it makes it clear that, before Aeschylus, tragedy consisted of a simple dialogue between the actor and the chorus. Aeschylus introduced a second actor and Sophocles a third. Aristotle also attributes to Sophocles the first use of painted scenery, but we have seen already that it is extremely unlikely that this had any great part in the production of classical drama.

Moreover, the *Poetics* for the first time dealt systematically with the relationship between the literary text and the performance: tragedy is for Aristotle primarily a literary work. The performance is considered merely a way of communicating the poetic text in exactly the same way as the rhapsodist would render an epic poem by his singing and miming.

Aristotle does not accord equal status to staging as such, but he does at any rate mention it. If, on the one hand, tragedy must arouse 'pity and terror', independently of its being actually performed or not, on the other hand, it is possible 'to obtain this result by means of a theatrical performance'. To Aristotle's way of thinking, this is the business not of the playwright, but of the *choregus*. He acknowledges theatrical tragedy, or tragedy written for public performance, as a particular species of tragedy, characterised by the abundance of its visual ingredients: stage-props, extras, scenery and such mechanical devices as were used, especially by Euripides, to resolve the dramatic enigma by means of a divine intervention—the *deus ex machina*.

Chapter 4

ARISTOPHANES AND GREEK COMEDY

The very last words of that portion of Aristotle's *Poetics* which is still extant read: 'Then, as regards comedy . . .' Unfortunately, his treatise on this subject has not been preserved. This deprives us of a valuable source of information. It is clear he thought of comedy as contrasting with tragedy, but as belonging, nevertheless, to the same category.

At least there is an obvious parallelism and contrast with his remarks about tragedy, when the philosopher from Stagira traces the origins of comedy to the *exarchontes* who intoned phallic hymns during a procession (*komos*, hence the word 'comedy'), which in historical times was held in honour of Dionysus, but undoubtedly goes back to seasonal fertility rites.

In Athens comedies were performed during the Lenaea, a Dionysian festival occurring in January and February, which enjoyed state patronage from 442 BC onwards. Later, comedy was added to the City Dionysia as well.

Philologists divide the history of Greek comedy into three periods: Old, Middle and New. Horace's well-known trio of authors, '*Eupolis atque Cratinus, Aristophanesque poetae*', belongs to the earlier period. The dramatic form is remarkably free at this stage. Its nucleus is the *parabasis*, some sort of procession of chorus and actors to the accompaniment of biting verses. Around this are grouped dramatic episodes in the full sense, as well as the *agon*—an interchange between two or more actors, or between semi-choruses.

Only the comedies of Aristophanes (450–388) have been preserved and their plot is extremely thin. In the *Birds*, Euelpides and Peisthetaerus set out to found a city, 'Cloud-cuckoo-land', between heaven and earth. In the *Lysistrata* the women refuse to make love with their war-mad husbands. In *Peace* Trygaeus goes up to heaven in search of the peace that has been lost.

On the other hand, the themes and contents of these plays are extremely rich. They are not dealing with myth, nor with the unending questions of the human condition, as the tragedies do. Instead, they tackle political and social problems directly, the specific day-to-day realities of the Athenian *polis*. There is a manifesto against war and the demagogues (*Acharnians*, *Peace*, *Lysistrata*), against Socrates and the Sophists (*Clouds*), and against new trends in tragic theatre (*Frogs*). It is open to discussion whether Aristophanes' position represents brilliance in the service of reaction or total dedication to a constructive criticism of social life as he knew it. The fact remains that his main preoccupation is the Athenian *polis*, occasionally idealised as the Utopian city of the birds, but more often presented in terms of its own everyday political, social and cultural reality.

So it is not surprising that Aristophanes frequently takes issue with his audience and makes a butt of them. It seems likely that their responses were not limited to laughter or applause. On occasion the actors probably served as vehicle for a genuine

An old actor looking at his mask. Fragment of a vase. Würzburg, Martin von Wagner-Museum

47

dialogue between the poet and his fellow Athenians. The accuracy of our imaginary reconstructions of the comedy of this period is helped considerably by an abundance of iconographic evidence.

If we examine the internal structure of Aristophanes' comedies and follow up his references and other evidence, we can see that the dramatic rôle of the chorus in comedy was even more marked and varied than it was in tragedy. In particular, it was more closely integrated into the performance as a whole. There was no break in continuity between the vibrant dialogues among the principal characters or with the coryphaeus on the one hand, and the chantings of the chorus, which also included dancing, on the other. The chorus as a whole also often broke in on the action. Such rhythmic movements were partly inspired by the actual lay-out of the Dionysian theatre *en limnais* ('in the swamps', a spot on the outskirts of Athens) in which the comedy competi-

tions were held. An unbroken flight of straight steps rose up facing the stage on the side opposite to that occupied by the pit, which was oblong. The chorus was constrained, in this setting, to open and close its ranks in front of the leading actors, to stand facing them in a line parallel with the stage, or to take up a position along the sides of the pit, occupying it completely from time to time. The chorus did not take part in the other actors' activities, but overwhelmed them as their own rhythmic movements grew in range and power.

Throughout the play it was usually the task of the chorus to evoke a feeling of the dramatic and fantastic. Sometimes, as in the *Frogs* and the *Birds*, this atmosphere also pervaded the text and underpinned the entire meaning of the play and its performance.

We can get an idea of this from a series of black-figured vases. The figures certainly refer to comic

acting, but before Aristophanes' day. On one of the vases, kept in Berlin, we can see a male chorus masked as cocks and enveloped in large cloaks over their heavy, thick-set limbs. They are moving forwards very slowly and with mock solemnity behind a strutting flautist. The cock-chorus is depicted as stationary, to be precise, but it is obvious that one moment of rest followed each step of the processional advance. We know from written sources that the members of a comic chorus took off their cloaks before dancing. This makes it very likely that these imposing figures, grouped together to form an inhibited and static mass, were suddenly unleashed and became light and full of movement as their initially slow-paced, comic solemnity was replaced by the confusion of a carefree chase round the sides of the pit. Such is, at any rate, the picture suggested by another lovely vase showing human figures with wings sewn onto their arms. This, of course, reminds us at once of Aristophanes' chorus of birds.

From a dramatic standpoint the chorus shared the nature of both man and beast and the actions of the main characters were inserted into and did not interrupt this dialectic. Their acting was caricature to a far larger extent than the text shows when taken by itself. Mimicry was intense and life-like, though not necessarily exaggerated or grotesque. The actors' costumes indicate this even more than their masks. Their stomachs and bottoms were padded out and enlarged, often with a phallic symbol as big as an elephant's trunk hanging between their legs. The grotesque element became dominant only in the bad characters, the targets of the author's politicial and cultural onslaught. On the other hand, the gestures and movements of comic actors gave sculptors plenty of scope for their impulse to put on permanent record the characteristic attitudes of ordinary people at their most spontaneous, although, of course, without

Dionysus watches an acrobat practising. Vase. Lipari, Museo
Eoliano

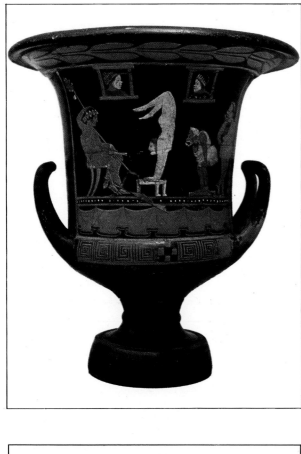

An old woman accusing a thief of having killed her goose. Phlyax
Vase no 24.97.104. New York, Metropolitan Museum of Art,
Fletcher Fund, 1924

Chiron being pushed up the stairs. Vase. London, British Museum.
These three vases belong to a large group of ceramics dating from
the end of the 5th century BC, painted with scenes from the phlyax
farces. Their abundance is evidence of the enormous popularity
of this sort of play

Middle Comedy characters. Greek terracotta statuettes. From left to right: nos 13.225.13, 18, 19, 24, 27 and 28. New York, Metropolitan Museum of Art, Rogers Fund, 1913. The second statuette from the right represents Herakles, while the third probably shows a parasite

laying any claim to factual accuracy.

Numerous statuettes representing characters in Old and Middle Comedy bear this out. Some of them remind us of Aristophanes' own unforgettable characters. Thus one cannot fail to see in the happy drunken couple in the Berlin Museum a memento of Dicaeopolis, the main character in the *Acharnians*. Despite all the soldiers and war-mongers, he celebrated his own private peace and sang the praises of the pleasures of life. Admittedly this reference is not as exact as that to *Ecclesiazousai* ('Women in the Assembly') in the extraordinary old couple exchanging juicy titbits of gossip. However, this does not detract from the value of these sculptures as evidence of the typical attitudes and mimicry of comic actors.

It is also necessary to add that ordinary men, and not imaginary or allegorical personages, make up the chorus in the majority of extant comedies (*Lysistrata*, *Acharnians*, etc.). This means that the actors' style of speaking and gesturing is adopted by the chorus. The unity between chorus and actors is reinforced. This happens the other way round in the frankly allegorical texts, such as the *Frogs* and the *Birds*. Here mechanical devices are often used to bring out the parody behind the plot.

The theatrical significance of the Old Comedy becomes clearer, if one also considers the themes and structure of the *phlyax* or Italic farce. This enjoyed tremendous popularity, possibly even in Greece itself, as is evidenced by the large number of vase-paintings referring to it.

The *phlyax* farces were performed either on a very small wooden stage set up in the orchestral pit of a theatre or, alternatively, in a public square. The rear of the stage was sometimes closed in by a small framework of light material which provided a backdrop. A curtain or painted cloth sometimes took the place of this. The stage rested on small pillars and there were hangings between these. Access to the pit itself, or to the square, was always by a small stairway. Thus the action could move continually between the pit and the stage and this compensated for the severe restrictions of movement on the stage itself. Theatre of this kind was at its height in the second half of the fourth century BC; by that time the *skene* of the tragic theatre may have come to be used as a raised stage and have been built in stone.

Similarity of theme links the *phlyax* farce with the *hilarotragodia* or tragic parody. It was, in fact, a mythological parody in which gods and heroes were ruthlessly ridiculed, although topics connected with the citizens' daily lives were also explored. Caricature here attained its most grotesque form. It only took three actors to fill the entire stage. Their features and general physical appearance were scarcely recognisable as human. Their acting was very much restricted in terms of space, but their gestures by contrast were emphatic and enlarged. Only at rare intervals did they settle down into stylised dance movements. Even the stage-props were designed to increase the sense of caricature and the grotesque—great Zeus himself appeared in one of these plays with very short legs and was made to sit on a throne much too high for him, like a baby in a high-backed chair.

The action knew no respite, save perhaps a short pause to underline one particular gesture as even wilder than the others. This seemingly uncontrolled explosion on the stage of man's animal energy makes the *phlyax* farces the most violent dramatic form known to antiquity.

The Middle Comedy probably coincided with a decrease in the importance of the chorus and an increasing concentration on the dramatic actor. As political and private polemics receded into the background, the actor became less of a caricature, until with the New Comedy he preserved no more than a slight twist of kindly irony.

The New Comedy centres on ordinary city-life: the escapades of hot-headed youngsters and money-grubbing fathers, happy endings and a ceaseless ringing-of-changes on an inexhaustible plot. Menander (343–291) was the principal representative of this school. Despite the popularity of his work, we have no more than two almost complete plays (*Dyskolos* and *Samia*), substantial portions of five others and large numbers of shorter fragments. Nevertheless, when Rome came into contact with the Greek way of life, it was the New Comedy which was in fashion. It therefore became the prototype of 'comedy' in the theatre of the Western world.

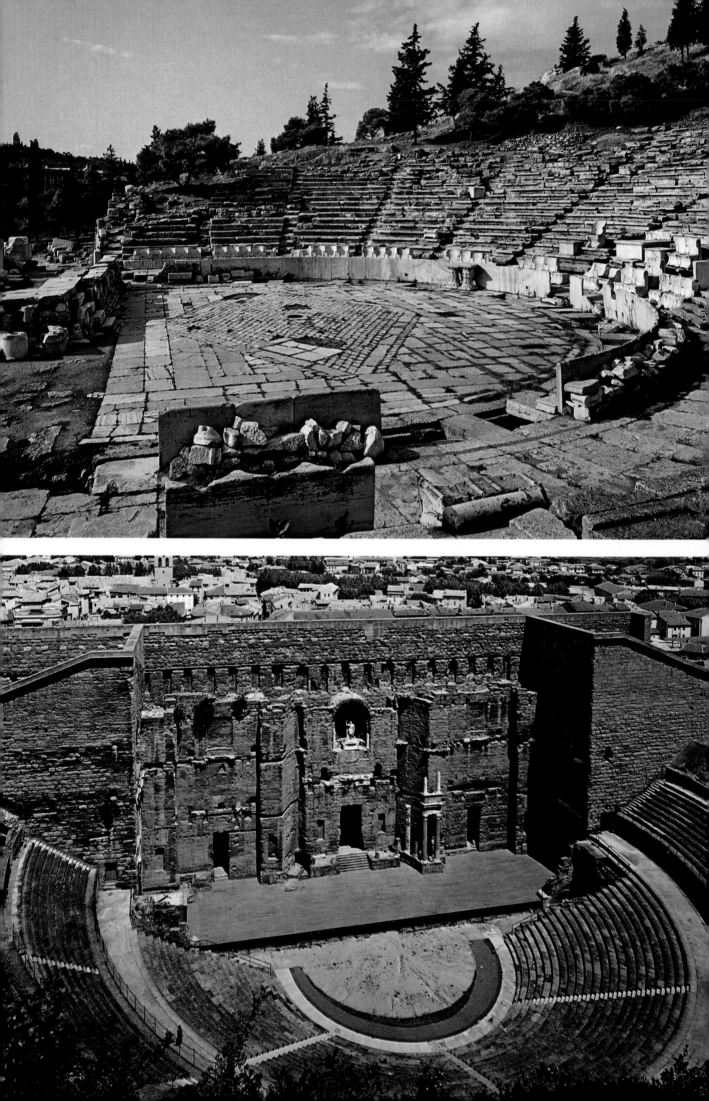

Chapter 5

THE ARCHITECTURE OF HELLENISTIC AND ROMAN THEATRES

A brief recapitulation of the main architectural features of the ancient theatre may help at this point. They were the pit, *cavea*, *skene* and *parodoi*. The central nucleus of the theatre was the pit, which began as a rather shapeless or roughly oblong plot of land, but had become by the end of the fifth century a circle marked out by a small stone perimeter, as can be seen in the theatre of Epidauros, the only one that has kept its original Greek form. The Greek word for pit is linked with the idea of dancing, and means 'place where dances are held'. As we have seen, however, the entire dramatic action was probably enacted in it in classical times. The *cavea* is a later Roman term for the range of steps provided to accomodate the spectators. It would be a mistake to regard the Greek word *skene* as strictly equivalent to our term 'stage'. In the Greek theatre this was a dressing-room for the actors, originally a mere hut, and it soon found an additional use as a backdrop for the dramatic action. The Romans called this backdrop the *scaenae frons*. Finally, the *parodoi* were ramps leading from outside the theatre into the pit. The same word, *parodos*, also referred to the entrance hymn of the chorus.

The architectural history of the ancient theatre reduces in practice to an account of the meaning, function and mutual relations of these four central features. Their relationship, in fact, was increasingly organic, but it took until the period of the Empire to arrive at perfect architectural integration.

In the beginning the *skene* was actually set at a distance from the pit in which the play was performed, but it is known for certain that before the middle of the fifth century it was providing the backdrop for the drama. The *cavea* may have been oblong at first, but because of the circular form of the pit, it very soon was arranged along the arc of a circle. The Greeks always took advantage of a natural slope to construct their theatres, both in the case of wooden tiers of steps and, from the fourth century onwards, of constructions in stone. The lines of the steps were set into the rising ground, and the pit was an open space at the bottom of the hill. This organic bond between the building and the surrounding landscape was simple and immediately striking to the eye.

The *skene* was also built in stone during the Hellenistic age. The façade was probably a sort of portico. *Pinakes*, or paintings placed between the columns, would serve to situate the dramatic action. There are various stories about these scene-paintings going back to the time of Aeschylus and it is hard to know what to make of them. Then, in classical times, the roof of the *skene* was used for divine apparitions and for any scenes that had to be seen as taking place on a higher plane. Later on, as dramatic festivals degenerated into model performances of existing classical works, the interest of the audience focussed on the actors. Accordingly, they started to perform on top of the *skene*, or, more precisely, on a new

Above: Athens: the Greek Theatre of Dionysus. The part shown dates from the middle of the fourth century. *Below*: Orange: general view of the Roman theatre with the *cavea* and the *scaenae frons*

57

Sabratha (Libya). Roman theatre built in the Imperial age. The *scaenae frons* has three rows of columns

feature, the *proscenium*, corresponding to the modern stage, so that the pit remained free for the chorus, whose rôle had dropped into the background. In this way the former *skene* became a two-storey construction, the façade supporting the *proscenium* offering a background for the choral performance, while the façade with painted scenes served as a backdrop for the dramatic action proper.

This is no more than the best available hypothesis. The only definite fact is that throughout the Hellenistic age, in other words from the third century BC onwards, the enlarged *skene* was a two-storey portico, and that large paintings were placed between the various columns. More often than not the lateral extensions of the classical *skene*, the *paraskenia*, are not found in these constructions.

The *cavea*, formed as a rule of more than two hundred steps ranged round a circular pit, tended to assume the shape of a horse's hoof and the pit itself was no longer precisely circular. In the Hellenistic age the chorus no longer could be said to act, but merely performed a few movements in unison.

Finally, the *parodoi*, which formerly served as entrance for both chorus and spectators, were increasingly used by the latter. They were levelled out and closed off by upright railings to either side, running from the extremities of the *cavea* to the enlarged *skene*.

Livy the historian (59 BC–AD 17) tells us that in Rome during the Republic the audience had to stand up in the theatre. However, his statement conflicts with certain indications in the comedies of Plautus (254–184 BC) and Terence (190–159 BC). The spectators were definitely seated on wooden steps in front of a stage which was probably no different than the one used for the *phlyax* farce. In any case, the structures were afterwards dismantled when the festival was over.

The first permanent theatre in Rome was of stone and was built by Pompey in 55 BC. It was the only theatre there for many years, being referred to quite simply as '*the* theatre'. Then came a second, that of Balbus, in 13 BC, and a few years later a third, the theatre of Marcellus. This is the only one of which very much remains.

A large number of entirely new theatres were built in the Imperial age throughout the Roman provinces from Gaul to Mauretania and existing Greek theatres in Greece, Asia Minor and southern Italy were adapted to the needs and tastes of the Romans.

What, then, are the main points of difference between the Greek and Roman theatres? An outstanding one is architectural—the Romans very seldom used the slope of a hill to take the rising steps of the *cavea*, but usually supported them above ground on a series of arcades, arranged one above the other. The lower arcade provided the entrance to the inside of the theatre, from which stairways took one to the very top of the *cavea*.

The internal features remained the same as in the Greek theatre, but their function and mutual relations were markedly different. The pit was halved and reduced to a semi-circle. The *cavea* naturally became semi-circular as well. The pit was no longer used by the chorus, which hardly ever featured in Roman theatre, but became a seating-area for dignitaries. Because the important people were in the pit, and a high *skene* would have spoiled their view, this was reduced to one yard in height, while in Hellenistic theatre its height was ten feet and more. One architectural feature that increased in importance during the Imperial age was the *scaenae frons*, the façade corresponding to the extended *skene* of the old Greek theatre. This was a series of colonnades, as many as four being set one above the other, with rich polychrome marble columns and pilasters framing decorative statues and paintings. It all reflected the Roman authorities' desire to make a big impression. For all its architectural grandeur, from a theatrical point of view the façade meant everything and nothing. 'The scene today represents Athens' or 'Today it represents Tarentum' we often read in prologues to comedies. The only functional thing about it was the three doors the actors used for their entrance and which might represent the homes of the main characters. The central door, which had always been particularly elaborate and impressive, was styled 'regal'. It was set in a huge doorway and opened inwards. It may be regarded as the focal point of the entire theatre. The two side-doors, the *hospitalia*, opened onto recesses let into the wall behind. From the sides of these, tunnels, known as *versurae*, allowed characters 'from the city' or 'from the port' to make their entrance, in keeping with a convention dating right back to the actual lay-out of the Theatre of Dionysus in Athens.

Originally the *scaenae frons* represented, both in function and design, the façade of a royal palace, this being the preferred setting for the action in most Greek tragedies and their Roman adaptations. Tragedy, however, was less commonly played in Roman theatres than comedy and farce, with the result that the original function was lost to sight and other features came to characterise its design.

It is hard to be definite about the rôle of painting in this connection. Vitruvius, an architect in the time of Augustus who made a detailed comparison of Greek and Roman theatre-buildings, mentions three sorts of painted scenery—tragic, comic and pastoral. As likely as not they were set between the various columns for purely ornamental reasons. Yet why should Vitruvius have given them so much attention? We cannot refer to a single figurative work that sheds light on this question, save in a negative sense. None of them shows these paintings at all.

In a way, the function of the Greek *parodoi* was shared by the *versurae* and the *vomitoria*, the vaulted passages through which the spectators made their way in and out of the theatre. These linked the stage-complex to the *cavea*, and unified the different architectural elements in space.

The provision of a large canopy to cover the whole theatre must have reinforced the feeling that it was a single, organic whole. The canopy extended from the small roof over the stage (erected mainly for reasons of acoustics) as far as the gallery round the top of the *cavea*, and was a fitting crown for the whole building.

Thus, there are many profound differences between the final Hellenic form of Greek theatre and the Roman theatre. However, it remains an inescapable fact that the Roman theatre was never a home-product, and never the normal meeting-place for the entire population. It was the skilful re-elaboration of a foreign culture, a place to wonder at, representing more a discriminating choice, than the fulfilment of strictly dramatic or theatrical requirements. In any case, it was a choice dictated by authority, to which all were required to adapt themselves, and did adapt themselves at the price of betraying their own nature. This is the explanation and the meaning of Roman theatre.

Chapter 6

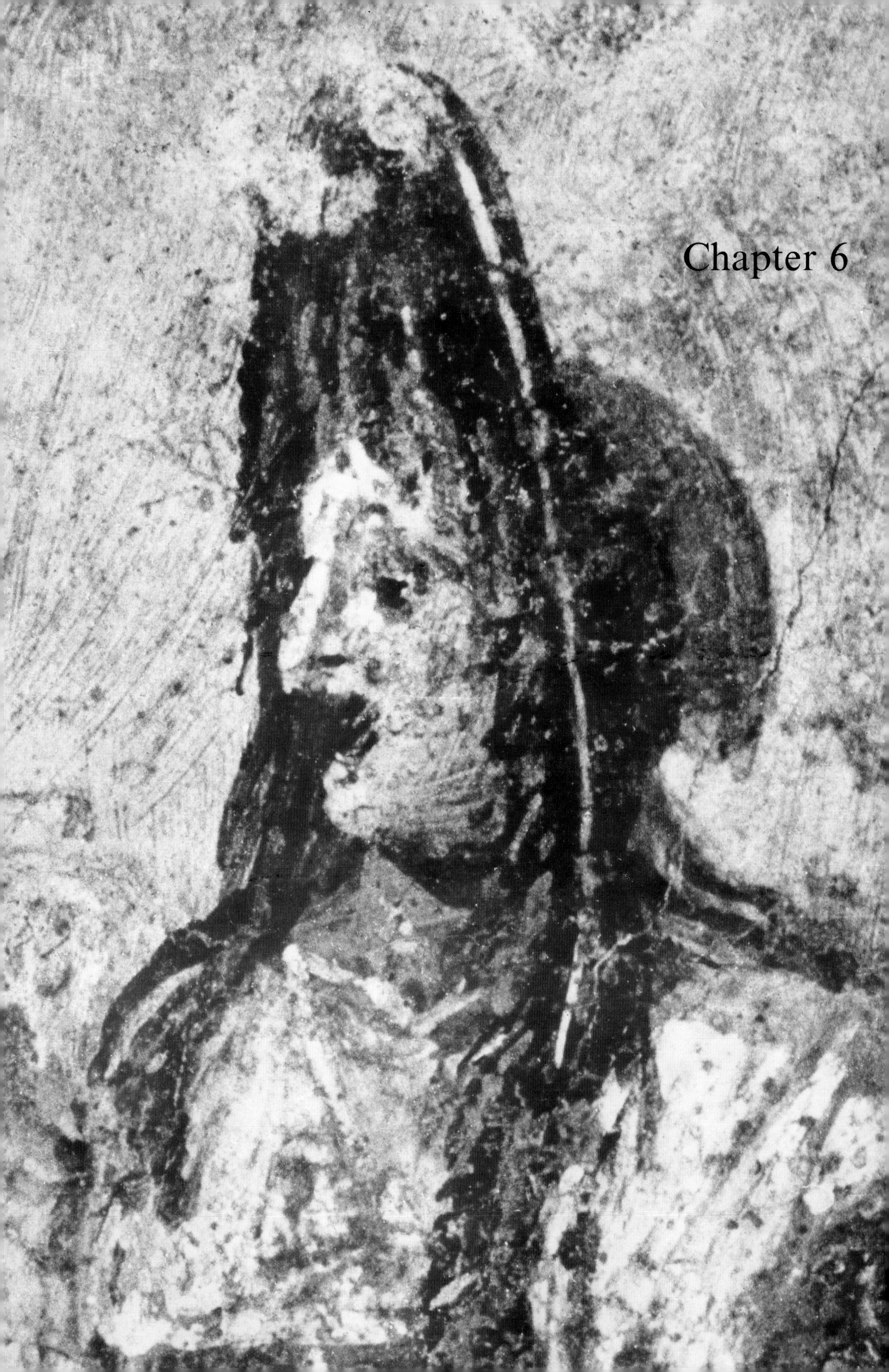

Scene from a tragedy. Wall-painting from the House of the Dioscuri in Pompeii. Naples, Museo Nazionale

ROMAN THEATRE

Today many would admit that the *Hecyra* is Terence's best play. He himself told the story, which is well-known by now, of how when it was being performed, the audience deserted the theatre twice—once to watch an acrobat, the second time to attend a gladiatorial show. This anecdote has invariably been interpreted as clear proof of the Roman audience's lack of cultural involvement. They preferred sporting events to the polished dialogues of the poet beloved of Scipio. This can hardly be denied, but there is also another point to the story, or rather, an alternative explanation

Like his predecessors Plautus and, in the tragic genre, Livius Andronicus, Terence was in the habit of constructing his comedies by borrowing from Greek models his plot, his characters and even his style and the details of his composition. A young man would be thwarted in his love by the prejudices of an ageing father or some similar set-back, which would be overcome thanks to the diplomacy of his servant, or because the real parentage of his girl-friend became known and acknowledged. Thus his main characters were young men in love, girls who had been raped, prostitutes, pimps, parasites and old men who were wise, or stern, or even more debauched than their offspring. His models were not the comedies of Aristophanes, but the romantic sketches of town-life composed by Menander. With very few exceptions, we find the same attitude to tragedy in Livius Andronicus and all Latin tragedians up to Seneca. They generally reworked themes already dealt with by the great tragic poets of Greece—the story of Thyestes, Phaedra's love for her stepson Hippolytus, Medea murdering her own children to avenge her husband's infidelity.

Obviously, this does not detract from the artistic and literary originality of the Roman authors, Plautus in particular, and neither does it take away from the high quality of the theatrical performances in Rome, which introduced radical changes into the Greek approach to stage-production, but it does serve to underline the difference in both meaning and function of the Roman theatre.

When the people of Athens went along to see a tragedy, they were taking part in the reconstruction and in the renewed interpretation of mythical and historical events that formed the essential nucleus of their cultural heritage. In the fifth century the theatre was an important, and probably the most important means of fostering, developing and preserving this native culture which was shared by the entire population. The situation in Rome was, in a sense, the direct opposite. Theatre became a means of dissecting and assimilating what was in reality a culture foreign to their own traditions, in order to adapt these latter to new social and political requirements. Naturally, only a restricted public was able to live through the incubation period of such an assimilation. The greater part of the population was simply offered a result it was quite incapable of either accepting or rejecting. Rome became the birthplace of classicism, the cult of constantly referring to a

63

supposedly ideal, ancient and foreign legacy of thoughts, images and frames of reference, knowledge of which was limited to a very restricted class of people. The logical consequence was a clear-cut break between one culture for the privileged classes, which they were then able to set before the people at large who had had no part in its elaboration, and another culture of the masses. At times this was a by-product of the first, in which case it was a mere caricature of a culture for the people, but at other times developing its own themes, despite its always being considered vulgar, inferior and alien to the very idea of culture. It was only spasmodically, when

the official product was at its lowest ebb, that this second culture rose vigorously on the rebound and staked its claim as an alternative. Unfortunately it lacked any basis in an effective transformation of social institutions and remained merely a passing episode of no consequence.

Roman theatre offers perhaps the first and certainly the clearest example of this sort of situation which has been repeated right up to our own times and is the besetting fault of Western culture.

Élitist literary works could address themselves exclusively to their particular readership, but theatre was obliged to a certain extent to take a much wider

Scene from a comedy. Wall-painting from the House of Casca Longus, Pompeii. In Roman comedy the acting of the main characters was often stylised and rather sad. Only the servant displayed any liveliness of expression and his mimicry was trenchant and vulgar

audience into account. Two roads lay open to curry its favour. The way chosen by Plautus was that of inserting themes and motifs drawn from the people's own culture into a neo-hellenic context. He became notorious for his *italum acetum*, spicing his characters with bitingly satirical overtones and using the different metres of popular songs. The other way was that of selecting topics and talking-points which seemed naturally likely to arouse surprise or some other superficial response. The Roman stage seems to have been built with tragedy principally in mind, yet this was the genre that found least favour. The works of Livius Andronicus, Naevius and Accius,

who wrote during the Republic (third to first centuries BC), have been lost without trace, and after their efforts we hear of very few other examples of the genre until the reign of Nero when, in about 50 AD, Seneca in his own dark and violent dramatic work began to re-work the classical themes of Greek tragedy.

Right from the time of the Republic the tragic mask based on Hellenistic models must have been quite large. The hair was normally very thick and arranged in curls which fell down over the brow and temples and framed the face. This made the mask appear even larger, and the impression it created was

one of affluence and splendour. The gaping mouth and the round eye-holes lent to the glazed features a look of shocked grief, and the effect created by the immobility of such a countenance on a scale larger than life must have been rather hypnotic. Nor was it only the face that was made disproportionately large. The Romans were not satisfied to leave the *cothurni* of the Greeks as richly ornamented boots, but turned them into the chief means of increasing the stature of the characters, so that they seemed to transcend the limits of humanity in royalty and majesty. It is not hard to picture these demi-gods exhibiting themselves to an astonished audience and strutting up and down the stage in the theatres of the Augustan age. A continuous pedestal supported the three door-ways and the colonnade of the *scaenae frons*, with the result that an actor had to come down a few steps to reach the stage. We can be certain, then, that the principal characters on coming on through the regal entrance would make a deliberate pause on the threshold, making of the whole vast colonnade no

more than a fitting niche for their own greatness. Then their slow, solemn movements and gestures, once they had come down onto the stage, were accompanied by outbursts of grief or anger in keeping with their rôle.

With the passage of time, this could not help but prove tedious. The façade of grandeur wore thin and the leading-actor's majesty aroused only fear. The striking quality of the central personage increased imperceptibly but relentlessly, and toppled over into mere horror. The displays of anger and grief passed the bounds of decorum, and in such ungainly creatures their expression was terrifying, unrestrained and dismal. Seneca had already transferred to the stage itself the violent episodes of murder and suicide which Greek tragedy had left to a messenger simply to describe in words. After his time stage-production occupied itself increasingly with an even bloodier rendering of events, so as to satisfy a taste for the macabre. The characters were sinister and perverted from the moment they came on stage and

Scene from a tragedy, possibly the *Medea*. Painted terracotta relief. Rome, Museo Nazionale

their appearance was almost grotesque. People either laughed at them, or felt disgusted. Lucian has left us this account of his revulsion with the tragic actors of the later Empire: 'When a man is decked out in such a way that his measurements change beyond all proportion, and when he is perched on tall clogs and given a mask that rises well above his head, with the mouth gaping open in an enormous yawn as if he wanted to devour his audience, the very sight of him is disgusting and alarming—and this without mentioning the padding-out of his chest and stomach to equip himself with the false and unnatural semblance of a body.'

Tragedy, once the perfect and best-loved form of drama, thus became a shoddy pastime for an ignorant and simple people, still capable in the provinces of fainting with fear in the presence of such horrible puppets. Meanwhile, the aristocracy was providing itself with another sort of theatrical entertainment. This was the pantomime, which preserved the themes and frequently even the text of tragedy, but

Actor in farce or mime. Bronze statuette no 12.229.6, New York, Metropolitan Museum of Art, Rogers Fund, 1912. In farce and particularly in mime the trend of caricature was towards a grotesque realism, not towards a standard type, as it was in the Atellan

Theatre-tickets in stone and carved ivory. Paris, Bibliothèque Nationale

excluded all the decadent features which had crept into its production. A chorus or a soloist would sing the finest passages from some well-known tragedy, while a single actor wearing a triple mask played all the principal parts, expressing their changing feelings by the vivid and astonishingly varied way in which he used his hands. Attention no longer focussed on the text, nor even on the artistic form, if by that is meant the plastic representation of an imaginary world. The virtuoso performer had to know how to make himself understood. He had, quite literally, to translate a verbal language into a sign-language. This was the important thing.

The story of comedy is less eventful. The tale of Terence's bad luck is perhaps proof enough that the public was never over-enthusiastic about comedy. On the other hand, it never got bored. The recipe was always the same—a love-story complicated by the use of disguises, mistaken identities, recognition scenes, and servants adroitly outwitting old men and pimps and spinning a web of intrigue to further their masters' interests. Yet it always seemed different. This was why, both as a literary genre and from the point of view of its stage-performance, comedy never really changed throughout the whole, long course of Roman history.

Masks, wigs and costumes were designed to create an impression devoid of personality, but somehow typical of the different characters. The facial expression, the colour of the skin, the set and tint of the hair, the beard and the style of dress all immediately indicated to the audience whether the character on stage was a servant, a pimp, a father or a hanger-on. The young man who was, at least nominally, the central character of the drama, since the action revolved round the satisfying of his desires, usually wore a delicately moulded mask, with a touch of sadness about it, and quite without any attempt at

Negro acrobat. Clay statuette. Berlin, Pergamonmuseum

Mime. Bronze statuette. Princeton University, The Art Museum. This figure from the later Imperial Age already begins to resemble a medieval jongleur

comic distortion. The same held true for the young girls. However, the characters of the two personalities between whom the real clash was taking place, the old man and the servant, were heavily emphasised. The servant had a mouth like a large funnel, through which the actor's face was showing, and the broad grin on the mask was partly sarcastic, partly terrified. The old man's facial expression was rather similar, and he was distinguished by his carefully groomed wig and his white beard. The range of gestures used by the servant seemed inexhaustible, but they were all typically timorous and sly. In fact, a later generation found it necessary to do away with the unvarying ambiguity of his mask, and replace it by one with two different expressions, depending on the side one was looking at. The servant's comic stooge was the parasite. He wore a red wig, which was always untidy, and the expression on his mask showed that he was permanently hungry. The part assigned to the parasite was made much of in the Imperial age, because of the scope for mirth created by his ceaseless endeavours to get himself invited to a dinner. Eventually his mask became the picture of an almost bestial greed.

By contrast with such erudite productions of works from the Greek, there were altogether three main forms of theatrical entertainment for the people: the Atellan, the Fescennine and the mime. The first two were of popular Italian origin, and so closer to the local customs of Rome. The Atellan was a rustic farce, in which the masked figures represented always the same characters, such as Dossenus and Pappus, who passed, seemingly unchanged, through an unending series of minor adventures. There was an élitist vogue for the Atellan in the Imperial age and it became popular with the upper classes. Interest in the Fescennine, a sort of dramatic satire, was of rather brief duration,

Comic scene. Terracotta relief. Naples, Museo Nazionale. A classic example of the acting in the New Comedy and in Roman comedy. The gestures of the young man in love are stylized, sweeping and rather sad. Those of the old man and the servant are brusque and comic

because of its political overtones and the tendency to make a butt of particular individuals.

The mime was originally Greek and flourished mainly in the Hellenic colonies of southern Italy. A few talented poets, such as Herondas and Epicharmus, cultivated the genre. The Roman version was connected with the Greek original by name and by a common underlying structure, but its contents were quite different in substance and, in reality, always changing. It was characteristic of the mime to develop themes taken from everyday, low-class town-life. Its use of actors, who played their parts with their own faces showing and without using any masks at all, was unique in the annals of ancient theatre. It was on this footing that the mime became the Roman people's favourite form of theatre. The mass of the audience could see itself reflected in the everyday characters. The unmasked actor showed the Romans their own aptitude for representational realism, their own taste for sharp and subtle imitative gestures. The limits could be pushed back towards the boundaries of caricature and the grotesque without taking away from the sense of realism, precisely because it was becoming increasingly hard to know how much belonged to the actor and how much to the character he was representing. After a short run of well written mimes, the meagre plot of this sort of theatre ended up as the mere setting for a string of snappy, comic interludes, and these often concealed an undercurrent of political poison. Eventually the mime probably became a variety-show, with coarse songs, dances and strip-tease. However, the character of the actor always dominated the scene, to such an extent that the words 'mime' and 'actor' seemed synonymous.

Probably when the rot set in, mime was the only form of entertainment to retain any life of its own. It, too, became corrupt and distorted, but it enshrined, if not the culture, at least the taste of the Roman people. Western history may seem to carry some ineradicable imprint given it by that people: that, however, was exclusively the doing of the Senate.

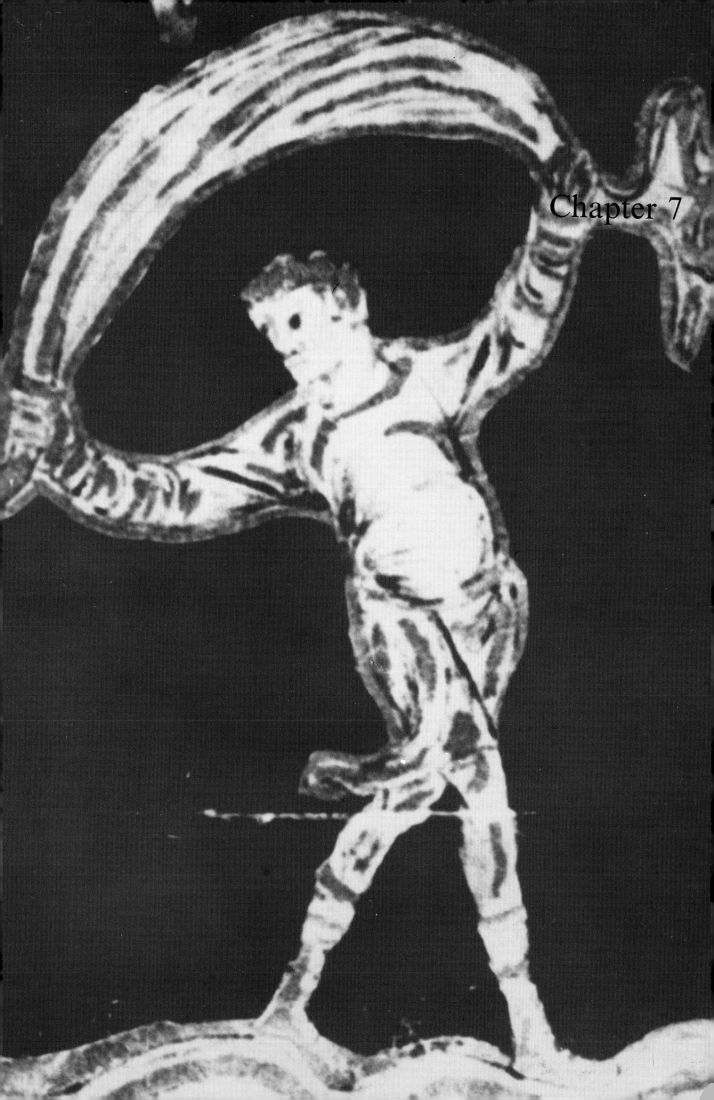

Chapter 7

EVERYDAY THEATRE IN THE MIDDLE AGES: MIMES AND MINSTRELS

One consequence of the fall of the Roman Empire and the barbarian invasions was a withering away of civilized life. Those forms of theatre which were technically the more elaborate and socially the most impressive also disappeared, but theatre did at least survive as a means of self-expression.

It is true that in the High Middle Ages the stage-production of works of literary merit was quite unknown, but the net result of this was merely to get rid of the dross from that complex phenomenon called theatre and to purify those elements which survived. The reading and copying of masterpieces of dramatic literature continued. They were still the theme of graphic illustrations and were even produced privately to some extent. On the other hand, opportunities for mime and other forms of theatre were never lacking.

The last reference to a genuine stage-production in Western Europe takes us back to AD 467. From that time on, for almost a thousand years, it becomes impossible to speak of everyday theatre except in a very vague way. We can do no more than delineate the main activities of the mummers who inherited the theatrical traditions of the late Empire, the jongleurs, as they were called in the 9th century, or minstrels.

The changing nomenclature only partially reflects a development of their rôle. No precise feature can be said to distinguish the jongleurs from the mummers. They were all ballad-singers, acrobats, conjurers, mountebanks and mimics in the modern sense of the word. 'Mummer' reminds us of a classic link with the activities of the professional entertainers in the Roman theatres of late antiquity, while 'jongleur' is a readily understood and more precise term, corresponding to the Latin *joculator* (he who plays). The idea of playing is at the root of many modern German, French and English theatrical terms and derivatives: *Spiel, Spieler, jeu, jouer,* 'play'. 'Minstrel' is a later, 12th century term, deriving from *minister,* which means 'man-servant' or 'official'. The expression referred originally to those jongleurs who worked regularly for some particular lord. Since their main function was to enliven the company at table with their singing, it was easy to regard them as musicians. In fact, as we shall see, it was precisely as musicians that they shared in the production of the later mystery-plays.

Our information about the activities of mummers and jongleurs derives mainly from the numerous condemnations pronounced against them by bishops and councils, following the example of the Fathers of the Church—Augustine, Tertullian, Jerome. These inaugurated the war that the Church waged for centuries against the theatre. The fight was still on in the 18th century, and its meaning is obvious from the start if we call to mind that Christianity originally attempted a cultural revolution by rejecting classical culture *en bloc*. It was in the theatre that this culture found its most worldly and diabolical expression. Among the condemnations may be mentioned those of Alcuin (*c* 791), the Council of Tours (813), Bishop Agobard (836), and the Synod of Eichstätt

'Charivaris'. Miniature in the *Roman de Fauvel*. Paris, Bibliothèque Nationale, ms 146, ff 36ᵇ and 34ᵃ. The contortions and grotesque or animal masks give some idea of the atmosphere of popular entertainment in the Middle Ages. Its essential ingredients were disguise, mimicry, dancing and rather cruel jokes. Jongleurs and buffoons were involved, but were not the centre of attention. The 'charivaris' or boisterous party-pieces to serenade sleeping widows were particularly notable among these popular pastimes

Musician. 11th century miniature from the *Tropaire de Saint Martial* (of Limoges). Paris, Bibliothèque Nationale, ms lat 1118, f 111

Dancing girl from the same codex: f 114. On the right—Flautist and young juggler: f 112. The jongleurs cultivated all aspects of showmanship: mime, song, dance, etc. The women *jongleresses* found that their audience liked them to 'specialise' in dancing

Minstrel and girl playing for a lord. 13th to 14th century miniature from the *Cancioneiro da Ajuda*, Ajuda Library.

(1435). They were not all equally decisive or all-embracing. Indeed, Thomas de Chabham in his condemnation (about 1300) distinguished between good and bad jongleurs, referring to them by a classical appelation, *histriones*. In this way the Bishop of Salisbury made it possible for us to bring their activities and capabilities to light. He put them into three categories. Some jongleurs change the shape and appearance of their bodies, gesticulate and leap about in a disgraceful fashion, go nude or wear terrifying masks. Others travel in the retinue of noblemen and tell wicked and shameful stories about people who are not there—these are the *scurrae vagi*. The *joculatores*, finally, sing to enliven the company at table, or celebrate the mighty deeds of noblemen and saints.

These then are the singers. Their repertory must have consisted of epic songs for the most part and it is not hard to suppose that most of their themes were drawn from the cycles of Charlemagne and King

PLAGITE

OFAG

& filio &

Sicut era

nunc & se

seculorum

A de leua

dilexit Dilexisti virtul ou bo

Arthur, especially when they were singing at court or on the occasion of some joust, tournament or other chivalrous festivity. During pilgrimages and on the feasts of patron-saints they would prefer to take subjects from the lives of the saints.

The *scurrae vagi* are real buffoons and in them there is no clear difference between their perform-ance and their ordinary manner of speaking. Their wit is impromptu and they are, perhaps, the satirical journalists of the Middle Ages. They are paid to smear, but often do so spontaneously and upon instinct, sticking their necks out because of their pungently critical spirit. They were probably not without learning and may have been none other than those wandering clerks (*clerici vagantes*) who hymned the pleasures of life, but felt obliged to pry into the affairs of those in high station.

In any case, it is the *histriones* belonging to the first category mentioned by Thomas de Chabham who are of most interest from the point of view of a history of the theatre. These dancers and mummers must have been the spice of every feast, although among the people rather than at court. The folk who had come to the fair would flock round them, while they in all likelihood tried to get an audience together whenever and wherever they could. Their speciality was dancing and miming, rather than singing or telling stories: these *histriones* were mimics first and foremost. Rather like the pygmies, whom we saw to be particularly talented in this direction, the medieval mummers covered their faces with masks to impersonate the lion, the wolf, the bear, the serpent and, of course, the human being. It was at this point that their act became a small play with several characters, but only one actor, as we gather from the Latin epitaph of the 9th century mummer, Vitalione: 'I used to imperson-ate the expressions, gestures and speech of my characters, and it might have been thought that a whole crowd was expressing itself by means of a single mouth [. . .] Thus, this fatal day has snatched away with me all those characters I embodied.'

After having been persecuted and denigrated for centuries, from the 12th century onwards the mum-mers, jongleurs and minstrels sought to defend them-selves as a profession and came together in guilds and corporations, such as the well-known 'Pui d'Arras' and similar fraternities in Paris, London and Chester.

Although the jongleurs mainly played an inde-pendent rôle, there were also instances of small companies, family groups for the most part. Both art and literature refer to the women jongleresses, who also performed. Real drama was, therefore,

Buffoon dancing. 16th century bronze statuette. London. Victoria and Albert Museum

E. Grassner. Buffoon executing a step from the Moresco or Morris-dance. Bronze statuette. Munich, Stadtmuseum

quite feasible. However, this is only a deduction supported, however, by the thought that unless a tradition of farce had been kept alive throughout the Middle Ages, it could never have reappeared so vigorously in *Maître Pathelin*.

During the Middle Ages the taste for mime was not confined to the West and may even have been more widespread in the Eastern part of the Empire. In Byzantium the mime was the focal-point of the shows in the Hippodrome. Short, realistic, light-hearted sketches were performed and, as had already been the case with the Roman pantomime, poems and even classical tragedies were performed in mime as a single actor recited the text. This emphasised even more that separation of gestures from words that the later Middle Ages came to regard as typical of all Latin theatre.

From the 13th century onwards the theatre was to be restored to its proper place in the official life of society. Nor were sacred dramas the only other theatrical shows: first, the farces and *sotties*, acted by companies of merry-makers (*les Enfants de la Basoche, les Sociétés Joyeuses*): then, the miracle plays and *Miracles de Notre Dame* in which the religious element was mimimal, consisting solely of the final, *deus ex machina* intervention of a saint or the Virgin Mary to provide the best possible solution to the dramatic dilemma: there were also the morality plays (*moralités*), in the allegorical vein of the *Roman de la rose*—in these all the characters personified something abstract, Death, Life, Vice, Virtue, etc; finally, other plays (*jeux*) performed many of them by jongleurs, such as the *Courtois d'Arras* and the *Jeu de la Feuillé*.

The famous *Jeu de Robin et de Marion* merits special mention. It takes its themes from country life and possibly exemplifies a breakthrough into literature of some popular, rural culture associated with May-day and the December festival. Such rural celebrations were often dramatic or nearly dramatic in character. At Lucca in Tuscany the 'maggi' or rustic festivities of pagan inspiration are still celebrated each May.

The scenery, stage-props and other apparatus available for all these dramatic productions must, with notable exceptions, have been scarce or non-existent. Of course, the jongleurs certainly had no need of scenery or stage-props.

Chapter 8

LITURGICAL DRAMA

The Christian Church offered spiritual rites of purification of her own as alternatives to wordly-minded shows. At least implicitly, then, in opposing pagan theatre and, indeed, theatre in general, her objectives were never merely negative.

Features reminiscent of theatre abound in Catholic and, indeed, all religious rituals. Besides this, the apex of the Church's liturgy, the Mass, holds quite a dramatic meaning, not merely because the text contains dialogues, but principally because it is a representation in symbols of an event: 'Do this in memory of me.'

Christ's human life and sacrifice is the central mystery in the Christian religion. The fixed part of the Mass derives its strong dramatic flavour from this fact. It is hardly surprising that the variable introductory and concluding parts of the service, which are designed to bring out the meaning of the central rite and make it easier for believers to visualise the event it represents, should also have a markedly dramatic emphasis.

The earliest theatrical embellishments of the ritual, according to most authorities, were the tropes: 'versiculi ante, inter vel post alios ecclesiasticos cantus appositi' (verses preceding, following or interwoven with official Church music). The Roman Office contained some music which was technically hard to sing, antiphonal music being notorious in this respect. To make the work of memorising it somewhat easier, a monk called Tutilo from the monastery of St Gall in Switzerland devised short verses

or tropes, composed in the form of a dialogue, to be sung by alternating choirs of priests or clerks, during pauses which were made in the singing of the office itself. These tropes were taken from or inspired by the Gospels via the Gregorian office. One of the earlier ones, the 'Quem quaeritis?' (Who are you looking for?), creates sustained dialogue from this text of the office: 'Angelus domini locutus est mulieribus dicens: Quem quaeritis? Jam surrexit. Venite et videte.' (The angel of the Lord spoke to the women and said: Who are you looking for? He is already risen. Come and see). Here is the trope:

Interrogatio: Quem quaeritis in Sepulchro, Christicolae?
Responsio: Jesum Nazarenum crucifixum, o Caelicolae.
Interrogatio: Non est hic. Surrexit sicut praedixerat. Ite et nuntiate quia surrexit.

Question: *Who are you looking for in the tomb, you Christians?*
Response: *Jesus of Nazareth who has been crucified, you heavenly beings.*
Question: *He is not here. He has arisen as he promised. Go and proclaim that he has risen indeed.*

Obviously it was no mere two-part song, but one calling for impersonation and a certain amount of acting. Fairly soon the two choirs singing the questions and responses were replaced by three clerics playing the women's part ('*in persona mulierum*') and

Holy Sepulchre in the basilica of Aquileia, Italy. 12th century. This is a reproduction of the Sepulchre in Jerusalem. Like the altar, it was a focus of the action in liturgical dramas

Constance Cathedral, Switzerland. Holy Sepulchre in the chapel of Saint Moritz, *c* 1280. *Below*: detail from the decoration on the sepulchre

a priest representing the angel.

As similar motifs developed, they grew into authentically 'liturgical dramas', so called because of their link with the ritual which they elaborated and of which they formed a part. It was often the same priests who both sang the office and acted in the drama. This might open and conclude with a liturgical procession. The choir making up the immediate audience of the drama, remained in the place it had for the recitation of the office itself and sang a commentary on the scene being enacted, or else took part in it.

The liturgical drama obviously had the same architectural setting as the rite it accompanied and, like it, abstracted from and passed beyond any merely concrete consideration of the possibilities offered by the particular locality, which was treated as just another instance of space as such, without being at all closely defined. All space was seen as vaguely symbolic and both ritual and drama were more often than not content to make use of no more than a part of the space available in the Church—the altar area, perhaps, or the choir-stalls.

The more straightforward sorts of liturgical drama were centred on a single reference-point, often the altar, which would symbolically represent the place of Christ's birth or of his burial, say. Very little attention was paid to the distance the characters had to traverse, or to the place from which they started, the sacristy, as a rule, or choir-stalls.

In most cases, too, the gestures were restricted to liturgical ones, although occasionally they had some symbolic and even theatrical significance, so that the performance became a self-explanatory mime.

Until very recently, we must add, the liturgical drama was operatic in form. The singing, which slowed down the action and movement, sometimes favoured a more sustained use of gesture and sometimes required its temporary suspension.

These remarks are, unfortunately, all very general, but we can provide a few concrete examples, based on particular 'performances'. In ritual, gestures are given as much importance as words, and so the rubrics that accompany a text, the stage-directions so to speak, are often much longer than the text itself. From our point of view, this is an advantage.

One of the most ancient texts, dating from the 11th century, so integrates ritual and performance that it is hard to say which is one and which the other. This is an Easter-day office used in the monastery at Neubourg. The drama it enshrines presupposes the performance of a ritual that is separated from it in time. In the course of the night

Plan of Lucerne market-place, Switzerland, with spots marked out for the 1583 performance of the Mystery of the Passion. Ms 137–138, Donaueschingen Library

Interior of the Basilica of St Zeno, Verona, Italy. 12th century

Christ riding on a donkey. Polychrome wood-carving from the 13th century, Zürich, Schweizerisches Landesmuseum. Both in the mystery-plays and the later liturgical dramas for Palm Sunday, a priest in the character of Christ came into the church sitting on a donkey. In some cases a wood-carving drawn on wheels was used, as is shown here

that ushers Easter in, before the bell rings for matins, the senior priest goes in procession with a small retinue to the altar of repose to remove the body of the crucified Lord from his sepulchre and makes a ritual adoration in the prescribed liturgical form. This, obviously, is pure ritual: a symbolic gesture accompanied by hymns and prayers. Later, however (the rubric says quite specifically: 'when he returns to the sepulchre for the second time'), a drama begins, or rather the rite takes on a dramatic form. The choir splits up into two sections and then sits down to listen to a sort of prologue or narrative: 'When the Sabbath was over, the two Marys brought some spices . . .' After this, two priests from one half of the choir take the parts of the two Marys, impersonating them dramatically and representing them. Although they wear liturgical vestments and do not change into costume, they are 'in persona mulierum'. They make their way into the sepulchre, not the altar of repose this time, but a special small house-like construction, still, by the way, an architectural feature of certain churches, or, alternatively, the crypt. Inside the sepulchre, in other words, out of sight of many of the people and even of the clergy, the central act in the drama takes place—the 'Quem quaeritis'. After this short dialogue, the priests playing the part of the holy women 'turn towards'

The three Marys at the sepulchre. 12th century miniature from the St Gall Liber Responsalis. St Gallen, Stifts Bibliothek, ms 391, f 33

the clergy and narrate what has happened. Clearly, this implies that they have made their way back into the church proper and are in the choir-stalls once more. Another chant begins at this point, and serves to introduce the second act in the drama: Peter and John—in other words, two more priests—repeat the action of the two Marys, but when they return and face the choir once more they show them the winding-sheet, as if the choir were the remaining apostles.

The Office of the Sepulchre used in Narbonne belongs to the same period, but its structure is quite different. The action remains uncomplicated, but utilises much more space and fills the entire chancel from the altar as far down as the pulpit, from which two canons, who impersonate the apostles ('tamquam apostoli'), question the two Marys. The amount of movement involved is quite slight. The Marys 'approach', but presumably do not reach the altar. An angel removes the veil from the altar to represent the rolling-back of the stone from the sepulchre ('in figura sepulchri'), turning to face the two Marys, the clergy and the assembled faithful. The Marys never actually make contact with the apostles, represented by the canons in the pulpit, but speak to each other and to the members of the choir, while all remain in their respective places. The fact that the whole action is static in this way gives added emphasis to the quality of the costumes, which, if not realistic, are strongly symbolic and theatrical. Thus, the angels wear a white alb and cincture, together with a red veil over their face and wings on their shoulders.

The Office of the Sepulchre used in Mont Saint-Michel also includes the 'Do not touch me', and the action is more complete and comprehensive. Although there is no break in continuity, the transition from liturgical chant to drama is clearly marked and unambiguous. As the choir comes to the end of matins, a monk crosses over the choir from his place in the stalls and makes his way back to the sacristy. He 'will be God', and wears liturgical dress, adapted to make his assumed character unmistakably clear—'an alb dyed the colour of blood, a crown, a beard, barefoot and carrying the cross'. In the interval of silence that immediately follows the singing of matins, simply and yet solemnly, the figure in red crosses the wide, empty space, in the half-light of early morning. His return from the sacristy is a symbol both of Christ's resurrection and of His ascension into heaven. Nothing could be less miraculous or more normal. The Marys then act out their part, along the length of the choir-stalls, between the main altar and the altar of repose or sepulchre. Their weeping is symbolised by a downward nodding of their heads. In front of the altar

Christ appears to Mary Magdalen and a concentrated mime follows. Other examples of the treatment of this scene and of Peter and John's race to the empty tomb also called for some use of mime.

The structure of the Office of the Sepulchre was paralleled in dramatic offices for Christmas. These came into use at a later date, since it is the death and resurrection of Christ, rather than his birth, which provide the dogmatic and liturgical focus of the Christian religion. Nevertheless, the faithful from quite early times preferred Christmas and enjoyed it more and the dramatic elaborations of the Christmas ritual were adorned with a variety of intensely theatrical motifs.

In Rouen in the Office of the Shepherds, the angel's heralding of good news from 'on high' was given by a boy high up in the choir to the fifteen monks and canons as they entered the choir in processional order and wound their way through the transepts, where other children sang the *Gloria in excelsis* from a place in the clerestory—'*in voltis ecclesiae*'. In front of the altar there was then enacted a short mime inspired by the *Quem quaeritis*, following which those who had impersonated the shepherds returned, like the three Marys, to their places in choir.

At Rouen there were also two other remarkable instances of this dramatic use of large spaces.

The Epiphany Office of the Star, although it derived its dramatic pattern from that of the '*Quem quaeritis*', was developed into some surprisingly complex theatricals. Three clerics 'dressed in the costumes of kings' made their way towards the high altar from three different directions. It seems likely that this silent journey, similar to that envisaged in the Mont Saint-Michel Resurrection Office, took up the whole transept area. In front of the altar the Magi gave each other the kiss of peace. They then formed a procession and made their way through the side-aisle of the transept to the head of the nave. A circle of candles hanging 'in a star arrangement in front of the crucifix' was then lighted and the Magi pointed to this star with their staffs. The procession then continued on its way to the Lady Chapel, which probably opened off the nave. The liturgical drama, thus, not only moved out of the chancel into a much larger area, but also involved the faithful in the action itself. A definite meaning was, moreover, given to the journeying of the characters (for such they clearly were) from the high altar to the Lady Chapel. It represented that part of their travels between their meeting each other and their arrival in Bethlehem. Similarly, the time taken up in going from the high altar to the Lady Chapel in procession, symbolized the time needed to travel from the place where they had met to Bethlehem.

This seemingly arid and contrived use of symbols was already surprisingly clear and precise in comparison with the earlier tendency to see all spaces and times indifferently and to remain completely vague about them. It contained the essentials of what would be later called 'simultaneous' staging. Anyone interested in the rhythms of history could point out at this stage a transition from a Romanesque to a Gothic way of interpreting events.

There is also a 'Mystery' drama, loosely linked to the liturgy, which takes the entire church for its setting and gives to the different places where the action develops, as well as to the distances between them, the same symbolic or representational meaning. The subject of the drama is no longer linked with the two central mysteries of Christianity, but is the conversion of Saint Paul. The rubrics are crystal-clear: 'A chair is made ready in a suitable place, *as if it were Jerusalem* . . . Two chairs are prepared some distance off, *as if in Damascus*.' The short distance between these simple stage-props represents the long journey that Paul will have to make from Jerusalem to Damascus, during which his conversion will be effected.

Strictly liturgical dramas never had this clear indication of spatial relationships even when their general development was quite complex. The somewhat late (13th century) Orleans *Mystery of the Resurrection* keeps to the language proper to liturgical drama. The narrative may be more sustained and the dramatic action is relatively free from refrains and repetitions, but the 'theatrical space' is still vague and undifferentiated. There is no idea of distance being travelled or of places as such in the progression of the drama, which focuses exclusively on the sepulchre. However, there are other respects in which this text comes closer to everyday theatre, especially in its abrupt and specific direction that the three Marys, in making their way slowly to the sepulchre, must approach it as if they were sad, '*quasi tristes*'. This is mime.

Chapter 9

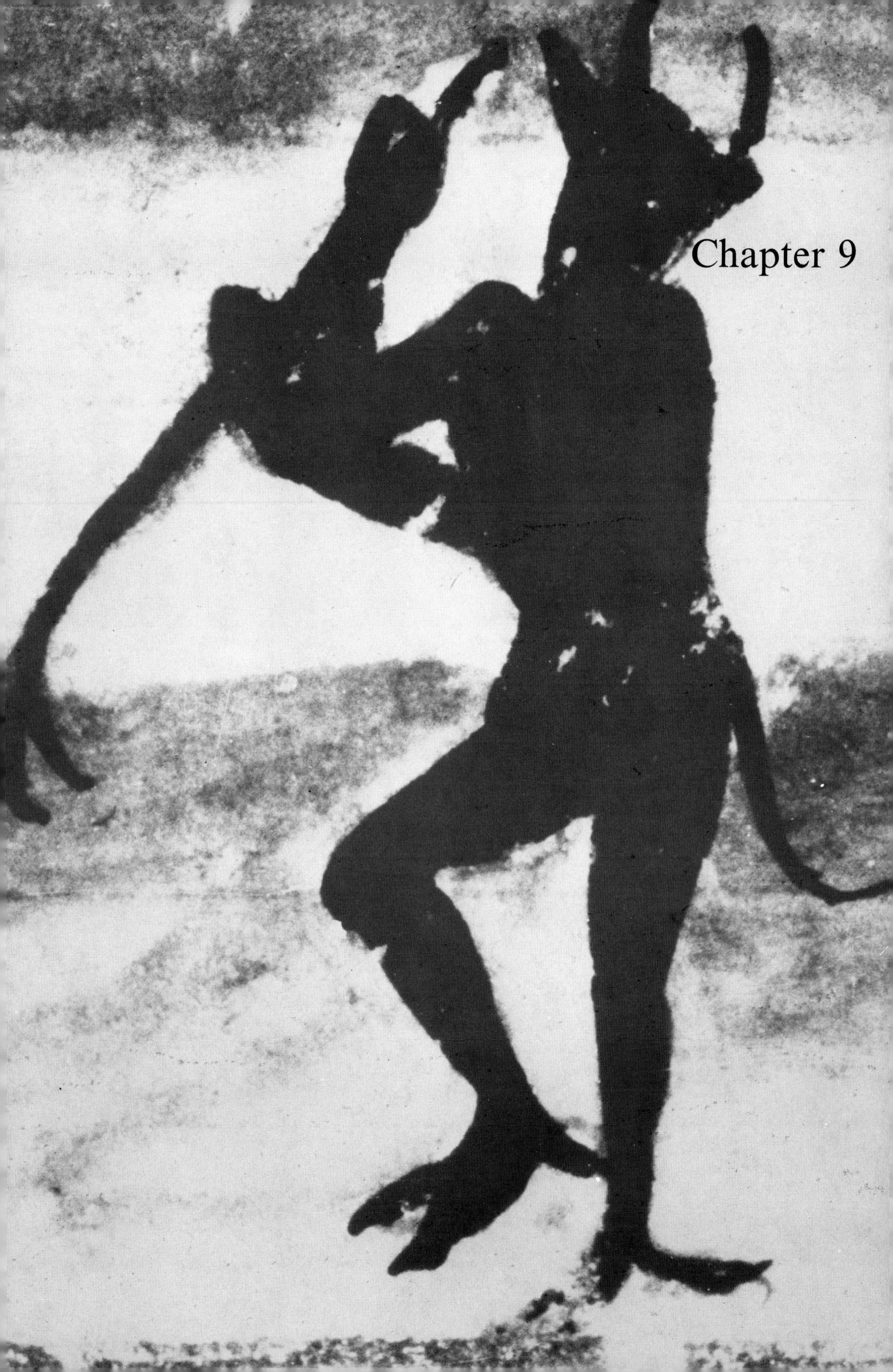

THE MYSTERY-PLAYS: RELIGIOUS THEATRE FOR THE PEOPLE

As the great mass of the people was no longer able to understand Latin, the liturgical dramas, which had grown to an extent that threatened to submerge the very ritual they were designed to interpret, became with the passage of time alien and almost meaningless. The Church found herself forced to choose between the purity of her own tradition, the preservation of which had become the clergy's peculiar duty and privilege, and some recognition of the ordinary believers' cultural requirements as a community. The Catholic church repeated the cultural schizophrenia of Roman antiquity by choosing the first alternative, while at the same time trying to keep control of those other, more popular manifestations which had, of necessity, to be staged away from the church. This may explain why popular religious drama was so short-lived, despite the ordinary man's involvement in its inception and its growth.

The first scriptural dramas, staged away from church-buildings and independent of any liturgical ceremony, were still produced by clerics or priests, so that stage-directions were in Latin. A residual link with the sacred precincts remained in that the stage was set-up in front of the cathedral which might, indeed, be used to symbolize heaven.

An unknown Norman, writing at the end of the 12th century, has left us a typical example of this sort of theatre—the *Jeu d'Adam*. Historians fond of clearly defined epochs in history have for long regarded his work as 'transitional'. The spatial relationships between the various locations are not made clear, but a new element emerges, which was to become basic to the structure of the great 14th and 15th century French mystery-plays. This was the complete representation of the universe, in other words, of earth, together with the heaven and hell that were its limits.

If from a literary standpoint the text exemplifies the Christian realism that is also a characteristic of the Gospels themselves, it represents the realism of townsfolk in opposition to chivalrous or courtly literature and, from the theatrical point of view, it is a fine example of a taste for the life-like expression of deeply moving emotions, not so much in words as by means of mime and gesture. The stage-directions are minutely precise about these and in their description of the stage-settings. There is a fascinating description of a sensuous heaven, flowing with milk and honey, but raised above the level of nature, as is indicated by the device of allowing the characters to be seen only from shoulder-height upwards.

We are familiar with the history of this form of medieval theatre from the fifteenth century onwards. It was very grand, and possibly the most highly developed form of theatre at the time, but its typical production did not spread throughout Western Christendom, and France was definitely the nation that gave it its final shape.

Nevertheless, the mystery-play is Christian theatre first and foremost. It can be summed up as a visual and dramatic presentation of the holy scriptures and

Scenes from Genesis: *above*, the Creation of the Angels, and of the Animals; *below*, the Expulsion of Lucifer, and the Creation of Eve. Miniatures from Gréban's *Mystère de la Passion*, Paris, Bibliothèque Nationale, ms fr 816, f 3

H. Cailleau, 'Le théâtre ou hourdement pour traict, comme il estoit quant fut joué le mistère de la passion.' General lay-out of the stage used for the Valenciennes Passion. The scenes shown in other miniatures and reproduced on the six following pages must be pictured as set in this background. Miniature from the Mystère de la Passion of Valenciennes, Paris, Bibliothèque Nationale, ms fr 12536, f 1ᵇ, 2ᵃ, 2ᵇ. There is another illuminated manuscript of the Valenciennes Passion in the Rothschild collection 1.7.3, Paris, Bibliothèque Nationale

the lives of the saints. For the medieval mind, then, it tended to be a universal history, showing the links in the single chain that was thought to connect all human events together from man's first coming into existence until his destiny found fulfilment in heaven.

This universal history, of course, is nothing other than the dialectic intrinsic to the eternal conflict of good and evil, and it is between these poles, represented by a heaven and hell that were believed to be also the physical limits of the earth, that the action of the play oscillates. Virtues, vices, angels and devils continually bring their energies to bear on and are directly embodied in the events of life on earth. Many of the texts, therefore, run in cycles and so, naturally, did many performances, although it was always possible to take the individual episodes one by one, since each embodied the same metaphysical themes and called in consequence for the same sort of stage-setting. When a major mystery-play required several days to perform, the meaning, arrangement and even the structure of the 'mansions' or 'houses' (the scenes represented in the action) might change, but heaven and hell remained fixed and unaltered, as the unique, eternal reality which alone made any sense of the incessant passage of earthly things.

The simultaneous structure of the scenery is the outstanding characteristic of mystery-play production. A variety of small features representing different places in which the action is to take place are placed next to each other on the same stage. Whether these places are near each other in reality or at a great distance from each other has no bearing on where they are fitted in on the stage. After all, the stage does not represent a particular extent of space within which the different spots are to be found, it is the entire cosmos. Nevertheless, the more or less equal distances used on stage to represent the effective distances between real places were, in the popular imagination, credited with geographical accuracy. The time it took to move from one spot to another was, in a similar way, thought to indicate whether the corresponding real journey was long or short. In other words there was a fluid relationship between real and theatrical time. The reality of space and time was merely empirical, never absolute, so that there was no need to represent them in terms of a stable reference-frame. On the other hand, they had to be given some sort of representation, since Gothic art was concrete in orientation and could not allow action to be represented without this dimension. Theatrical space, too, was quite elastic, and not just because different distances were represented on

different scales. The whole unoccupied part of the stage in front of the row of 'mansions' served now as one place, now as another, just as the action required. In other words, not just the space in front of any particular place represented on stage, but the stage as a whole could, by its imaginary relationship now to one such place and now to another, be accepted as either that place itself or as a spot bordering on the territory that the place in question occupied.

The stage-set for the mystery-plays must have seemed a confused, unending swarm of leading characters and extras, constantly coming and going. All the actors were always on stage, so that they at least brightened it with their presence, even if they only

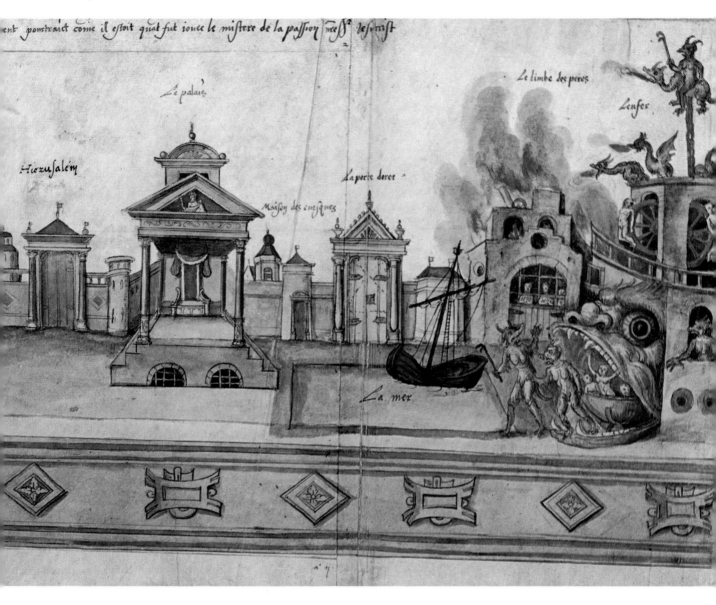

sat down and remained in their own places whenever they had nothing special to do. The movements were further complicated by the simultaneous presentation of complementary or else of totally separate scenes on different parts of the stage which, in the mystery-plays, became an image of the restless toings and froings of men on earth.

Undoubtedly, however, the main significance of such displays was that they brought before people's eyes that sacred history, which the medieval Catholic believed contained all he needed to know. Thus, they served the same function as the *Biblia pauperum*, but were infinitely more popular and effective. Their structure was that of a continuous narrative which

explicitly conveyed an appreciation of how all the different pieces in the drama belong together. This was the fruit of the idea of using a simultaneous scene technique.

There is a further way in which the mystery-plays differed from the *Biblia pauperum*, and this was in their rendering explicit something that the Bible in general, and the Gospels in particular at least implied, that is the presence of an intimate link between God's intervention in history and everyday human events. There was, of course, a literary development. Scenes of everyday reality taken from the bible narrative or from the lives of the saints would be filled out and developed in detail well

95

1

2

4

1. f 2bisᵇ—3ª: *From left to right*: God with Mercy, Peace and Truth; Truth coming down to earth; Marriage of Joachim and Anne; Charity of Joachim and Anne; Joachim expelled from the Temple; Joachim and the Angel; Meeting at the Golden Gate. A rubric says: 'Here Truth comes down and travels through the world obviously searching for someone. Meanwhile, the devils talk about it'
2. f5ᵇ: Birth of the Virgin and Mary's Presentation in the Temple
3. f29ᵇ: Zachary's prayer; the Annunciation; Meeting with Elizabeth
4. f42ᵇ: Nativity of Christ; Vision of the Shepherds; Angel appearing to the Three Kings; Circumcision
5. f53ª: The Three Kings offering gifts to Jesus; Flight into Egypt; Massacre of the Innocents; Herod's suicide
6. f66ʰ: The new King; Return from Egypt; Jesus among the Doctors; Judas as an unwanted baby
7. f77ʰ: The King's debauched life; Preaching of John the Baptist; Jesus is baptized

beyond the limits of the passing references to such events in the original texts. The lives of the saints were accepted as representing the final stage in a universal history that had already had its culmination in the Saviour's sacrifice on Calvary. They were also regarded as an 'imitation' of the life of Christ, just as the Old Testament was interpreted as its prophetic anticipation. More than this, however, in the mystery-plays Christ's own sublime gestures were acted out with the very same realism and sensitivity as were, although with much more impact,

everyday ale-house scenes. So close was the link between God's operation within history and everyday routine living.

The acting of performers of mystery plays, while no doubt inspired by deep reverence and a literal acceptance of the stories which they were enacting, must clearly have been highly expressive, carried out not only with the arms and face, but with the entire body in a highly varied range of attitudes. Thus, in the *Jeu d'Adam*, we can mention Adam and Eve's violent outburst of grief, throwing themselves down

5

6

7

to the ground, beating their breasts and hugging their thighs. Obviously when actors were called upon to impersonate the great ones of the earth, their expression became unnatural, rhetorical and only in a strained way sublime. The costumes always had to match the character. Costume-design was left to each individual actor to attend to according to his taste and resources. This ensured a certain distinction in the costumes of kings and princes, since their parts were given to the more affluent citizens.

We know that the visual presentation of the sacred narrative was given at least as much importance as its dramatic interpretation, because, in the early fifteenth century, mystery-plays were staged in silence: *sans parler* or *par signes*. The audience's grasp of what the story was about might be helped on by the use of large cards (*tituli*) which described the situation or contained the main character's words, like the captions to a silent film. Sometimes, too, the mystery-plays were simply a series of *tableaux vivants, sans parler ni signer*. This was the case, for example, with one played in Paris in 1424,

8

9

10

11

12

13

14

15

16

8. f89ᵇ: Judas killing the son of Iscariot; Devil tempts Christ; Wedding-feast at Cana

9. f102ᵃ: Herod has John the Baptist arrested; Calling of the Twelve Apostles; Sermon on the Mount; Miracle

10. f115ᵇ: The paralytic man is let down through the roof so that he can be cured; Mary Magdalen is converted; Girl brought back to life

11. f126ᵃ: The dinner in the Pharisee's house; Samaritan woman at the well; Centurion's son

12. f136ᵇ: John the Baptist is beheaded; Multiplication of the loaves and fishes

13. f147ᵇ: The woman taken in adultery; Cure of the man born blind

14. f156ᵇ: The argument about traditions; Cure of the girl possessed by a devil; Transfiguration

15. f166ᵃ: The resurrection of Lazarus; Jesus in the home of Zacchaeus

16. f175ᵃ: Jesus in Simon's house in Bethany; Entry of Jesus into Jerusalem

17. f183ᵇ: Parables; Council of the Jews and the treachery of Judas

17

18

18. f193ᵃ: Jesus and Mary are separated; Last Supper; Garden of Gethsemane
19. f204ᵃ: Jesus praying in the Garden; Arrest of Jesus; In the house of Annas; In the house of Caiaphas
20. f216ᵃ: Jesus before Pilate; Jesus brought before Herod; Judas repents; Judas commits suicide
21. f225ᵃ: Jesus and Barabbas; Scourging and crowning with

thorns; 'Ecce Homo'

22. f240ᵃ: The ascent to Calvary; Crucifixion; Taking Down from the Cross; Burial. The rubric says that as Jesus dies, he bows down his head, the earth trembles, the dead come back to life, the veil of the temple is torn in two and rocks are broken open
23. f254ᵃ: The Resurrection; The three Marys at the Sepulchre; Jesus appears to Mary Magdalen; 'Noli me tangere'; Other appearances of Jesus

19

20

21

22

23

24

25

24. f264ᵃ: The guards tell Annas and Caiaphas what has happened; On the road to Emmaus; Appearance to the Apostles and to St Thomas; Appearing to St Peter

25. f280ᵃ: Final appearance to the Apostles; Ascension; Pentecost; St Peter beginning to preach

in which it was specified that the characters should
arrange themselves like statues standing with their
backs to the wall.

The leading French mystery-playwrights were
Eustache Marcadé (d 1440), Arnoul Gréban (1420–
c 71) and Jean Michel (d c 1501). They were talented
and long-winded versifiers of sacred history and their
productions were simply immense—more than forty
thousand lines, while a classical tragedy had rarely
exceeded one thousand five hundred. All three men
staged the Passion, and in practice took in the whole
life of Christ. In 1547 a new production of their work
for a relatively small stage was given in Valenciennes
and took twenty-five days. Each day, however,
involved only a few hours of theatre, while the
original productions of mystery-plays had normally
made use of all the daylight hours available. The 1547
production was called the *Mystery of the Birth,
Passion and Resurrection of Jesus*, and we know quite
a lot about it, thanks to the miniature paintings of
Hubert Cailleau, who '*a peint les histoires sur chacune
journée de ce livre, comme aussi il fut joueur audict
mistère de plusieurs perchons, entre lesquelles il veult
representer l'ung des trois Roix, assavoir le nègre . . .
Il donna aussi le portrait du hourdement du théatre
avec Jacques de Moelles comme il se veidt en ce
present livre.*'

Cailleau, then, was both actor and scene-painter
and has left us pictures of different scenes from the

mystery-play, as well as of the stage as a whole. The
architectural style of the settings is already that of
the Renaissance. The theatrical meaning and, in
some respects, the actual appearance of the stage
obviously changed between the artist's beginning his
work and bringing it to a conclusion in the course of
a large number of short sessions. This, for instance,
is why there is no mountain in his general view of the
stage and why this differs in several particulars from
his miniatures relating to individual days in the development of the plot. In any case, the miniature paintings do not purport to be a photographic record, but
strike a middle note between a documentation of the
actual theatrical and a visual illustration of the
artist's own powers of fantasy.

On the other hand, the general view is undoubtedly
a faithful reproduction of the actual stage-setting for
the production of the play. Instead of the various
'mansions' being simply placed next to each other in
a single row, they were arranged in a double row.
Places such as the temple or the palace stood out
towards the front of the stage, while an unbroken
line of wall with towers and gates formed a sort of
background. This latter could also serve an independent function and represent the city seen from
the outside.

We cannot say this sort of feature was common to
all productions of the mystery-plays. Yet it was
used in Italian religious theatre and it became

indispensable whenever a siege was being staged, for example, in the mystery-play of the *Vengeance of Our Saviour*, which showed the destruction of Jerusalem.

In the mystery-plays, as well as such incidents as sieges and battles, there were sometimes other episodes of a highly theatrical nature which called for the use of lots of extras, special effects and mechanical devices.

This was certainly the case, for example, when, a few years before the Valenciennes production of the *Passion*, L Choquet staged the *Mystery of the Apocalypse*. All sorts of natural and supernatural wonders were made to accompany St John's fourteen visions. The production also offers a good illustration of the parallel staging of different themes, since, while St John was having his visions, other events were taking place in Rome.

In Gréban's *Mystery of the Acts of the Apostles*, produced in Bourges in 1536, the apostles' separating to go their several ways made it clear that the stage was being used to represent the whole world. Simon Magus was also shown flying through the air, only to fall suddenly down to the ground as a result of the prayer of St Peter.

On the other hand, if the demands of the subject went beyond anything that available theatrical techniques made possible, producers never had any hesitation about using the very simplest conventions. Thus, six painted canvases served to show the six days of creation.

To produce a mystery-play was an event for the whole town. The two, three or four days required for one complete performance in the great 15th century productions were holidays for the entire population. Before the play, all the actors walked in procession wearing their costumes. Since they were townsfolk themselves and known to all their neighbours, this created a special relationship between them and their audience, and this was carried over into the whole atmosphere of the production, although, of course, everything was taken quite seriously.

With the exception of short interludes during which a few of the actors, and especially those playing the parts of devils, mingled with the crowd, the space set aside for the actual performance, usually a large stage, was, in the French mystery-plays, kept quite separate from the area accommodating the public. The audience would be in front of the stage, more often than not in a public square, but sometimes in the *cavea* of an old Roman theatre.

The situation was quite different in the northern countries. The 'mansions' for the actors were erected here and there in the public-square, and there was no large stage to serve as a unifying element. Any movements from one location to another were, therefore, kept to a minimum and when they could not be avoided, were rather like a procession through the crowd, which was able to watch it go by, but usually preferred to join in its progress. Since the performance of the mystery-plays was still regarded as being in some way linked with the church services, this participation of the audience in the procession took on almost a double meaning.

In Germany the audience probably did not assist at all the events represented in the course of the performance. In many instances an individual spectator was unable to make his way across the square from one 'mansion' to another. This did not seem strange. In the French mystery-plays the whole universe was tied together and summed up in a single, integrated tableau. For the Germans the theatre was a little world that mirrored the real scattering of different events in time and space. They belonged together in some absolute sense, but in relation to any individual the appreciation of their unity and his own participation in them was necessarily conditioned by his own nature, as a being living at a particular time and in a particular place, and not otherwise.

Destruction of the Temple. Woodcut based on a play representing the *Life of Saint Apollonia*. Italian religious theatre often staged the Destruction of the Temple

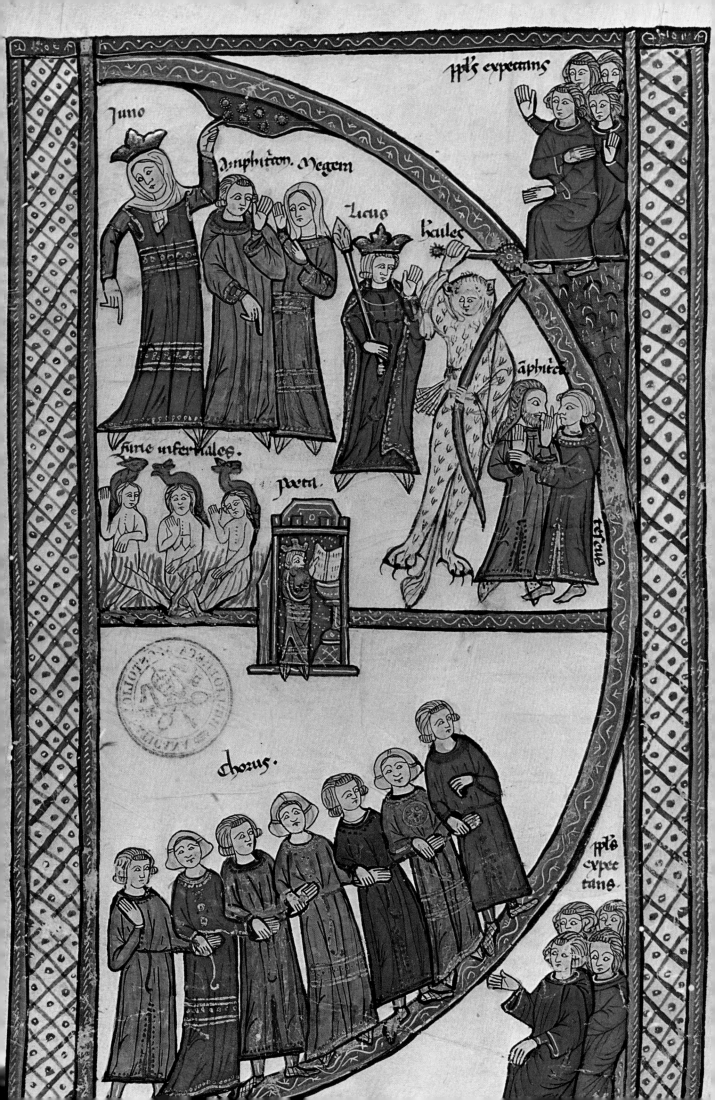

Juno

Amphitron Regem

Iuno

hailes

Ihs expectans

āphites

furie infernales

poeta

chorus

Ihs expectans

In England scriptural drama was characteristically organised into series of plays constituting entire cycles, the performance of which would take several days. Performed on separate stages, these plays gave a cosmic view of the fate of mankind: Creation and Fall, the Nativity, Passion and Resurrection of Christ, the Last Judgement. Four of these cycles are still preserved (the Chester, Wakefield, York and the so-called N-Town Plays), but there must have been many more in different parts of the country which are now lost.

In Italy the scriptural drama took the form of the so-called *sacre rappresentazioni*, which might at times be small-scale performances, but which at other times were elaborate spectacles designed to be played to large crowds. Thus, a performance in Milan in 1476 drew as many as 80,000 spectators. The actors were frequently boys who belonged to religious confraternities.

The 'mansions' were identical with those represented in the French mysteries: the temple, the palace, the mountain and also Rome or Jerusalem. A crenellated wall provided the background and gave a sense of unity to the whole. As time went on and the performances were given indoors, this wall enabled actors to move conveniently from one 'mansion' to another. However, occasionally one is struck by the absence of two basic 'mansions' for the mysteries: Paradise and Hell—which would mean that the stage now represented part of the world rather than a metaphysical and moral universe.

A favourite theme was not only the life of Christ but the lives of saints, such as St Theodora. In these the saint was the protagonist of romantic adventures in an uninterrupted journey, with the 'mansions' as its various stages.

Because they were on a small scale only, the Italian productions had greater freedom. Quite apart from heaven and hell being sometimes left out, there are plays which involve only a few 'mansions', and others which multiply them within the confines of a particular imaginary city and then, of course, there has to be quite a degree of realism about the stage-sets, so that the audience can identify the different places without difficulty. In this way the saints' restless adventures are kept within the horizons of the ordinary citizen's limited vision.

It was quite easy to think of the different 'mansions' as the dwellings of the principal characters, and from that it was a small step to adapt the settings for these religious productions to the staging of classical plays.

Chapter 10

THE HUMANIST REVIVAL OF ANCIENT CLASSICAL THEATRE

As a first stage in the process of her own self-affirmation the Church had adopted towards classical culture an attitude that was undisguisedly and emphatically hostile. By multiplying her own rituals and developing them along theatrical lines the Church attempted to cater completely for all aspects of the spiritual life of believers, including elements that would today go under the heading of general culture or simple recreation. Thus, during the Middle Ages, on fixed days in the liturgical calendar the ritual was supplemented by or transformed into a festive display inside the church. This was meant to provide some outlet for the people's animal energies and it included a sort of theatre in which the rites of the Church were parodied or otherwise made fun of, together with dances and games which, in the opinion of some authorities, often degenerated into straightforward orgies. The Church was either unable or unwilling to acknowledge these developments and give them a permanent place. Instead, she chose to re-affirm, though it might be more accurate to say inaugurate, the exclusive purity of her own ritual. She put a drastic stop not only to the parodies and theatrical diversions, but also to the existing dramatic extensions of the liturgy. Liturgical drama was abolished, and the mystery-plays were banished from the sacred precincts. In addition, Latin, by now an unknown tongue to the ordinary people, was chosen as the language of the liturgy, with the natural result that the ritual came to occupy a world apart, accessible only to the educated. The most the illiterate believer could do was just to be there. In the cultural sense, the Church was no longer an *ecclesia*, a community.

In the theatrical world religious culture survived this development for a considerable time. The Church renounced her former hostility to classical culture, and the mystery-plays, miracle-plays and other forms of religious theatre separated from the Church that had first shaped them. They retained their popularity.

In Italy religious theatre did not have either the scope or the appeal it had in other countries. This very fact, coupled with its being the principal, if not the only form of theatre during almost the whole of the fifteenth century, may explain its influence on the growth of the new theatre—the learned, classical theatre.

The renaissance of the ancient world was an awe-inspiring project that consumed Italy for two hundred years, and produced a culture that was frankly aristocratic and élitist. This involved a complete review of theatre from the point of view of literature, architecture, scenery and production.

The study of theatre as literature was part of the humanists' immense philological undertaking to bring to light, publish and provide commentaries to all the works of the ancient writers. Lovato Lovati (1241–1309) and Nicolò di Trevet (1259–1329) contributed outstanding studies of Seneca,

Roman theatre. Miniature. Frontispiece to the *Térence des Ducs*, Paris, Bibliothèque de l'Arsenal, ms fr 664. The upper portion of the miniature offers a good idea of how late medieval scholars imagined ancient Roman theatrical performances: the actors, dressed as jongleurs, mime the action in front of the stage, while a reader declaims all the words of the text. It is like a puppet-theatre. The audience, the *populus romanus* gathers round the actors

Theatrum. Woodcut. Frontispiece to the 1496 Strasbourg edition of Terence's *Comedies.* Vienna, Bildarchiv der Österreichischen. Nationalbibliothek. The audience is shown in a quite impracticable hanging loggia, and the whole picture is a fantasy, but some realistic features are shown—the actors in modern dress and a stage-setting with three niches

Coliseus, sive theatrum. Woodcut. Frontispiece to the 1497 Venice edition of Terence's *Comedies.* While the engravings of the individual comedies derive from those in the 1493 Lyons edition, this is the first picture of the ancient theatre to present it in humanist terms: a *cavea* for the audience, and stage-sets rather like bathing-huts

and the discovery by Nicholas of Cusa of previously unknown comedies of Plautus in 1425 was especially important.

The rebuilding of theatres in accordance with the ancient designs was given a similarly scientific basis in an archeological survey of existing remains, witness the numerous reports of research-projects and excavations. Flavio Biondo's *Roma triumphans* contains a quite exhaustive description of the Roman theatre, but an even more painstaking treatment of the question we owe to Leon Battista Alberti, who based his work on archeological surveys and also on a study of the fourth book of Vitruvius's *De Architectura,* which is in part about the building of theatres.

Alberti's own architectural treatise, *De Re Aedificatoria,* suggests that the *cavea* of the theatre was surmounted by a loggia, which was open on the inside, but closed at the back. Both the *cavea* and the

stage were set around the pit, which was, therefore, the focus of the entire theatre. Thus, its dimensions determined those of the other architectural features, just as its shape determined their position and design. Like the Roman theatres it was semicircular, but its limits were extended by two parallel lines, and the stage together with the *skene* building were accomodated in the resulting area. The *skene* building rounded off the internal architectural composition of the ancient theatre and also served as a façade. Alberti, rather surprisingly, then proceeds to reject this theory in favour of a *skene* of two or more superimposed colonnades, arranged 'to look like houses'. In other words, he attempts a synthesis between the *skene* of classical times, of which he retains the regal door, 'adorned like the doors of a temple', and his appreciation of the need to provide both comedy and tragedy with a more realistic, concrete and functional theatrical setting by means

Three scenes from the *Adelphi.* Miniature. Rome, Vatican Library, ms vat lat 3868. Evidence of a probably continuous tradition in illumination, these miniatures are from the early 9th century. We know of eleven similar codices dating from between the 9th and 12th centuries, all derived from a 4th century original

reſpicit noſ; SOS properatu mea canthara curre obſtetricem arceſſe ut cū opuſ ſit
ne in mora nobiſ ſiet;

DEMEA   SENEX

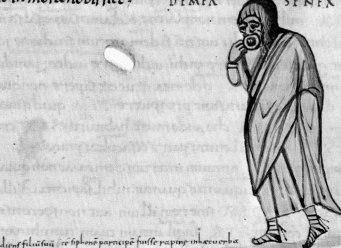

enea audienſ filiū ſuū teſiphonē participē fuiſſe rapinę in haec uerba
rupit

EM diſperij cteſiphonem audiui filium una adfuiſſe in raptione cum aeſchino; id miſero reſtat mihi
maliſ illū poteſt quia licui rei eſt & iā ad nequitiā eum adducere, ubi ego illū quaerā credo ab
ductum in ganeum aliquo pſuaſit ille impuruſ ſat ſcio ſed eccū ſyrum ire uideo; hinc ſcibo iā ubi ſiet;
atq̄ hercle hic de grege illo eſt ſi me ſenſerit eu quaritare nūquā dicet carnifex, non oſtendā id me uelle;

SYRUS   SERUUS·   DEMEA   SENEX

opera ſrre nunc uiuo feſtiuum caput quin omnia ſibi poſt putarit eſſe p meo co modo.
maledicta famam meum amore & peccatū in ſe tranſtulit nihil ſupra poteſt; quiſ nā
forer crepuit SYR mane mane ipſe & it foraſ;

AESCHINUS   CTESI PHO II   SYRUS   SERUUS SAN NIO II
ADULES
CENS

ubi eſt ille ſacrilegus SAN men quaerit nū quid nam effert occidi nihil uideo;
hem opportune te ipſū quaerito; quid fit cteſipho in tuto eſt omniſ reſ, omitte uero triſt

The Adelphi. Woodcuts from the 1493 Lyons edition of Terence's *Comedies.* Vienna, Bildarchiv der Österreichischen Nationalbibliothek. The illustrations follow the action of the drama, developing from scene to scene. A character is sometimes (e.g. 10) shown twice, obviously to reflect his movements during that scene. Clearly, then, the illustrator's aim was to show the possible course of a real or imagined theatrical production. This is more than proved by his repetitious use of the same stage-setting, although he varies the decoration slightly. These woodcuts may have inspired or have been inspired by humanist productions at the time

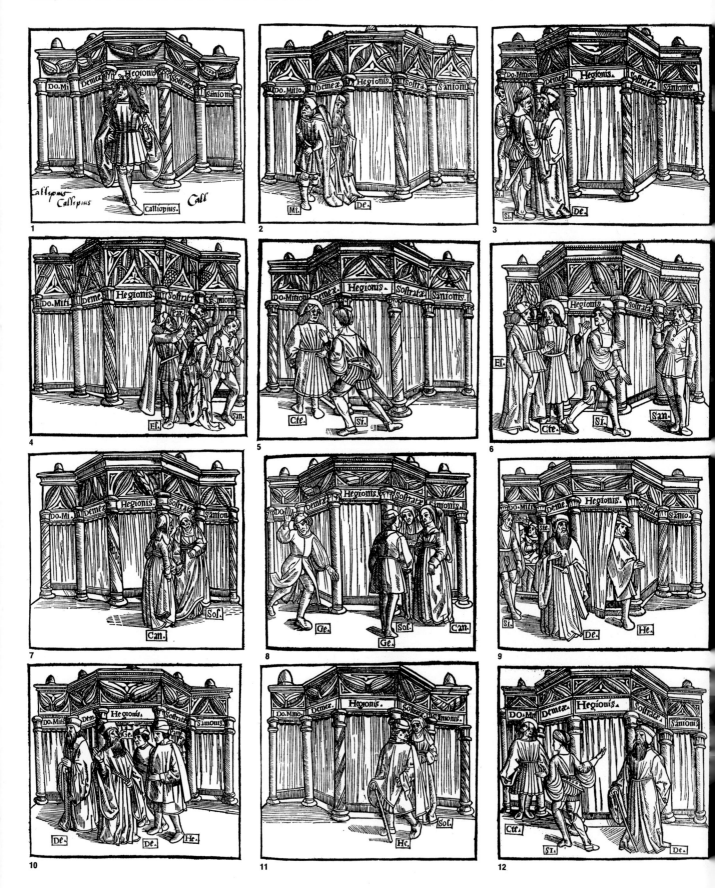

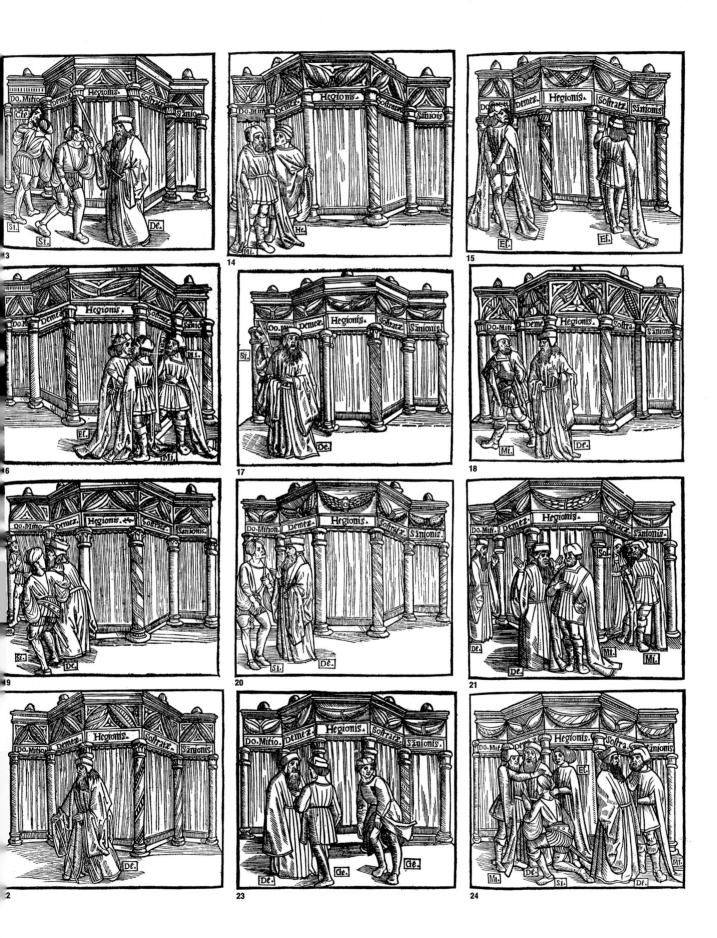

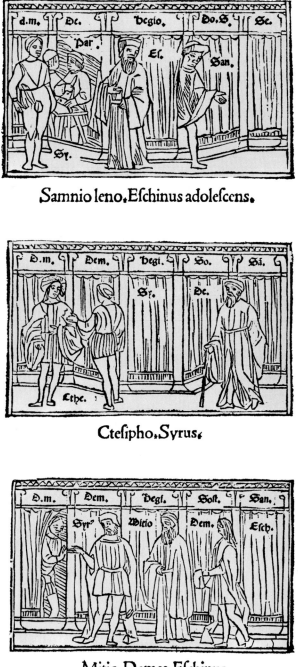

Samnio leno. Efchinus adolefcens.

Ctefipho. Syrus.

Mitio. Demea. Efchinus

of houses representing the homes of the main characters.

Alberti's ideas about theatre-buildings were collated and revised in a small, still unpublished treatise by Pellegrino Prisciano, a humanist in the service of the court of Ferrara, who no doubt played an important part in organising the production of Latin comedies in Ferrara in the last fifteen years of the fifteenth century.

Some have referred to these productions as the Ferrara 'classical festivals', and they were the first attempt to tackle the central problem, that of actually interpreting a classical text on the stage itself. Duke Ercole d'Este was the heart and soul of

A scene from an illuminated *Terence*, ms lat 7907 f 18ᵇ. Paris, Bibliothèque Nationale

these productions, which were continuous from 1486 until 1493, and from 1499 until his death in 1505, with sometimes as many as five or six plays in one season. The main plays of Plautus and Terence were performed. In 1486 the *Menaechmi*; in 1487 the *Amphitruo*; in 1490 the *Menaechmi* again and, perhaps, the *Curculio*; in 1491 the *Andria* and the *Amphitruo*, and in 1493 yet again the *Menaechmi*, a play which enjoyed tremendous success and not only in the fifteenth century; and then in 1499 the *Trinummus*, the *Poenulus*, the *Eunuchus*, etc. The lay-out of the *skene* did not vary much: a row of small buildings, painted to resemble brick houses and provided with doors and windows in working order. A line of

117

battlements ran along the top, so that the overall appearance was that of a castle or a crenellated wall. The front of the stage was also probably painted to resemble bricks. Alberti's debt to Vitruvius is clear in this application, and Prisciano is also obviously influenced by contemporary religious theatre with its rows of scenery and its mechanical devices. Thus, a ship would sail across the courtyard of the castle of Ferrara while the *Menaechmi* was being performed and in the *Amphitruo* Jove was seen coming down from heaven.

The audience sat on large steps prepared as carefully as the performance itself and often covered with rich velvets. At Ferrara the classical Latin comedies were performed in an Italian translation, often rhymed in triplets, and the theatre became the vital nucleus of court festivities. Classical culture was looked upon as indispensable in an aristocrat. It is an exaggeration to say, as some have done, that there were five hundred guests at a time, but they were certainly very numerous and gathered in the hall in which the theatre had been set up only after prolonged festivities and dancing. The play was, it must be added, not the only feature in the theatrical display. It was often preceded by a procession of people in costume, which served to show the splendour of the court since no costume was ever repeated. Even to represent such characters from the comedies of Plautus as 'Greek slaves, servants, masters and merchants', contemporary costumes were used which, despite the far from affluent town settings of the plays, were always made in a luxurious style of the finest materials: satin, rich brocade, silks, the best of linen. Between acts and at the end of each play there were mimed or danced short theatrical interludes representing light-hearted or pastoral themes. The characters for these might be boys and girls enjoying their local harvest-festival, or nymphs and shepherds or other country-folk. It was quite rare for the Olympian deities or those allegorical figures who became so popular in the ensuing century to appear on the scene.

It is hard to imagine how the comedies were actually performed. Court scholars took the leading rôles and even played the female parts. However, the interludes had to be light in tone and paced to convey the sense of a child's dream-world. They were more obviously theatrical and this may be why they were soon preferred to the comedies, the impact of which was dulled by poor translation.

At Ferrara classical theatre was grafted onto the cultural life of the upper classes. There, too, in 1471 the first 'pastoral' play in Italian literature was apparently performed, the *Orpheus* of Angelo Poliziano. Thus the way was open for the production of Italian comedies inspired by Latin models. However, at about the same time the real humanist attempt at a full-scale restoration of classical theatre was being carried forward in Rome, in an academy founded by Pomponio Leto. He was an unusual combination of the scholar and the adventurer. Today he is remembered mainly for his work for the theatre and for his conspiracy against Paul II. Despite this accusation, his contemporaries found him a fascinating and learned teacher and his epigraphical and topographical studies were well-known.

Pomponio Leto's stage-productions were linked quite explicitly with the work of Vitruvius. Sulpizio da Veroli, a humanist friend of Leto, in his epistle of dedication to the *editio princeps* of the Roman architect's writings, recalled how Cardinal Riario had been the first 'to show our generation the horizons of that painted world (*picturatae scenae faciem*) in which Pomponio's actors had played their rôles'.

Pomponio Leto's theatrical activities were within the framework of his life as a scholar. There had been similar attempts before. For instance, Tito Livio Frulovisi (d 1440), author of a Latin life of Henry V, who taught in Venice in the early part of the century, had had the original Latin texts performed on stage by his pupils. However, no one equalled Leto in his attention to detail. The works of Plautus, Terence and Seneca were produced in Latin, using a text that had been critically established. Leto, good teacher that he was, made sure the pronunciation was precisely correct, even to the point of pedantry. The only reference we have to his stage-settings is Sulpizio da Veroli's phrase, '*picturatae scenae faciem*', and '*picturatae*' in this context could refer to painted scenery or else to a backdrop with paintings hanging on it.

However, there are many grounds for thinking that the woodcuts in the late 15th century editions of the comedies of Terence, and particularly in the 1493 Lyons edition and the 1497 Venice edition, were at least indirectly inspired by Pomponio's productions. Any interpretation of the woodcuts must also consider the tradition of miniatures with which they belong. The Middle Ages have left us various codices of the works of Terence and Seneca with accompanying miniatures to illustrate the text. One 9th century series of such codices derives from an older, late Roman source. Terence's characters are shown in the attitudes adopted by Roman actors of the 3rd and 4th centuries AD. Their mimicry is lively and intense and the gestures are broad and

---

Characters from plays by Terence. Woodcut from the 1496 Strasbourg edition of his comedies. Vienna, Bildarchiv der Österreichischen Nationalbibliothek. The upper portion shows the opening scene from the *Heautontimoroumenos*

Above: further characters from the Strasbourg edition of Terence. The illustrations to individual comedies consist of groupings of small wooden blocks, each depicting one character or one decoration

Miniatures from the *Térence des Ducs*. Paris, Bibliothèque de l'Arsenal, ms fr 664. In the *Térence des Ducs* miniatures the stage-settings vary all the time. Apparently, the illuminator was not deeply interested in theatre as such

sweeping. The actors are wearing classical masks, and the only bit of scenery is a square door.

From the 14th century, by contrast, we have the brilliantly illuminated manuscript known as the *Térence des Ducs*. The frontispiece is a large miniature illustrating the late medieval idea of a theatre in antiquity. The actors are jongleurs. They are miming their parts in a convulsive, almost frenzied dance-rhythm, while a reader recites the words of the text. He is Calliopius, who was made responsible for the prologue in many 15th century woodcuts. However, these figures have vanished from the miniatures illustrating particular scenes from the comedies. Instead we have 14th century characters elegantly dressed in Burgundian style, whose extensive yet restrained gestures clearly convey the sense of the immediate situation. The setting is mainly made up of small houses, open at the front, and reminiscent

main characters. Their use of gesture follows the *Térence des Ducs* fairly closely, though in a more restrained way. Their position on stage as well as their use of mime is carefully shown: their costumes are modern.

Pomponio's actors may very well have used this sort of setting—since the portico seems a scaled-down version of Vitruvius's idea—although in practice it may not have been so very elaborate, but merely a simple row of wooden columns arranged in a straight line with a flat roof overhead.

The guiding ideals of Leto's academy become much clearer when we turn to consider the humanist school's main theatrical production, the staging of the *Poenulus* of Plautus in a theatre specially built on the Campidoglio. This was during the festivities in connection with the conferring of Roman citizenship on Lorenzo and Giuliano de' Medici in 1513.

of the individual 'mansions' used for scriptural drama.

It is probable that this tradition was familiar both to the editor, Jodocus Badius Ascensius, and to the artist whom he commissioned to design the woodcuts for the Lyons edition of Terence, yet his own work reflects a real or imaginary theatre of a very different sort from the ones pictured in medieval miniatures. On stage he shows a portico, with curtains between the various columns. These are the homes of the

Classical drama formed an integral part of a ritual designed to celebrate a purely political occasion. The producer of the play was a pupil of Pomponio Leto, Pietro Inghirami, better known as Phaedrus because of his outstanding performance in the title-rôle of Seneca's play of that name when it had been put on by his master many years before. In all probability he was also the inspiration behind the great wooden theatre which his contemporaries regarded as the eighth wonder of the world. The

The setting for *La Betia*. Venice, Biblioteca Marciana ms 6370.
This drawing is in the manuscript of *La Betia*, a comedy by Angelo
Beolco, called Il Ruzzante. It gives a rough idea of the stage used
in Ferrara for the classical festivals. Instead of the neutral if rather
grand, settings of the humanists, there was a move towards
realism

description of the theatre is quite clear and the plans were recently discovered by Cruciani. The oblong building comprised a clear central space, with tiers of steep broad steps on three sides. The remaining wall, unencumbered by steps, served as the setting for the performance. It, like the other walls, was decorated with pilasters, and large paintings filled the upper spaces between these, while six door-ways closed off by gold hangings occupied the space underneath. Obviously, the structure was similar to that shown in the illuminations of the works of Terence, and it seems clear that both were inspired by Pomponio Leto's study of Vitruvius. Young pupils of Inghirami acted the *Poenulus* in Latin. The costumes were luxurious and of modern design. The chroniclers tell us it was a delight to see these children dressed as lovers or adults and reciting their parts with suitable gestures and an excellent pronunciation.

This performance was no more than one item of central importance in the festitivities both inside and outside the theatre. Mass was celebrated on an altar erected in the middle of the stage, almost as if a Christian ritual was being enacted on the *thymele* of an ancient Greek theatre. There was a banquet with the more notable guests sitting on the stage itself. Long speeches followed. As far as we can tell, there was no discrimination about the issuing of invitations, and it is hard to guess how people reacted to this grandiose philological and archeological attempt to bring the Roman *ludi theatrales* back to life—what we do know, is that the majority could not understand Latin!

Chapter 11

fondo del teato

13

LEARNING, SPECULATION AND ARCHEOLOGY IN THE RENAISSANCE

The preceding chapter has mentioned the great influence of the technical writings of the Roman architect, Marcus Vitruvius Pollio, on the thinking of those who re-introduced the classical theatre. He described this theatre in detail. The plan was derived from a circle, representing the pit, in which were inscribed three squares, in planning a Greek theatre, or four triangles, for a Roman theatre. He discussed the actual stage, the superimposed colonnades, the fitted *periaktoi*, or revolving triangular drums with a different scene painted on each side—one tragic, one comic, the other pastoral.

During the Renaissance the impact of Vitruvius upon architecture was similar to that of Aristotle and Horace upon poetry—they served both to orientate artistic practice and to stimulate aesthetic reflexion. Vitruvius was issued as a plain-text in editions by Leon Battista Alberti and by Sebastiano Serlio, and in editions with commentaries by Cesare Cesariano and by Daniele Barbaro. The recovery of the text was important both for an understanding of the text itself and for its relevance to the problems of contemporary stage-production. Not only were Vitruvius' architectural ideas valuable but also the 'laws' upon which they were based.

The study of Vitruvius's text was complemented by archeological digs which provided confirmation of laws of this kind. However, the archeological findings also needed interpreting in both theoretical and practical terms. Like Vitruvius's work, they helped build up an ideal picture of an architectural style, of ancient architecture in a particular interpretation. This could guide, but could not give a precise form to contemporary endeavours, which were necessarily linked to a different mentality, served a different purpose and satisfied other needs.

The re-discovery of ancient theatre lacked this final operational stage. An operational interpretation of antiquity would have required a context and a tradition ready to receive it. Because these were lacking, it almost remained an abstraction.

Its meaning and value are better appreciated if we remember it was the achievement of artists and scholars who considered theatre as one element in a much vaster canvas. It was not the work of theatre people. In the 15th and 16th centuries there were no real experts on theatre in the specialised modern sense. The only person to devote himself, if not exclusively, at least in the main to a study of theatre was Leone de' Sommi, a Mantuan Jew.

Interpretations of ancient theatrical architecture were the fruit of a view of Roman classicism as having created majestic and imposing buildings, and of an intuition of the likely function for a theatre-building in such a setting. It would be a place where an ideal people could gather together, hierarchically divided into various classes. In it they would celebrate their festivals. Hence they would need to be able to go in and out and to find their proper place without any confused mingling of different age-groups, sexes, or social classes. The idea of a dramatic presentation would never be uppermost—people

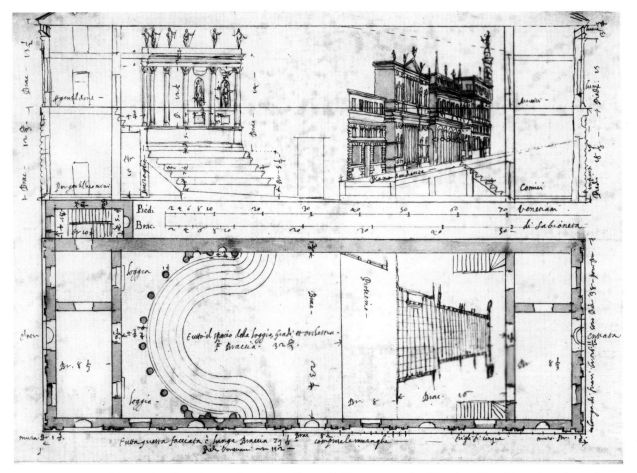

were there to celebrate by listening to fine rhetoric,
so that voice-production was all important and
acoustic considerations would be the ones that
shaped the development of ancient theatre.

These twin strands of thought governed the
development of Vitruvius's passing references to
ascending flights of steps dividing the theatre into
segments, to the portico, the *praecintia* and echo-
chambers. New questions emerged about the out-
ward appearance of the theatre and it was to answer
these that people looked at the ruins of the Roman
theatres. Other questions concerned the entrances,
the inside stairways, etc. Finally, in 1521, Cesariano,
author of the first translation of and commentary on
Vitruvius, strove for solutions to the strictly technical
problems of theatre construction.

It should be clear from all this why the question of
the stage itself seemed secondary to the authors.
Cardinal Barbaro, who wrote a commentary on
Vitruvius and a treatise on perspective, was the very
first to really grasp the importance of the *skene* as an
integral architectural feature of the theatre as a
building, on the evidence both of Vitruvius and of
the archeological remains. The earlier failure to
make this connection is best illustrated by a drawing

of Francesco di Giorgio. For him the *skene* is a
triangular stage, a *periaktos* perhaps, which can be
thrown down anywhere at all inside the huge circular
building. The ground plan and Vitruvius's rather
academic arrangement of triangles inscribed in a
circle were the only things seen to have any bearing
on the *skene-cavea*-pit relationship.

Nevertheless, the most original thinking in such
treatises may be found in the short passages that
deal with the *skene* and may even be due to this
erroneous interpretation. After all, it is only logical.
If the *skene* is not an organic constituent of the
theatre-building, it can be abstracted from it, taken
by itself and related to contemporary problems in
stage-production. People might not appreciate the
theatre as a building, but they did understand how a
stage served as the setting for a theatrical event. The
only exceptions to this were the theatre built in the
Campidoglio in 1513 which expressed the idea of a
theatre as a place of celebration, and the Teatro
Olimpico in Vicenza built in 1582, after almost a
century of theorising had worn itself out.

In general, the *skene* issuing from meditation on
Vitruvius was open to the influence of sacred theatre
and we can recall the work of Leon Battista Alberti

126

Ground-plan, elevation and cross-section of a Roman theatre. Engravings from Cesare Cesariano's 1521 annotated and illustrated edition of L Vitruvius Pollio's *De Architectura libri decem . . .* Milan, Biblioteca Nazionale Braidense

Comic, tragic and pastoral stage-settings. Engravings from *Second Book of Perspective* by Sebastiano Serlio of Bologna published in Lyons in 1545. Milan, Biblioteca Nazionale Braidense. These are perfect examples of 16th-century stagecraft

Meneur du Jeu. Miniature from the *Mystère de la Passion.* Paris, Bibliothèque Nationale, ms fr 2675. This is one of the first pictures of a 'director' at work during rehearsal, holding the script in one hand and his baton in the other. Some directors of mystery plays were laymen, as in this illustration, others were clerics like the *meneur de jeu* of the *Martyrdom of St Apollonia* (see page 105). This theatrical figure was to be defined in his function by Leone de' Sommi's famous treatise in Italy

and Pelegrino Prisciano in this connection. It could, in other words, take the form of a row of houses, or of a long portico embellished with Roman sarcophagi in imitation of Vitruvius' supposed ideal, or of a 15th century perspective scene justified by a stretched interpretation of passages in Vitruvius referring to shaded paintings, which applied rather to the *periaktoi* and the three sorts of scenery.

The exegesis of these passages was responsible for the most creative and forward-looking developments in the stage-design in the Ferrara festivals and in Pomponio Leto's Roman academy, as well as for the definitive treatment of the theory of perspective scene-painting in Sebastiano Serlio's second book of architecture, published in 1545. He deals with perspective in general and devotes a special section to perspective in scenery.

Court festivals and academic productions need only a bare minimum of accommodation for spectators. Thus the theatre buildings remained a dream which kept close to ancient ideals. The stage, on the other hand, was a tangible reality, fulfilling a new function

il est a notter que pour faire
leurs despenses et ordonances de ladicte
passion, lesdictz compaignons donne…

and projecting a new image, nourished by knowledge of the classics, but deriving their life and meaning from contemporary experience alone.

In the 16th century as well as studies of Vitruvius there were many treatises based on an analysis of Aristotle's writings about literature. Since the most important of these writings, the *Poetics*, considered the structure of tragedy, most 16th century treatises, being written by poets and literary experts, finished up having some direct connection with theatre. The precise and definite rules which governed play-production in France and Italy for centuries issued from these studies. In particular they established the three notorious unities of time, place and action. Every comic or tragic text was to keep its development within these strict limits. The characters had to be concerned with one single question and to act within a single environment for a period of time not exceeding twenty-four hours in imagination.

These rules, we have said, held equally good for both comedy and tragedy. Aristotle had said that tragedy was the most sublime literary genre, with the result that every competent writer felt obliged to compose one. An enormous number were written in the course of the century. Nevertheless, it was the comedies which proved successful on the stage. There were probably several reasons for this. Theatrical productions were almost always part of some secular festivity and it was difficult to feel at home with tragedy in the gay atmosphere characterising such an occasion. Comedies were also easier to produce, since their themes belonged to everyday life and reflected the citizen's familiar surroundings. The Ferrara productions of Plautus and Terence in Italian translation proved that classical comedy was theatrically viable.

Sixteenth century Italian comedies based themselves on the plan followed by these two Latin authors. Their works were re-written and their themes re-explored. The characters' names (Erofilo, Calandro, etc.) indicate the intention to preserve established characters, while endlessly ringing the changes on the details of their adventures. Yet it was not long before the characters operating within this classical scheme began to change their names, their rôles, their external trappings and finally their personal characteristics, which became more contemporary—the old men becoming merchants and the young men very often students. As the characters changed, so did their social context, no longer just some ancient or imaginary city, but a precise location, Florence, Venice or Cremona. There was also a slight change in the plot. The typical story had been that of the young man helped by his servant to win his beloved despite obstacles from her father, a ruffian or a charge of rape. This came to be complemented or replaced by another story, in the telling of which the Tuscan novelist Boccaccio had anticipated his 16th century compatriots, a story in which some jealous husband was suitably made a fool of. This provides the theme, in fact, for some of the few masterpieces out of all this comic production. In Niccolò Machiavelli's *La Mandragola* ('The Mandrake'), old Sir Nicia allows his wife to sleep with her young lover because he thinks that the death of the first man to make love with her is among the side-effects of a fertility-drug she has taken. In Giommaria Cecchi's *L'assiuolo* ('The Horned Owl') an old, jealous, profligate husband is tricked out of his assignation with a girl, remaining locked out in the cold all night, while a young man sleeps with his wife. This change of plot meant farewell to such important features of Latin comedy as the final recognition scene—the Aristotelian anagnorisis. The latter had often allowed some girl, stolen in childhood from her real parents, to marry her lover, because it showed she was not a slave, or that she was of noble birth. This *coup de théâtre* was resorted to so often that one of the most brilliant sixteenth-century writers of comedies and short stories, Anton Francesco Grazzini, felt he had to oppose it outright. He complained that comedies: 'are never without a recognition scene, and this annoys and disturbs the audience, who, as soon as they hear about babies or children being abandoned or getting lost in the taking of this city or during the siege of that castle, know that they have heard it all before.' Nevertheless, despite the novelty of certain modern, realistic features, the basic structure of ancient comedy remained unchanged. The action unrolled with a precise and abstract logic and did not seem to need particular characters or a special setting, but only stereotypes and a vacant space. What was said about events off-stage continued to be more important than what took place on the stage itself and the original division into acts was retained, with each act having its invariable, specific function. It was for this reason, and not just to distinguish it from the more plebeian *commedia dell'arte*, that Italian comedy got the name of 'regular' or 'learned comedy'.

The first regular or learned comedy we hear of, was performed in Ferrara. This was in 1508 and the comedy was a prose-work by Ludovico Ariosto. Latin inspiration was evident in both plot and title: *La Cassaria*. Two young men are in love with a couple of girls under the control of a pimp, and smuggle a chest full of valuables into his house as a pledge in exchange for one of the girls. They hope the pimp will be arrested when the watchmen find this treasure in his possession, but it is eventually the father of one of the young men who has to redeem the pledge.

It so happens that our first sources of information about the newest development in stage-setting, namely perspective scene-painting, refer to this first regular comedy production.

Perspective painting around a common focus, that is with one central vanishing-point on which all the lines in the composition converge, was the great formal achievement of the 15th century, thanks to Leon Battista Alberti and Filippo Brunelleschi who promoted it, and to such artists as Paolo Uccello and Piero della Francesca, who both used it in practice and theorised about it. Perspective painting came to be regarded as the application of the laws intrinsic to human vision to the field of figurative representation. Therefore, if it was properly used, such vision could be reproduced with the maximum exactitude, and one could create an imaginary space capable of producing the illusion that it was an extension of real space, into which it could be integrated without any break in continuity. For three hundred years the decoration of walls with virtuoso examples of such deceptive paintings was to be a specialised art even the experts found hard. On the other hand, since perspective science was based on an analysis of monocular vision, the mathematical and visual space it created did not coincide with the empirical reality of psycho-physically normal, binocular vision.

Because perspective had these two meanings, the theatrical application of perspective painting was bound to develop in more than one direction. Yet it undoubtedly brought about a complete revolution

Baldassare Peruzzi, Setting for a tragedy. Siena, Istituto di Belle Arti

in the very notion of stage-production. Perspective scene-painting found its justification, if not its inspiration, also in Vitruvius, in the passage where this Roman architect analyses the three sorts of scene-painting: tragic, comic and pastoral. In his opinion, scenery should barely suggest a place. Sixteenth-century scene-painters, starting with Pellegrino da Udine, who designed a well-known set for Ariosto's *La Cassaria*, and on until Vasari, Lanci and Buontalenti, preserved this pictorial feature of the Roman theatre, but abolished its architectural proportions, which Pomponio Leto and his pupils had preserved, though on a much reduced scale. The Teatro Olimpico in Vicenza, inspired by Daniel Barbaro's researches and brought to completion by Palladio, was to restore the ancient architecture as if by magic as the century drew to its close. The perspective scene-painting of the sixteenth century

which we are discussing was, of course, no simple backcloth. It was not the sort of perspective painting that furnished only a background but not a setting for the dramatic action. Instead, the scenery comprised a series of flats set at an obtuse angle at either side of the stage and all painted in perspective. Some were set parallel with the line of the proscenium, while others were arranged obliquely relatively to the centre of the stage and ran in towards the back of it. The doors, windows and ledges were only paintings, but the canvases formed a real three-dimensional structure and only the final, distant scene at the back was simply painted on a single canvas. It was not a background, but a setting, and yet a painted rather than a constructed setting and, in a sense, both. It was a real illusion. This remains the paradox of perspective, on stage as well as off it. Both the contradiction and the ambiguity perfectly

Baldassare Peruzzi, Setting for a tragedy. Florence, Uffizi Gallery

The *scaenae frons* of the Teatro Olimpico in Vicenza. The perspective backgrounds are by Vincenzo Scamozzi. Palladio had planned merely painted perspectives mounted on *periaktoi*

suited the purposes of contemporary comedy. The artificiality of perspective painting made the scenery reflect the artificiality of the plot typical of that dramatic form—a comedy abstract in its vagueness as to time and place, but realistic in its respect for the psychological and social authenticity of its characters and in its use of normally accepted Tuscan forms of speech.

The relationship between the abstraction and the reality varied both in nature and in content. Essentially the stage-setting sought to create in the audience the illusion that they were themselves in a place opposite that in which the drama was unfolding. When Cardinal Bibiena's comedy, *Calandria*, was performed in Urbino in 1514, Baldassare Castiglione tells us that the scene was 'one of the last streets between the city-wall and the last houses. The wall itself with two large towers was very convincingly represented by the front of the stage down to ground-level. . . . The auditorium was left as a dry moat, with two walls or aqueducts running across it.' In other words, the scene on stage represented a street or square in an imaginary town somewhere near the walls, which were represented by the front of the stage and imagined to be cut through at a certain level, like the fourth wall in naturalistic theatre. The auditorium itself was arranged to give spectators the impression of not being in a theatre, but in a dry moat surrounding the town. In contrast with this, various features which were introduced into the furnishings of the auditorium and into the disposition of the stage, such as the use of grotesque decorations along the front of the stage and the provision of a proscenium arch by Vasari, apparently in 1565, served to cut off the space reserved for spectators from the abstract, make-believe world of the stage itself.

Turning to the actual choice of scenery, the 16th century set represented a city street or square, a place where all the characters would have to go and in which they could conveniently meet. This street or square might be left rather vague, or it might be one the audience would recognise at once. Thus, among extant 16th century sketches for stage-settings we do find some that most faithfully reproduce some well-known and definite place. When a comedy by Giovanni Battista Cini was performed in Florence in 1569, Baldassarre Lanci prepared scenery showing the Piazza Signoria, a spot well-known to all the citizens. Twenty years previously the Bolognese architect, Sebastiano Serlio, author of the first and most complete treatise on perspective scene-painting, drew sketches for scenery to represent the square in front of Saint Mark's in Venice.

Baldassare Lanci, Setting for Giovambattista Cini's *The Widow*,
1569. Florence, Uffizi Gallery

BALDAS... LANCI DA URBINO INGEGNERE

Francesco Salviati, Perspective scenery. London, British Museum

However, other sketches show unrecognisable places in well-known cities, synthetic presentations, as it were, of the city as a whole. Finally, most of the sketches depict no specific place at all, but just a nondescript street in an unidentified town: a location that is generic but typical—a street that today may be in Ferrara and tomorrow in Cremona, as Ariosto remarks in one of his prologues. Obviously this meant that the spectator's bewitchment and involvement in the illusion varied in degree.

How did gesture, mime and speech fit into this setting? What were their characteristics? We really know very little, since the chroniclers were more interested in the *décor* and the intermezzos, while the scholars concentrated on textual criticism and problems of scenography. It was not until 1556 that Leone de' Sommi of Mantua wrote what we can describe as the first treatise on production and direction in the history of theatre. This was the third of his *Four Dialogues concerning Theatrical Performances*. As well as describing how de' Sommi set about staging a play, it contains interesting observations about the actors' performances.

To begin with, we must remember that it was almost always amateurs who acted in learned comedies staged at court or in the academies. In the 16th century the ruling class was inclined to arrogate to itself all responsibility for cultural activities and to be an intellectual was often synonymous with being a courtier. Painting, however, not being numbered among the liberal arts, was left to professionals. Professional theatre developed out of the culturally inferior, purely recreative, productions for the people. Men played the women's rôles and de' Sommi emphasises the need for each actor to have physical characteristics well adapted to his part. A lover should be handsome, a soldier robust, a hanger-on corpulent and a servant rather thin, while anyone playing a woman's part should, obviously, not have a deep voice. De' Sommi's ideal in acting seems to call for more harmony between ancient and contemporary approaches to character-casting in comedy and increased sensitivity to the individual actor's personal adaptation to his rôle. The latter has not merely to embody attitudes typical of the character he is interpreting—a miser, for instance, must never let go of his purse—he must also draw attention to the immediately relevant circumstances with suitable gestures. Thus, if a servant 'is made the victim of a playful prank, he must know how to respond at once with a graceful leap. In time of grief, he should tear his handkerchief with his teeth. In moments of despair, he will take off his hat.' What is wanted is not realism, but ways of avoiding static immobility

and of varying the action on stage as much as possible. De' Sommi, in fact, prefers clarity of diction to realistic intonation, rich costumes to realistic apparel. Hence, actors must always speak their parts slowly, and though no one except a servant can be permitted to wear 'a ragged old tunic', even he can be dressed in velvet, provided his master wears brocades and so maintains his proper station. This liking for luxurious and variegated theatre is behind his suggestion that every character's costume should be completely different from all the rest, because this will also give greater clarity to the unfolding of the plot.

In comedy the scene could be any more or less convincing city cross-roads. In tragedy the street was always entirely imaginary and the houses to either side had to be the luxurious apartments of those magnificent characters who had been made its protagonists. Tragic performances were rare in the 16th century, and the best known of these did not use perspective scenery. It was not a new production, but the classic tragedy of them all, *Oedipus Rex* by Sophocles, played to inaugurate the Teatro Olimpico in Vicenza in 1582 and produced by Angelo Ingegneri. He was the author of several comedies and pastoral sketches and had also written a treatise just as valuable as de' Sommi's, though it came much later. However, perspective scenery was used in Reggio Emilia in 1568 for the stage-production of another tragedy, called *Alidoro*. Other 16th-century-style productions of this sort became quite a regular feature in the 17th century, one that should be mentioned being the famous staging of Prospero Bonarelli's *Solimano* in 1619.

These tragedies, whether produced in the 16th century or the 17th, whether in a setting of perspective scenery or in front of the imposing *skene* of the Teatro Olimpico, all had certain features in common. De' Sommi and Ingegneri in their treatises had considered these of fundamental importance. The production of a tragedy had to have a splendour and dignity in keeping with the majesty of the characters involved in it, as well as of the princes and lords who, as generous patrons, made the performance possible, being themselves the modern heirs of those great ones from the past. The costumes had to be magnificent, although, as in comedy, social distinctions

137

had to be maintained. Gesture and movement had to be most dignified and solemn. Even in their most violent emotional outbursts the characters, especially the leading characters, had to preserve their decorum and grandeur. A variety of costumes was believed to be just as important in tragedy as it was for comedy, in order to lend clarity and interest to the performance. Nevertheless, the audience showed a keener interest in exotic or barbaric costumes because of their greater novelty. *Solimano* was a classic proof of this.

The small number of characters allowed in the closely knit development of any tragedy conceived along Aristotelian lines could not possibly produce all this solemnity and grandeur. For this reason, extras, almost unknown in comedy, were increasingly made use of. However, in 16th century tragedy the extras were not a confused, indiscriminate mass, a crowd, or the people, they were almost always regular rows of persons in uniform, soldiers quite often, and their task was to provide an escort to accompany the main characters and so reflect their grandeur, since each one's escort was proportionate to his rank. A scene involving three characters, therefore, called for three bands of extras, three colourful groups, moving about, mingling together, or opposing each other in a controlled fashion that formed, as it were, a further setting for the main action. For his production of *Oedipus Rex* in Vicenza, Ingegneri relates that for Sophocles' nine characters he used one hundred and eight extras, twenty-eight of whom provided the escort for the actor playing the leading rôle.

Vitruvius listed a third sort of play as well as comedy and tragedy, namely satire, and he may have been referring to the satyric dramas which were the concluding feature of the Greek tetralogies. The satyric scene was set in the forest. Vitruvius mentions trees, caves, hills and other pastoral features. Sixteenth-century scholars had no difficulty in adapting scenery of this sort to a new type of drama, the pastoral romance. The most successful example of the genre was Torquato Tasso's *Aminta*, inspired by the *Orpheus* of Poliziano. With disconcerting monotony these pastorals follow the ups and downs and the intrigues of the love-life of Arcadian nymphs and shepherds. Their popularity in court circles was partly due to their intimations of a completely care-free dream-world beyond the reach of time, their emotional gaiety and escape from the realities of life. It was also due to certain features of the scenery, principally the interpretation of a natural setting in contrived and artificial terms. For, in pastoral stage-settings, the painted scenes were supplemented and

might, indeed, be dominated by some definite three-dimensional feature, such as trees with silken leaves arranged in the middle of the stage. Alternatively, everything that separated the audience from the spectacle might be done away with, as when *Aminta* was played in a natural setting in Cornelio Bentivoglio's park near Ferrara, so that all the spectators had the impression of having made their way into the magic world of Arcadia itself. Even the shepherds were sometimes of noble blood, since otherwise their nobly born audience could not have regarded their life as an ideal, and the costumes of these, like those of the wandering nymphs, were exotic in a way that was carefully contrived and belonged to no special period or locality. Ingegneri described this particular garment as nymphal. The text was always in verse and lyrical in tone, though often in a forced sort of way. Movement and gesture would be in keeping with this lyricism, light and measured, rather like a dance.

Sixteenth-century theatrical productions were presented in the main by learned academies or at court. In the latter case, they were not usually isolated events, but the comedy or pastoral was staged as part of a much more complex programme arranged to celebrate the coming of a distinguished guest, a birth, christening, marriage or other important event. This restored to theatre that Aristotelian sense of occasion which, in quite a different way, it had enjoyed in the Middle Ages and, prior to that, in the Athens of Pericles. Theatre, in other words, was a single phase in an integrated festival that also comprised banquets and balls, as well as other theatrical displays such as processions and parades of allegorical floats, decked out for the occasion with authentic scenery and props. This could involve the entire population. Now, the performance on stage was often the high-point of all these manifestations and, obviously, a straightforward comedy, no matter how luxuriously it was produced, did not fit the bill. This is why the intermezzos were developed considerably during the 16th century. They had featured in the Ferrara productions of the works of Plautus and were mainly short mimes including some dancing, though solo or choral songs might also feature in them.

However, while the intermezzo in the late 15th century Ferrara productions had kept within the limits we described, and did no more than offer elegant, light entertainment between acts, their 16th century counterparts, especially in Florence, became increasingly ambitious in design. Their subject would be mythical or allegorical—peasants being changed into frogs for offending Latona, the allegory

of Calumny as described by Apuleius, or even Virgil's fourth eclogue. They were often produced on a lavish scale in a way that was highly dramatic. Naturally, this was not always the case. The dramatic action might frequently be limited to all the characters coming on stage together and arranging themselves in a row, as happened by way of intermezzo in the 1567 Florence production of *Calumny*, when the characters were ranged in a half-moon round King Midas. A famous painting by Botticelli treats the same subject. Again, there might be nothing more than a short theatrical mime, like that of eight nymphs dressed in silver returning from the hunt (Florence, 1539). Alternatively, there might be songs and dancing. Nevertheless, in other instances quite impressive stage-props were involved, such as the floats also used for the allegorical parades. In Florence in 1569 a group of boys and girls were shown going to meet the float of Hunger followed by all the famous men of antiquity. In Parma that year and in Reggio Emilia the year before, floats representing the four elements, Fire, Air, Earth and Water, were used. Other effects arrived on the scene thanks to some mechanical magic and either covered or partially concealed the setting for the comedy itself. Such was the huge dragon's mouth representing the jaws of hell from which men notorious for their lives of vice stepped forth (Florence, 1567). Vasari, too, made Mount Helicon rise up from beneath the stage in the last of a series of intermezzos presenting the story of Eros and Psyche. In the first of these,

Venus came down from heaven on a cloud surrounded by a retinue composed of the Graces and the Hours. This was the traditional way for divinities to put in an appearance and was obviously the most spectacular, not only because it used all three available dimensions of the stage-setting, but because of the wonder aroused by the complexity of the apparatus. Prior to Bernardo Buontalenti's magnificently staged intermezzos of 1585 and 1589, such 'engines' were not much used, but, at least on one occasion, the changing and moving, coloured, papier-mâché clouds filled the whole stage and became a performance on their own account. This was in Florence, for the intermezzo between the second and third acts of Giovambattista Cini's *The Widow*, staged in a setting designed by Baldassare Lanci to represent the Piazza Signoria. Sixteen boys personifying the winds suddenly emerged from under the stage. By blowing, they filled the sky on stage with multi-coloured clouds, and on each of these a girl was sitting. It is obvious that such large-scale props changed or masked the view of the setting for the main comedy. In any case, in this very same 1569 performance, for the intermezzo about Latona and the peasants, the appearance of the main scene was itself transformed and the Piazza Signoria became a pleasant stretch of countryside just outside Florence. The flats may have been mounted on those triangular drums that Vitruvius named *periaktoi*, which could be swivelled round to show a different surface to the audience.

Chapter 12

Prospettiua
Della metà del Teatro, che serui
al Torneo Festeggiato in
Bologna l'Anno
M. D. C. XXXIX

A. Machina ... rappresentante la Sicilia
B. Vltima Machina con VI Deità à VIII.
C. Ponte per il quale scesero i Caualieri nel piano della sala d. del Podestà.
D. Proscenio alla parte verso Leuante
E. Iride che scese dal Cielo nel mezo della Sala che da Ponente hauea un altro simile Proscenio.

F. Piano nel quale si ormeggiò a piedi & à cauallo.
G. Luogo per i Sig. Cardinali Ducchi et Prencipi.
H. Luogo dei Sig. Antiani e Confaloni
I. Ponti 160. in uno per i spettatori ...

THE BAROQUE VOGUE FOR OPERA

The intermezzos began as secondary features in the programme, complementary to the main play, but ended up as the central climax of the dramatic performance. They provided a focus for the growing taste for pure theatre, in which what happened on stage was not subordinated to spoken words, but became self-sufficient as a vision of life in motion on a scale that grew incessantly in grandeur and complexity. Intermezzos sometimes told a story. For instance, we have mentioned some in 1565 that related the story of Eros and Psyche. Even when they did not, they could still have a single theme running through them. Thus, in the end, the several acts of the main comedy became the intermezzos in a performance composed of intermezzos.

At Florence in 1585 and 1589 two performances were arranged which allowed full scope to this sort of production and thus were established the salient thematic and linguistic features of opera. In both instances a learned gentleman of the Medici court, a certain Giovanni de' Bardi, devised the intermezzos, while their actual production was entrusted to the court architect, Bernardo Buontalenti, who had made his reputation in Florence by putting up some of its most elegant buildings.

In each of the performances the scene changed completely for the intermezzo and changed back for the next act of the comedy. Intensive and continuous use was made of 'engines' permitting the main characters to fly through the air on trails of clouds, or to spring up from below stage sitting on the gentle slope of a hill. The actual movement of the characters on the stage itself was reduced to a minimum. The theme, too, was new and had important implications. In the 1585 production there were, as usual, six intermezzos. The first and last featured as prologue and epilogue. The other four depicted the four elements that go to make up the universe of Aristotelian physics: Water, Air, Earth and Fire. The way chosen to portray these on stage was not allegorical, but the successive presentation of the four kingdoms —the Sea, the Sky, the Earth and the Underworld. In other words, the entire universe was shown, as if to affirm the theatre's unlimited capacity as a medium of interpretation.

The theme of the intermezzos accompanying the presentation of Girolamo Bargagli's comedy, *La pellegrina* ('The Pilgrim') in 1589 was the effect on the world of music and rhythm. The four central intermezzos, which again ran through the four kingdoms, illustrated the theme with stories from ancient mythology. The first intermezzo, however, took the audience to the very centre of the universe, showed them the vast heavens composed of four series of clouds carrying the heavenly Sirens and the planets, in their orders, all converging on the throne of Necessity. It was the universal harmony of the Platonic and Pythagorean myths, the originating vortex for the music of the spheres.

All three classical forms of theatre survived into the 17th century, but only just. Themes from the preceding century were kept going or timidly devel-

Theatre for tournament-opera built in Bologna by Francesco Rivarola, called the Chenda. Miniature from *Insignia*. Bologna, Archivio di Stato

Bernardo Buontalenti, Delphic couples, costumes designed for the third intermezzo of a performance staged in Florence in 1589. Florence, Biblioteca Nazionale. Notice the exotic features in these supposedly Greek costumes

Bernardo Buontalenti, Venus' costume for the first intermezzo. Every detail of this costume has some symbolic meaning

oped. The three unities were gradually abolished. Changes of scene became admissable. Each act in a comedy or tragedy could have its own stage-setting and location. Prose productions of learned theatre aroused little interest and no amount of concentration on exotic dressing availed to remedy the situation. The literary output was still prolific, but information about actual performances is very sparse. The 17th century was the century of opera, which spread from Italy throughout the whole of Europe. Italian scene-painters, authors, musicians and singers became the centre of foreign court festivals, especially in Austria and Germany. Throughout the century theatre outside Italy underwent important developments, as we shall see, but in Italy 'learned' theatre wore itself out.

Modern opera was born on a definite date and in a specific place, but very soon lost its original

character. It sprang from the last gasp of pure, cultural humanism, the result of the efforts of a group of Florentine intellectuals, members of the Camerata dei Bardi, to effect a complete restoration of Greek tragedy. They believed that in antiquity the text of this had been sung.

The stage-settings for the Camerata dei Bardi's performances were rather like those for pastoral romances. This was because the selected operas had themes which, while tragic, were also bucolic: Apollo and Daphne, Orpheus and Eurydice. Although this lyrical and dramatic form called for plaintive solo-singing, other theatrical requirements, already more than catered for in the intermezzos, continued to make themselves felt.

Almost immediately a new unity emerged. No later than 1600 Buontalenti produced in a highly theatrical way an opera that had been set to music by Giulio Caccini, one of the greatest exponents of monodic composition. The outpourings of Buontalenti's lively imagination, hungry to expand the horizons open to its own creativity, quite overwhelmed Caccini's dream of Grecian purity. The courts consummated this sacrifice of the humanist ideal. At court, theatre just had to be luxurious, grandiose and bombastic. Opera became the favourite way of satisfying these needs. Aristocratic society found there its own reflection and also its apotheosis. The gods of Olympus were summoned to visit, reverence and exalt the protagonists, heroes whose adventures were unfolded as ways of dealing with some complicated love-affair that embraced all four kingdoms of the Aristotelian universe. Aristocratic social life in the 17th century was largely a matter of such passionate pastimes, but it had needed Buontalenti's research to translate the universe into theatre.

The most obvious external features of court operas were the frequent changes of scene and the use of mechanical devices. Towards the close of the century

Bernardo Buontalenti, *Music of the Spheres*, 1st intermezzo, London, Victoria and Albert Museum. *The Myth of Arion*, 5th Intermezzo, London, *ibid. The Demons of the Air in Hell*, 4th Intermezzo, Paris, Louvre. *The Challenge of the Muses and the Pierides*, 2nd Intermezzo, London, Victoria and Albert Museum

Vulcan's Workshop, stage-setting by Giulio Parigi for the 4th Intermezzo of *The Judgment of Paris*. Engraving by R Cantagallina, Florence, 1608. Florence, Uffizi Gallery

Closing Ballet in Heaven, Alfonso Parigi's stage-setting for Coppola's *Marriage of the Gods*. Engraving by A Parigi, Florence, 1637. Florence, Uffizi Gallery

Cupid raising a Storm, Alfonso Parigi's stage-setting for A Salvadori's *La Flora*. Engraving by A Parigi, Florence, 1628. Florence, Uffizi Gallery

Procession of Coaches, Francesco Santurini's stage-setting for F M Piccoli's *Avenging Berenice*, Piazzola, 1679, Florence, Uffizi Gallery

scene-changes became one mad rush. The apparatus caused a stir of admiration for the skill with which the illusions were created and allowed movement on the stage to vary and take place on a much vaster scale. By comparison with the preceding century, the layout of the stage-settings was simplified considerably. Easily manoeuvrable painted scenes were used instead of flats set at an angle with certain features standing out in relief. These simple scenes were fitted together to give just one overall effect. The mechanical devices enabled the characters to fly on clouds, chariots or winged horses, but also made possible other miracles—the sudden appearance or disappearance of particular persons or entire palaces, the raising of mountains, unleashing of tempests and swaying of the ocean. Thus, as well as mythological marvels, there was the whole range of natural phenomena from the rising and setting of the sun to the first burgeoning of spring. It was all part of 17th century theatre.

The description of natural phenomena was almost made the main subject of some productions. A typical instance of this is Andrea Salvadori's *Flora*, produced by Alfonso Parigi who, along with his brother Giulio, followed Buontalenti as scene-painters to the Medici court. The crowning moment in the show was precisely the blossoming of the flowers in spring, as a result of the Zephyr's tears of joy, in his happy love of Chloris—for so the story goes.

In the first half-century, and especially in Florence, other productions developed cosmological subjects from Buontalenti's intermezzos into stories with a single thread holding them together. Thus, in *The Wedding of the Gods*, directed by Alfonso Parigi

The Favour of the Gods. Apollo sees Daphne on the bank of the river Alpheus. Stage-setting by D Mauro, Parma, 1690. Parma, private collection

himself in 1637, the love-affairs of Olympian deities served to lead the audience through the kingdoms of the universe.

Subjects of this sort occurred only spasmodically in the second half of the century and featured in opera more for the sake of variety and as an act of homage to tradition than out of any inner sense of their suitability or necessity. What Marivaux would have called the game of love and chance definitely became, along with a taste for characters who showed their feelings, the central focus. The new themes expressed an underlying concern for high society and its characteristic life-style. In Piazzola a Venetian courtier, Marco Contarini, arranged a performance in which the worldly life of the aristocracy was portrayed, with special attention to the essentially theatrical elements it contains—hunting, coaches in a hurry, theatre itself. In a sense, then, the gap between theatre and social life disappeared. Gian Lorenzo Bernini achieved the same result in a performance about which the record is incomplete— he portrayed on stage an audience watching a theatrical performance. For Bernini, however, the abolition of the distinction between life and theatre was not a fact to celebrate. It was a tragedy—not far removed from the idea of his great Spanish contemporary and dramatist, Calderón: Life is empty; like theatre, it is a dream.

Scenery, which so dominated 17th-century theatre, was naturally affected by this shift in interest. Landscapes were used less and less and eventually almost disappeared. Their place was taken by fabulous palaces, regal courtyards, gardens of delight, places that seemed more fitted to welcome blue-blooded

The Coronation of Phaedra. The Royal Palace of Neptune. Stage-setting by Francesco Santurini. Engraving by M Küssel, Munich, 1662. Munich, Kunsthistorische Bibliothek

Temporary amphitheatre built in Bologna in 1627. Miniature from Volume V of the *Insignia*. Bologna, Archivio di Stato In keeping with a tradition dating back at least as far as the festival in Rome to celebrate the conferring of citizenship on Lorenzo and Giuliano de' Medici in 1513, although the background is a scene painted in perspective, the temporary amphitheatre was real enough to accommodate diplomats being fêted or who were presenting their credentials, and this was often its main purpose

Overleaf: Ferdinando Bibiena, *A Place of Magnificence*. Terlago, Collezione Cesarini Sforza. Typical example of rococo scene-painting. The subject was almost always a vast hall and several vanishing-points were used. Decorative motifs became oppressively rich
Below: Ferdinando Bibiena, sketch for a garden scene. Munich, Staatliche Graphische Sammlung

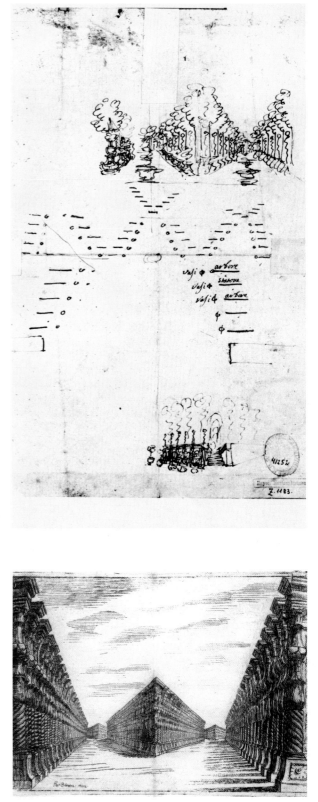

principal characters carrying the names of the heroes of old. The incessant scene-shifting no longer created an impression of a variety that was both disconcerting and relentless, but seemed rather the invariably insecure modulation of a single theme. Ludovico Burnacini's scenes for performances at the Viennese court are the most celebrated cases in point.

Scenery with architectural subjects attained its greatest heights in the following century, however, thanks mainly to the achievements of the Galli Bibiena family. Ferdinando, the head of the family, became famous throughout Europe for introducing to scenic design angle perspective, or perspective with two vanishing-points. This allowed a complete break away from the monotonous symmetrical arrangements that had been dominant for most of the 17th century.

The dramatic action was in the 17th century restricted for the most part, being confined within the framework of the proscenium arch. This made it abundantly clear where was the boundary between the real world of the audience and the imaginary world of theatre, which often mirrored that of the audience. Occasionally, however, the boundaries were not respected, and the theatrical world occupied the territory reserved for the audience. This was usually to make room for some ballet, tournament or joust of arms called for by the plot of the opera. The ballet-dancers or the combatants would use ramps to make their way down from the stage into the pit, where they would play out their rôles. Opera of this sort, especially when it linked together a tournament and a sung performance, was tremendously popular in court-theatres in the second quarter of the century. Francesco Guitti's production of Claudio Achillini's *Mercury and Mars* to inaugurate the Teatro Farnese in Parma in 1628 was remembered as outstanding in this respect. A patrol of soldiers was supposed to have been imprisoned by Mercury, who was afraid Duke Farnese's fascination for warfare would take him away from his writing and, at the end of every scene, these were set free by a god summoned by Mars and made their way into the pit, where there was a joust. The whole performance concluded with the most terrific *coup de théâtre* Baroque theatre had ever dreamed of—the pit was completely flooded and the final combat took place on an island.

Rather similar spectacles graced the boards of Buontalenti's now-completed Teatro degli Uffizi, where performances were held for the Medici court. Nevertheless, Giovan Battista Aleotti's grand Teatro Farnese remains the only outstanding example of this sort of theatre-building to have been preserved.

Didio Giuliano. Open galleries. Stage-setting by Ferdinando Bibiena, Piacenza, 1687. Bologna, Liceo Musicale. This was among the first instances of angle perspective in scene-settings and may be regarded as a paradigm case

Its towering, steep rows of steps were able to accommodate an enormous number of spectators, leaving the vast expanse of the pit quite free, so that, from above, it looked like a large piazza, while the proscenium arch, opening in the middle of an inclined architectural composition and set at a distance, seemed the mighty portals into a world that was far away. The later theatre-buildings of which we have pictorial evidence, those of Ferrara, Padua and Bologna, replaced the steps with small boxes in a series of balconies arranged one above the other. This was the final form of the Italian theatre-building. The oldest example of this still standing is the Teatro Comunale in Bologna, erected by Ferdinando Bibiena in the 18th century, but such boxes were

154

The Teatro Farnese in Parma built by Giovan Battista Aleotti in 1618

quite frequent in 17th-century theatres.

Boxes became indispensable when opera left the court and became available to any audience able to pay for it. This happened in Venice in 1637. Because of the new situation Venetian productions streamlined their design, became business enterprises and relied less on mechanical miracles and extras in rich attire and more on the singing ability of individual virtuoso performers, as well as on frequent changes of scene, Giacomo Torelli favouring them with his talent as one of the greatest scene-painters of the century. Since, then, the theatre was now open to all who could afford to buy a ticket, the building had to provide means of avoiding an indiscriminate mingling of the different social classes. The pit was reserved for the lower orders and separate boxes prevented rich merchants from rubbing shoulders with the nobility. Furthermore, especially in the 18th century, the stage itself became a sort of home from home: guests were received, refreshments taken conversation went on and only during solo arias was any heed given to the performance. All this afforded great scandal to foreign travellers, but there was nothing at all unique about it in the annals of theatre.

The success of Italian opera and of its characteristic way of using scenery was widespread, especially among the aristocracy and at court. As well as Ludovico Burnacini's productions in Vienna, we must mention those of Torelli in Paris and of Santurini in Munich. As well as this, German, French and English scene-painters soon learned the Italian techniques.

The most outstanding case of Italian inspired theatre being grafted onto the trunk of local tradition is probably provided by the masques staged by Inigo Jones, architect and painter at the Stuart court, and immensely fond of Italian art, having even made an educational tour of Italy round about 1613.

The English masque was an allegorical drama featuring the King, personifying Goodness, Beauty and Truth, as triumphant over his enemies, personifying Evil. The finale frequently included a magical transmutation of the jaws of hell into the Palace of Fame, with the coming down off the stage and into the auditorium of such allegorical and mythological characters as Beauty, Oberon the King of the Fairies, and various British heroes. The ensuing ballet then developed into merry-making all round.

In the 16th century the scenes did not all follow one another on stage in the same central location, but were ranged round the festival hall in a series, following the medieval idea of simultaneous settings —here was a grotto, there a hut, further on a temple or a wood. The same happened in France for the

Costume design by Inigo Jones for a masquer lord in Thomas Campion's *The Lords' Masque* (1613). Chatsworth, Duke of Devonshire Collection.

155

court ballet. Thus, the well-known *Ballet comique de la Royne*, danced in 1581, was produced with this technique.

It was, in fact, Inigo Jones who unified on the stage as a succession of scenes what had been previously scattered in space, though there had been temporal simultaneity. He introduced the Italian techniques of scene-shifting. At first, however, the composition and the subjects of his scenery were inspired almost exlusively by English sources—rock-faces which opened to disclose enchanted palaces, with no attempt to use perspective to create an illusion of depth. This was in his work for the theatre before he went to Italy and was almost entirely in connection with Ben Jonson's masques, *The Masque of Blackness*, *The Masque of Queens*, *Oberon the Fairy Prince*, etc. Afterwards the situation was entirely different. The influence of Giulio Parigi became so obvious that in some instances Jones's sketches are just copies of those of the Florentine master. Rocks give way to tastefully arranged country settings, perfectly harmonised and shown in perspective, framed by the proscenium arch. The scenes for *Florimene* (1635) and *Britannia Triumphans* (1638) bear this out. In England, too, therefore, Italian stage-settings, after their first appearance in the court theatre, supplanted the original, native, theatrical, scenic compositions which had established themselves in public theatres during the reign of Elizabeth.

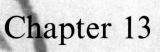

Chapter 13

Pantaloon's Serenade. Painting, Stockholm, Drottningholms Teatermuseum. This work showing a typical *commedia dell'arte* scene, the comical serenade followed by disaster, seems in some way related to a series of engravings, two of which are shown overleaf

THE COMMEDIA DELL'ARTE

If grand opera in the Italian style became the highlight of the court festivities of the aristocracy of Europe and, once it had overflowed into the public theatres, was also a very popular form of theatrical entertainment among other social categories, there was also towards the close of the 16th century another and vastly different, very unpretentious form of theatre spreading throughout Europe among every class of person. The amusement it offered was easy to appreciate and was totally free of pomp and ceremony in any shape or form.

There is, from the point of view of its production on stage, nothing simpler than the *commedia dell' arte* which involves no more than the actors' own performance. However, if we stop to unravel the cultural elements it brings together, we are faced with a complex phenomenon that is extremely difficult to understand.

Its history embraces a period of almost three hundred years, running more or less alongside that of opera, with the 17th century as the period of its most extensive influence. Even today theatre people and scholars continue to find it fascinating. It is a live issue. *Commedia dell'arte* is frequently quoted as an unrivalled example of pure theatre. It has been even defined as 'popular Italian comedy'. It really was, indeed, an expression of the people's own theatre. Unlike opera, particularly in the 19th century, it was never something ready-made offered to the people, who liked it a lot and so made it their own. On the contrary, its very roots lay deep in the culture and traditions of ordinary people, while its growth carried it up to the highest levels of the social scale, so that, even if noble intellectuals might despise it, they could never ignore it. It was a striking instance in the history of Western culture of the 'other' theatre, the one representing the lower classes, setting itself up as an alternative to the theatre of an intellectual and social élite.

Territorially speaking the *commedia dell'arte* sprang from fairs both large and small in which acrobats, mountebanks and ballad-singers liked to set up their little stage. It was on this that, prior to the attempted sale of such doubtful wares as the elixir of love or something to prolong one's life, the acrobats showed their skill in sketches and mimes, often with one and sometimes with more characters, while the ballad-singers accompanied the recital with a mime of their own, possibly almost a running-commentary on that of the main characters. In a sense, they were all carrying on the jongleurs' tradition, if only because their very survival was so closely tied to the people's good-will. They did not share with them membership of the same social class, since they were vagabonds, but they all shared the same poverty. It is hard to say how, when and under what conditions these mountebanks and acrobats began to assume their characteristic appearance and rôles as established personalities within popular tradition. However, when this process of integration was complete and both mountebanks and acrobats, conscious of the success of

Jacques Callot, *The Two Captains*. Engraving from the series: *Sfessania's Dances*. The grotesque, violent yet firmly controlled pose of the characters was typical of late 16th-century *commedia dell'arte*, especially in southern Italy

A Scalzi, *Pantaloon the Warrior*. Fresco. Landshut, Trausnitz Castle. The frescoes in Trausnitz Castle, especially those of the *Narrentreppe*, seem inspired by Massimo Troiano's amateur troupe, which was active *c* 1570 (*on right*)

Pantaloon the Ladies' Man. Engraving. Cambridge, Fitzwilliam Museum. This Pantaloon bears no resemblance to the impotent dotard of a later period; he is alive, robust, even athletic and brutal

their mimed dialogues, had ceased to work alone and had united in small groups or formed family companies, even before their theatrical efforts were divorced from the sale of love-potions, the *commedia dell'arte* was already a definable phenomenon. This was before the middle of the 16th century.

The essential elements in the definition of the *commedia dell'arte* are professionalism, the use of masks and improvisation.

The term *arte* (art) is not used in the modern sense, but with the medieval meaning of trade and even of guild or association. Thus, in Florence the trade-guilds were called *arti* (arts): the art of wool-traders, of doctors, of herbalists, of saddlers, etc. In the case of the actors, their guild did not exist as an organised structure, but was rather the shared consciousness of exercising a specific trade with,

later on, roots in a common tradition. In the 16th and 17th centuries the actors in learned prose theatre were amateurs, and among 'respectable' people the tradition of amateur theatricals has continued right up to the present-day. In countryside festivals, such as May-day games, Carnivals, and other fertility feasts, all of them quite closely related to the *commedia dell'arte*, the actors are amateurs. Operatic performers and virtuoso singers were professional people, but their professional association was run along quite different lines, since they were engaged individually and at a fixed rate, for a period of varying length by a court or by an impresario. The *commedia dell'arte* players, instead, spontaneously drifted together in travelling companies, whose composition was relatively stable. Their earnings depended on the fluctuating fortunes of their way of

Harlequin Bringing Columbine's Children to Pantaloon, and (*right*) *Harlequin Disguised as a Warrior*. Engravings from the Fossard Collection, Stockholm, Drottningholms Teatermuseum. A series of 18 prints recently arranged by F Mastropasqua, who discovered they all show scenes from the same comedy, probably one given by the Gelosi in Paris *c* 1580

Commedia dell'arte Characters. Oil on canvas. Béziers, Musée du Vieux Biterrois

French and Italian Actors. Painting, 17th century. Paris, Comédie Française

life and they either owned everything in common or arranged to share their profits. Most of them were of low birth and lived in poverty, which may explain why the actor's profession was automatically the butt of scorn and derision, though this did not prevent kings from fawning over famous actors.

A few scholars, however, interpret *arte* in another sense, as 'expertise', 'capacity', 'skill', and this would imply a professional sense linked to the possession of specific skills and so dependent on training. Actually, of course, a good actor not only needed acting ability, but had to be athletic, since leaps, capers and contortions were all part of the stock in trade needed to present certain characters. Naturally this interpretation describes a type of theatre more than it sets limits to the actors, who very soon took the opportunity to play parts in learned theatre, comedies, of course, but also tragedies and pastoral romances. For also in such situations their skill and professional training stood them in good stead and gave them an advantage over the aristocratic amateurs, whose only talent was a courtly elegance of delivery.

The *commedia dell'arte* is often called the comedy of masks. This is to look at it from the point of view of its inner nature and of the characteristics and idiosyncracies of the stock characters taking part in it. For the characters are established types, defined by special masks which covered only the top-half of the face leaving the mouth free, as well as by a special, immediately recognisable costume. Each character had his own name and his individual personality and, like his mask and costume, these never changed, whatever the differences in the situations to which he was exposed in different plays. It has been called impossible to think of Hamlet apart from that particular story in which his life revolves, but Harlequin is open to anything that comes along.

The Zanni were the original group of masked characters for the *commedia dell'arte*. (It is no accident that the English word 'zany' is derived from this popular buffoon.) Although they immediately took on servant-rôles, their own origins go back to remote times, and so prove the extent to which the *commedia dell'arte* has its roots in popular culture. The Zanni are characters in north Italian folklore

163

Rosaura. 18th-century Venetian statuette, Milan, Museo Teatrale della Scala

connected with propitiation rites and celebrations similar to the modern carnivals. Originally they represented the demons of the earth. When they took over this old character, the *commedia dell'arte* players preserved his external features almost intact —the devilish black mask and ample white gown made him immediately recognisable to the audience, at least in villages and hamlets. They then gave him a new identity as a servant-porter, the lowest form of life in working-class townships, and almost the proclamation of the common man's predestined condition of servitude. This profound meaning, flowing from the character's primitive ambiguity, continually comes to the surface as permanent hunger, conflict with his master, village wisdom and the need to make a come-back which, even when it comes off, never really lasts. Later the Zanni were either replaced or accompanied by other masked characters from the same background: Harlequin, the diabolical figure of rural French folklore, and Punch are the best known. During the 17th and 18th centuries these gave rise to a whole range of other characters—Truffaldino, Fritellino, Mezzetino, etc. The original characters also changed their own appearance, as their costumes and gestures became stylised and their particular character was fixed as either crudely exuberant or sadly thoughtful. Their rôle remained essentially the same, but the sense of their remote origin was inevitably lost.

Inevitably, too, the servant had to be provided with a master. This was Pantaloon the Magnifico, a Venetian merchant and head of the family. We cannot be as certain of his diabolical origin as we are with regard to the Zanni, but it is certainly possible considering his black mask and red costume and also because, while he is a lecherous old man, he need not be impotent or senile, but often remains violent and energetic. It was only Goldoni's emphasis on middle-class virtues which in the 18th century transformed him into a prudent and slow-moving character, a father much more than a master.

A modern mask added to these traditional ones is that of the Captain (Captain Courageous, Captain Matamoros, Captain Crocodile). Some have considered this a revival of the old Roman *miles gloriosus* or swaggering soldier, with the task of mirroring the situation of an Italy occupied and troubled by Spanish armies.

To these basic masks others were gradually added by a process of rôle-sharing. The Zanni was aided and abetted by a servant-girl, called Columbine or Franceschina. Old Pantaloon was accompanied by the erudite caricature of the Bolognese Doctor Balanzone. And so on.

P L Ghezzi, *Harlequin, Punch, Pantaloon*. Drawing in red chalk. Rome, Raccolto Teatrale Burcardo. The Roman painter, Ghezzi, lived from 1674 to 1755 and painted scenes for opera and for carnival floats. He took a keen interest in the *commedia dell'arte* and has left a very fine series of drawings of masked characters

No sooner, however, were these groups of acrobats transformed into theatrical companies, with the objective of offering the public an integrated performance instead of a series of intermezzos, than other characters were added to the masked ones and these did not belong to the popular tradition. Even though the lovers always used the same names, they were personalities and not stock characters, because their real faces were not hidden, their dress followed the fashion and their psychological traits varied and followed literary instead of popular tradition. The *commedia dell'arte* was born in the hot climate of the Renaissance. It offered itself as an alternative to learned comedy and learned theatre in general. Yet its exponents did not hesitate to borrow from the latter any features that might help to broaden the scope of their own masked performance and to give it some order, because they were certain, even recklessly, that their theatre would still keep its own identity. Plots became adventure stories, full of *coups de théâtre* and misunderstandings, and right from the start the servant had a respectable position and a rôle of his own. Additional characters were the lovers: Lelio, Isabel and Flavio, whose tearful or lyrical interludes afforded relief from the exuberant acting of the masked characters, while still belonging to the main lines of the plot.

Improvisation was the whole foundation of the acting technique in *commedia dell'arte*. This explains the name 'improvised comedy', just as its origin explains the name 'clowns' comedy'. The players familiarised themselves with a rough plot which was sufficiently detailed to specify the successive phases of the action and sometimes to summarise the individual scenes, or alternatively contented themselves with an overall idea of the dramatic development. They then improvised their rejoinders, always varying their handling of the plot, but remaining faithful to the known character of the mask representing their assumed personality. This made their dialogue fluid, spontaneous, sparkling, alive with delightful comments (*lazzi*) which were often very down to earth and must frequently have jolted the audience. The atmosphere of theatre was kept at high pitch. Scenic artifice was totally excluded. Indeed, there was often no scenery at all, or if any it was of the simple stock kind. For all that, the audience felt they were participating in the life of a real event, since the words they were waiting for came to life for the first time on the actors' lips. Of course, such improvisation was not without preparation. The actor needed a long apprenticeship to feel certain of never being at a loss for a word and of always leaving his partners with an opening for further comment. This was the origin of such aids for the actor as repertoires and miscellanies. It also made it necessary for each player to specialise in a single character, something that was logical enough considering the way comedy was structured.

The story of the masks is, therefore, identical with that of the actors who brought them to life and who were more often called by the name of their masks than by their baptismal names. Thus, Alberto Naselli started as Zan Ganassa and then became perhaps the first Harlequin. Francesco Andreini was Captain Courageous; Simone da Bologna, Pantaloon; Tristano Martinelli was renowned as Harlequin; Molière's teacher, Tiberio Fiorilli was Scaramouche; in the second half of the 17th century Mattia Barra was Punch, already played in the Neapolitan style; towards the end of the 17th century Domenico Locatelli was a most refined Trivelino; a hundred years later Carlo Bertinazzi played Harlequin without a mask, to please his Parisian audience, already devoted to the *Comédie italienne*, as they called it. Women had been severely banned from learned prose theatre, though not from opera, but played an important part in the history of the *commedia dell'arte*. The earliest and most famous names recorded in this connection are those of Isabella Andreini and Vittoria Piissimi. The history is also that of the acting companies and we know the names and the membership of the more famous ones. In the 16th century the names are similar to those of the contemporary academies (the Gelosi, the Desiosi, the Confidenti): later on, they took the name of their leading player. There was also probably an enormous number of companies which never went outside Italy and whose reputation died with them. Indeed, it may have been with these that the direct links with popular culture and traditions were preserved best and longest—things the bigger companies gradually lost as they mixed with the aristocracy and sought a perfect and refined ideal technique, discovering too late that it was devoid of content. Technically perfect performances became boring in the end and the people's comedy, reduced to a caricature of its former self, became very short of cultural inspiration.

Chapter 14

Gros Guillaume.   Gilotin.   Guillot Gorju.

FRENCH PROFESSIONAL ACTING FROM FARCE TO TRAGEDY

Angelo Beolco, the Ruzante, one of Italy's greatest playwrights, has been regarded quite wrongly by some as a precursor of the *commedia dell'arte*. The company he directed was active in Venice about the beginning of the 16th century. The first professional companies of actors were also being formed in France at about the same time. Thus we learn that in 1512 Jehan de l'Espine was acting as a vagabond all over France, moving here and there along with the other members of his family.

The references begin to become more frequent in the second half of the century, as they do in Italy, but the French professional companies and strolling players were organised on a very different basis from their Italian counterparts and developed along different lines. Thus they did not grow almost spontaneously out of the short sketches of acrobats and mountebanks, nor were their members identified as wearing character-masks. Instead, they were born of associations catering for recreational activities, which gave to theatre a more or less prominent place in a variety of ways. To opt for the stage as a profession was a free choice and implied the renunciation of an earlier trade.

The associations that produced France's first professional actors varied considerably. They might be lay confraternities entrusted with the organisation of religious drama—mystery-plays, miracle-plays, or morality-plays. The Parisian *Confrérie de la Passion* was the best known of these and, during the 16th century, it did devote itself precisely to producing the Mystery of the Passion. In the next century, however, it was organising, and more often exploiting the various theatrical performances in the capital. More often than not, however, they were purely recreational or cultural associations: *sociétés joyeuses*, *sociétés des sots*, student societies or workingmen's groups. The societies of fools sometimes derived from the medieval practice of allowing deacons to celebrate certain religious or countryside festivals inside the churches. Among the student societies were the *Enfants sans souci* and the *Clercs de la basoche*. Such societies may very well have had a jongleur on their pay-roll, who may have taken those keenest on theatre with him when he left, attracting them, no doubt, with the prospect of an adventurous, bohemian life.

In France, then, professional theatre was born in the town. Althought its initial repertory reflected a bourgeois culture, it was easy to broaden it quite soon to take in suggestions from humanist or aristocratic circles. Thus the French classical repertory from Hardy to Racine was developed and consolidated mainly thanks to the productions staged by professional acting companies.

That was to come in the 17th century, but already in the course of the preceding fifty years a repertory was built up in which farces, *sotties* and morality-plays were listed alongside the comedies and tragedies of the new school, in other words of the works of such humanists as Jodelle, Joachim Du Bellay, Jean de la Taille and Robert Garnier. These come-

Maître Pathelin in the Shop, *Maître Pathelin feigning sickness*.
Engravings from one edition of the farce. Paris, Bibliothèque
de l'Arsenal

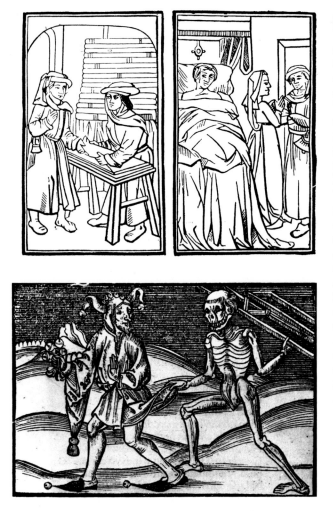

dies and tragedies were in the Italian style. Their
first performances were arranged at court or in
university-colleges. The stage-settings were also
based on Italian originals, introduced to France
indirectly through the reading of Serlio's treatise on
perspective or directly through the Italians' famous
production of *Calandria* at the French court in
Lyons in 1548. It was only four years later in Rheims
that Jodelle had his *Cléopatre captive* produced 'in
the antique mode' with magnificent pomp, while, in
1558 he staged his comedy *Eugène* in the Collège de
Boncourt. These performances were followed by
many others. For the court theatre, Italian perspective scenery was invariably used, but the university
productions had a simpler setting of hangings draped
round three sides of the stage.

The scenery used by the vagabond companies
certainly was closer to the university practice than
to that of the courts. For comedy, for tragedy and

Death and the Fool. Engraving for S. Brant, *Stultifera navis*,
Strasbourg, 1487. Vienna, Bildarchiv der Österreichischen Nationalbibliothek. The Fool here represents mankind, as he frequently
did in the *sotties* played by the *sociétés des sots*

for farce it was no more than a simple backdrop.
The only difference between the costumes and everyday wear was one of poverty, very soon to be the
actors' most faithful companion. It was only in the
second half of the 17th century that the best known
actors were able to escape this miserable condition.
The social status of the character represented was,
therefore, indicated by some trivial accessory.
Sixteenth-century professional tragic productions
may not have been much different from the one
described by Scarron in his *Roman comique*, although
he was writing about the situation in about 1650: In
the courtyard of an inn *'l'assemblée qui s'était
grossie, ayant pris place en une chambre haute, on vit
derrière un drap sale que l'on leva, le comédien Destin
couché sur un matelas, un corbillon sur la tête qui lui
servoit de couronne se frottant un peu les yeux comme
un homme qui s'éveille, et récitant du ton de Mondori
le rôle d'Hérode ... L'empâtre qui lui couvrait la
moitié du visage ne l'empêcha pas de faire voir qu'il
était excellent comédien. Mademoiselle La Caverne fit
des merveilles dans les rôles de Mariane et de Salomé;
la Racune satisfit tout le monde dans les autres rôles
de la pièce ...'* Perhaps, in the period of which we
are now speaking, tragedies were not performed for
riotous audiences in public-houses, but for more than
a hundred years the characteristics of the vagabond
companies certainly remained unchanged: masks,
accessories, no real scenery, a restricted number of
actors, insufficient for the number of characters.

However, the bulk of the actors' repertory was
undoubtedly made up of morality-plays, *sotties* and,
especially, farces. It was to produce such plays that
these companies had come into being and these were
still the staple diet of the townsfolk's recreational
associations. In Paris the last *prince des sots* was
elected in 1608, but he is mentioned in the provinces
as late as 1660.

The morality-plays had been produced principally
by the confraternities and began to disappear in the
16th century. Their characters stood for abstract
qualities, so that the action on stage was at a minimum and extensive use was made of emblems and
symbols. The *sotties* were not notably different,
since a considerable rôle was still assigned to allegory
and some suitable moral lesson, although the presence of the *sot* or joker did modify the plot. He wore
a costume similar to that of the jongleurs set off by a
hat like the one worn by the joker in French playing-
cards. Although his speech seemed incoherent, this
character hit out vigorously against the vices of
individuals and groups—it is the fool's privilege to
say what he likes. He was quite capable of filling the
stage by himself, and the *sotties* were often stream-

L Caullery, *Strolling Players giving a Performance in the Country*,
1598, Drawing. Cambrai, Bibliothèque Municipale

P J Quast, *Farceurs Dancing*. Painting on wood. Paris, Comédie
Française

lined as monologues. We can fancy him laughing and prancing about with extremely varied gestures not the least restraint, passing from paralysis to frenzy, from a whisper to a roar, making it his only rule to follow no rules at all.

The characteristic stage-production in French theatres at the end of the 16th and the beginning of the 17th centuries was farce. It called for very few characters, usually not more than four, though *Maître Pathelin* has five. The first travelling companies were obviously formed for just this sort of play and, whenever they wished to play tragedy or comedy, they were obliged to play two parts or more. A farce seldom ran into more than 500 lines, but apart from the length of the text, the metre and the number of characters, it is not easy to define it in theatrical terms. It can come close to the allegorical abstract character of the morality-play, or achieve the realism of middle-class comedy. This is exactly what happens in the most famous example of all, *Maître Pathelin*, where both the crooked lawyer's joke at the merchant's expense and that played by the peasant on the lawyer are brought down to the solid ground of everyday life, with the haggling in

Above: *Grotesque Pastoral Scenes*. Engravings. Stockholm, Drottningholms Teatermuseum. In both these engravings the simultaneous presence of Agnan and Harlequin suggests Agnan's company played in association with Italian actors

Agnan's Acting Company. Painting on wood, late 16th century. Paris, Comédie Française. Agnan was one of the first professional actors to devote himself by preference to short farces with 3 to 5 characters. These were among the more successful forms of French theatre, not so much on account of any literary merit, as because of the forceful, exaggerated acting

the shop and the wife's complaining about her husband's sickness, which is all a pretence because he doesn't want to settle his debts. Farce occasionally proves quite violent and grotesque—the shoemaker and the milk-maid have no scruples about killing the sergeant tied up in a sack. On the other hand, it may dissolve in laughter, as when, by interpreting his dreams, a mother, improbably but very cleverly and without malice, persuades her son he is destined to be Pope and then brings him back to his true position as a poor, ignorant, little priest. There is no recipe for farce, as there is for classical comedy and even for the *commedia dell'arte*. Apart from the quick moving development and the smooth running of the action, when action there is, farce is remarkable for the complete absence of moral overtones and for its prompt focussing on political and social issues—typical are the townsfolk's campaigns against the clergy, against the way justice is administered and against corruption. Farce is typically caught up, too, though this is a more indirect consideration, in the citizen's simultaneous attraction towards good behaviour on the one hand, and a life of self-indulgence and chicanerie. Even if it usually remained

La Farce des gueux. Engraving. Paris, Bibliothèque de l'Arsenal. An ordinary curtain was the scenery for farce, as it often was for Italian comedy. Thus all attention was on the action. Note the realism of the argument between the two gossips. Below are the backs of the heads of the audience

Above: Agnan's company performing two episodes of farce. Stockholm, Drottningholms Teatermuseum

below the surface, this appreciation of live issues was essential to farce. Thus, when Valleran Leconte, the first of the great French tragic actors, appeared on stage alone at the end of his performance, and told stories about what was happening in Paris and gave the latest gossip, his act was called a farce.

The instinct for the immediately relevant was probably most evident in the productions on stage. To take issue, even in general terms, with a priest of flesh and blood who is actually present, is a far different thing from expressing criticism of the Church allegorically. There is also a difference between having some fool point out women's shortcomings and actually showing them up in their behaviour. This was what made Molière the real heir to ancient farce.

Our ideas about the stage-production of farce during the 16th century cannot push back beyond the final decade or so, but do make us aware of its rapid development at the start of the 17th century. Agnan Sarat and his company, in association with some Italian actors, probably the Gelosi, were active and organising a few shows in Paris in 1578. The engravings that document one such performance show how varied were the costumes and gestures, with no stereotypes at all. A comparison with the studied gestures, contrived groupings and emphatic mime of contemporary Italian comedy is enough to make this clear. Agnan's actors might so use hyperbole as to leave reality behind, but the coarse gesture was never dignified by style. Compare Agnan's throwing himself at Peronne, when his mother is trying to restrain him, with the corresponding behaviour of the Italian Pantaloon: even if his body looks deformed, Pantaloon remains an athlete performing some graceful exercise; Agnan however has no coordination at all and seems to fall on his face in a rage, chewing the fingers of one hand, while with the other he pushes Guillemette away from him. No veils conceal the crudity and violence of his emotions. The same applies to the other scene, where the characters are shown in stylized poses, but are really only making a grotesque attempt to look graceful; any style there is belongs to the theme, not to the way it is being handled. When one considers how the lewd gesture of the figure on the right (p. 173) is not that of a woman, but of a man in drag, one will appreciate the degree of realism and energy these great actors must have reached. In less than a century the ideal of the theatre they represented was to become 'respectability', the exclusion not only of the slightest whisper that seemed coarse, but simply of anything at all that was less than noble (Desdemona's handkerchief!).

The meagre information we have makes it impossible to establish whether or not Agnan always acted in the same costume or used the same name. At any rate, he never brought into being a masked-character properly so called, since the performer's identity was never divorced from that of the actor. The same holds true of the three great Parisian actors who continued the tradition of farce, though, possibly as a result of having been influenced by Italian comedy, the trend toward stylization in their characters was more marked.

At the close of the 16th century Robert Guérin was performing in the Hôtel de Bourgogne and, until his death in 1632, he served that theatre faithfully. We shall have more to say about the theatre itself. Guérin assumed the professional name of Gros-Guillaume, and created this character. We know little of his psychological make-up, if there was anything fixed about this, but his appearance was that of a huge, fat man with a sad, chalk-white face. This does not seem like a violent or abnormal perversion of reality. This rôle was reserved instead for Hugues Guéru, who acted in farce under the professional name of Gaultier-Gargouille, and often played the part of an ageing citizen, miserly and bilious, bitter in his moralising and deservedly the victim of cruel pranks. Guéru's way of acting was exclusive to himself, inspired by his lean, skinny figure, and relentlessly worked at and polished. No detail escaped his attention, either of costume or gesture. His mask, his long pointed beard, his flat black skullcap, his black shoes, his red sleeves were the fruit of research. He had perfect control of his movements: 'all the parts of his body obeyed him so well that he really was a marionette', the super-puppet of whom Gordon Craig was to dream 300 years later! Yet, despite all this, his character bore the authentic stamp of the individual and reacted with the violence of real life, much more than it conveyed the impression of acting out the stock attitudes of the mask. On the other hand, the character created by Henri Legrand really was a mask: Turlupin. Turlupin came much closer to the Italian Brighella. He was the nimble deviser of a thousand traps, and spun webs of intrigue for Gros-Guillaume and Gaultier-Gargouille to fall into.

For eight years, from 1615 until 1633, these three actors were to appear together in the royal troupe at the Hôtel de Bourgogne. They restored and enriched the traditions of middle-class farce, the audience for which was by now decidedly lower class. The public was able to identify with the cruel thrust of the satire and to forget their own misery in the heady abstractions of the *turlupinades*.

Chapter 15

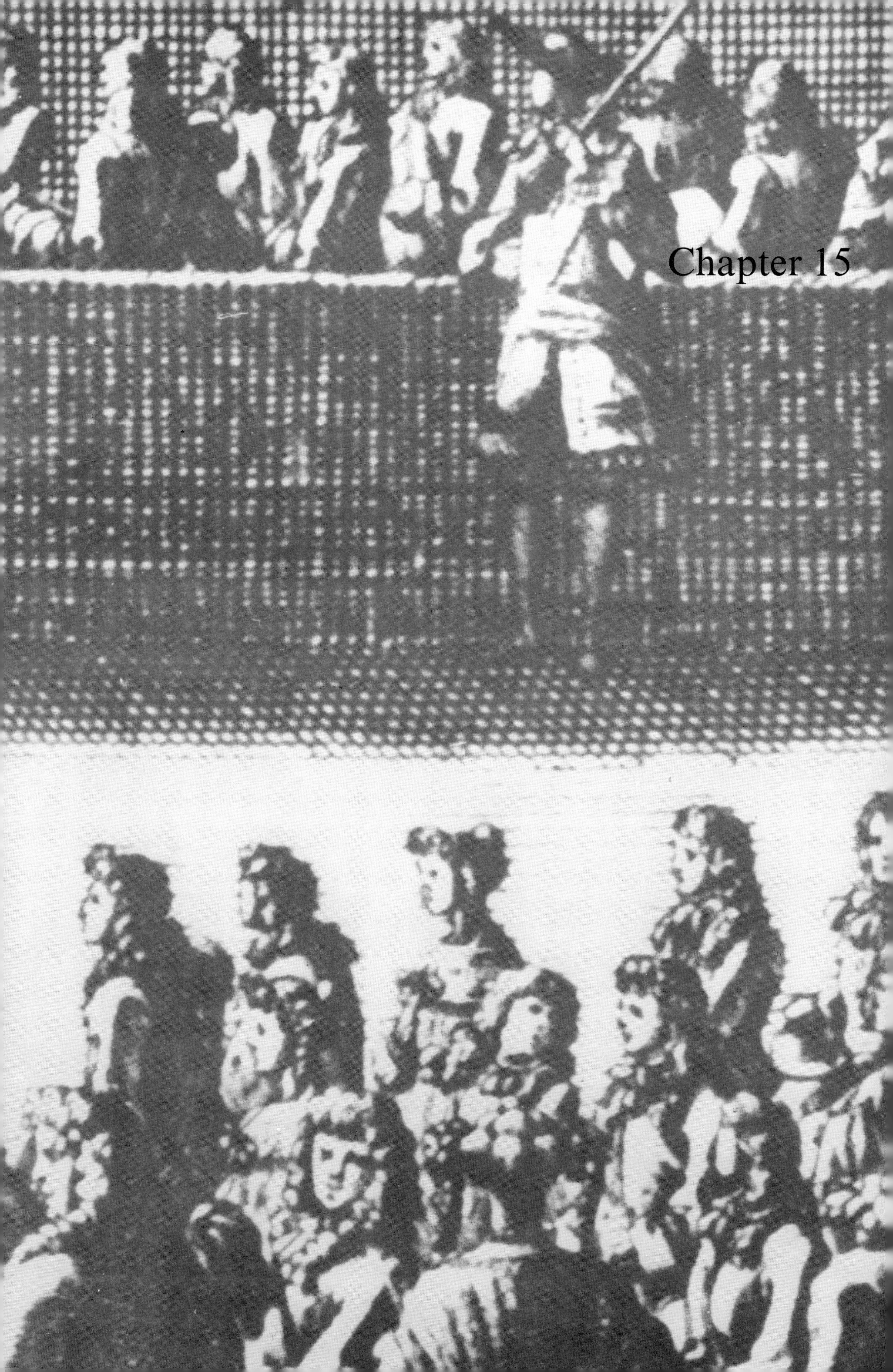

Les délices du genre humain. French farceurs and Italian masked actors. On the extreme left—Molière. Oil on canvas. French school, 1670. Paris, Comédie Française

THE COMÉDIE FRANÇAISE IN THE SEVENTEENTH AND EIGHTEENTH CENTURIES

As tragic actors Robert Guérin, Hugues Guéru and Henri Legrand were known to the public by other stage-names: La Fleur, Fléchelles and Belleville.

The French actors very soon began to produce the Aristotelian tragedies of the new humanist school and to add them to their original repertory of farce. It is hard to know why: the lower middle-class background of some of them may have had something to do with it, possibly suggestions made by the authors themselves, who introduced them to a more select sort of audience. It does not really matter. The astonishing fact is that the companies of actors literally forced tragedy on their audiences, which were mixed but mainly composed of simple folk, in the *jeux de paume* or indoor tennis-courts of the capital and in the provinces and eventually drew out a new audience of middle-class and aristocratic people, who had traditionally avoided the public theatre. Oddly enough, this proved harder in Paris than in the provinces and the achievement is linked not only with the names of the actors and companies who carried it off, but with that of the place where it all happened: the Hôtel de Bourgogne, one of the first permanent theatres in history, soon to be joined by the temporarily more successful Théâtre du Marais.

The Hôtel de Bourgogne belonged to the Confraternity of the Passion, who used it in the 16th century for the performance of morality-plays, farces and especially mystery-plays, admittedly for profit. Towards the end of the century, having obtained the privilege of being exclusively authorised to stage dramatic performances inside Paris, the Confraternity stopped producing plays itself and, on a purely economic basis, became the trustees of the theatrical life of the capital. Anyone who wanted to put on a show had either to rent out the Hôtel de Bourgogne or to pay a tax to the Confraternity.

This led to endless wrangles and a whole series of law-suits. Still, towards the end of the 16th century and around the start of the 17th, the Hôtel de Bourgogne witnessed the performances of many visiting companies—French, and also Italian, Spanish and English. However, Valleran Leconte's troupe was the first to install itself there on a regular basis. He tried his luck several times in Paris, in 1598, in 1606 and in 1612, but was never too successful. Alexandre Hardy, graced with the title of *poète aux gages*, belonged to the troupe and wrote comedies, pastoral romances and especially tragedies. His observance of the allegedly Aristotelian unities of time, place and action, which had regulated 16th century Italian drama and its French imitations, was never too rigid. Indeed he indulged his taste for romantic adventures meandering in space and time. Nevertheless, his steady elegance of phrase, his purity of language and his efforts to give his characters a more convincing and even individual psychology placed him on a cultural plane far different from that to which the Hôtel de Bourgogne audience was accustomed. The theatre had been traditionally patronised by the dregs of Paris—servants, porters,

179

idlers and prostitutes. Farce may not have been an expression of their own life-style, but at least it had met their cultural needs. Such an audience was not disposed to accept the more rarefied atmosphere and the considerably restrained theatrical presentation of Hardy's tragedies. All it could do was suggest keeping on with the old repertory of farce and this, of course, put off people of higher social backgrounds who would have appreciated a more refined sort of production from patronising the Hôtel de Bourgogne. Obviously Valleran could not eliminate farce overnight; indeed, he acted it himself. It was he who established the famous comic triad, but he did try to give it only second place, with tragedy as the central feature of his repertory. With admirable consistency

he persevered on this course, but, at least in Paris, he never had his ideas accepted. The 'new school' only came into its own with the opening of another theatre, the Marais.

But how were Hardy's tragedies produced? We have abundant evidence about the stage-settings, although it refers to a period after Valleran's death, when Pierre Le Messier, the Bellerose, his favourite pupil, had taken over the direction of his company, by that time the *troupe royale*. It is, in any case, quite likely that Valleran used the same sort of setting, which may, in fact, have been devised by him and Hardy. At all events, the evidence is that of a manuscript, entitled *Le Mémoire de Mahelot, Laurent et d'autres Décorateurs de l'Hôtel de Bour-*

gogne. This contains sketches of scenery and jottings about the scenery, accessories and costumes for plays put on in the Hôtel de Bourgogne from 1622 to 1635. It is a curious medley, a juxtaposition of 'mansions', the characteristic scenic features of simultaneous scene-settings in the mystery plays, with Serlio's sort of perspective stage-settings. The various 'mansions', painted on canvas in all likelihood and only of limited practical use, were arranged around both sides of the stage and along the back, leaving a central area free for the action. The location of the action at any given moment was indicated, as in the Middle Ages, by the point from which the actors made their way on, but, as in Italian theatre, they left the stage once they had played their part. A strange mixture, as I have said, that must have been wearying to the eye—the sketches are very poor as drawings, which does not help—but it suited Hardy's sort of theatre well enough, romantic, but tending towards the closely regulated patterns of classical drama. From a historical point of view it also makes sense that this sort of compromise was arrived at, since the Hôtel de Bourgogne had been until a short while previously the setting for religious dramas staged by the Confraternity of the Passion, so that the audience probably found it easier to interpret simultaneous stage-settings than successive scene-shifts. Moreover, it seems unlikely that even for the Confraternity's productions the 'mansions'

had been all arranged in a single straight line parallel with the front of the stage, since this rose up at one end of a rather narrow hall (60 by 100 feet), and would not have been large enough to accommodate very many. The more frequently mentioned 'mansions' are the cave, the marriage-bed and the palace; but the sea, a shop and the woods are also there. Usually, however, the palace is by far the dominant feature, and this helps to distract from the incongruity of the arrangement.

Valleran was certainly one of the first of the actor-managers to set about teaching young people stage technique and he cultivated the tragic style of acting before anyone else did. Two of his own advantages were a powerful voice and a magnificent presence, even if, in the opinion of his contemporary Tristan l'Hermite, his facial expression fell short of nobility. Valleran worked hard at the different shades of tragic pathos, frequently going too far, but by all accounts striving to vary its degree of intensity and avoiding the monotony of 'invariable grandeur'. As well as concentrating upon voice-production he had to pay great attention to gesture and posture, especially as tragedy was often played with the face covered by a mask—this, at least, being Hugues Guéru's practice.

In one *jeu de paume*, we are not sure which, but it may have been the one in which the Théâtre du Marais was inaugurated five years later, the company

Hésione, sketch by J Bérain. Stockholm, Nationalmuseum. The Académie Royale de Danse was founded in Paris in 1661 with the monopoly of opera-production. Jean-Baptiste Lulli became manager in 1672. Even his stage-settings followed the best Italian traditions. Stage-settings were produced jointly by J Bérain and Carlo Vigarani

led by Charles Lenoir and Guillaume Desgilberts, or Montdory, performed in 1629 with tremendous success *Mélite*, a tragi-comedy by Pierre Corneille (1606–86).

Corneille was the first on the scene of the three great French dramatists of the 17th century, and in his characters the tragic upheaval they experience is regrettably often grounded in a rather abstract confrontation between psychological stereotypes. The example of *Le Cid* is classical and characteristic. The protagonists are faced with a choice between the demands of honour and those of love ('*contre mon propre honneur mon amour s'intéresse*'); the dilemma for Rodrigo is such that either choice is fatal—he must avenge an insult: '*mon père est l'offensé et l'offenseur le père de Chimène!*'

It was in 1637 that the 'miracle of *Le Cid*' was performed, as people put it at the time. It is undoubtedly one of the most brilliant of Corneille's tragedies. *Mélite* retained the looser composition of Hardy's tragedies and the theme itself was romantic, while *Le Cid* was constructed according to Aristotle's rules, though not too rigorously; but the subsequent tragedies, and those with Roman themes in particular (*Cinna*, *Horace*), were kept within the strict limits of the unities of time, place and action.

In keeping with this it seems probable that, while the earlier plays were produced in settings no different from those in use at the Hôtel de Bourgogne, the later ones had alternative stage-settings. These were possibly Italian-inspired and, in a few instances of which *Le Cid* might well have been one, possibly just represented 'a room in a palace', which later became standard procedure. This suggestion is borne out if one turns to consider A. Bosse's engraving (see pages 174–75). On the other hand, the theatre was much more confined than the Hôtel de Bourgogne, only 35 feet wide and 100 feet long, and since the stage had an upper floor resting on pillars, it is even possible that no definite scenery was used at all.

At all events, Corneille's fortunes were for a long time linked with those of this theatre and of the company which made it their permanent base from 1634 on. Guillaume Desgilberts, known as Montdory, was their most outstanding actor. His most widely acclaimed performances were as Don Rodrigo in *Le Cid* and as Herod in Tristan l'Hermite's *Mariane*. Everyone tried to imitate him. Scarron's anecdote in this connection has already been cited. Montdory's own way of acting was violent and emphatic, but there was nothing superfluous about it, nothing superficial. Thus, Tallemant des Réaux, the shrewd and celebrated chronicler of Louis XIII's court, believed his imagination was so highly

developed that, '*il croyoit quasy estre ce qu'il representoit*'; there is also a story that he got an attack of paralysis when he was playing Herod, precisely because he was putting so much feeling and energy into his performance, and it was this that forced him to retire from the stage in 1637.

Scarron described the oldest member of a company of strolling-players as a poor, unfortunate who had grown old at his trade without making any fortune and who had been obliged to turn his hand to quite a variety of things from cashier to singer, acting in farce with a chalk-white face and taking parts in Hardy's tragedies: '*il jouoit en fausset, et sous les masques, les rôles de nourrice*'. To give vent to his feelings he would speak badly of established actors. Montdory was coarse, Bellerose too affected and Floridor too cold. The latter was the stage-name of Josias de Soulas, who became manager of the Marais after Montdory went down with paralysis. Scarron probably made use of this old actor's biting tongue to define in his own way the characteristics of

the three leading actors of his day. They did, in fact, originate different schools of interpretation with regard to the key-notion of noble tragedy. For Montdory this meant an intensely emotional form of expression, while Bellerose and Floridor saw it rather as a restrained elegance in speech and gesture. In Bellerose, moreover, such elegance became a studied imitation of the gestures of that high society which he never succeeded in winning over, while his diction focussed more on the rhythm of the verse than on the meaning of the sentence. This is not meant as a criticism, since metre can, indeed, modify the literal meaning and bring to light some deeper, poetic significance. On the other hand, Bellerose's style really must have been too artificial, since it seemed more like the aping of genteel folk's behaviour than any sort of restrained expression of noble feelings. Tallemant des Réaux, indeed, considered Bellerose a foppish actor who looked twice before putting down his hat for fear of spoiling the feathers and who lacked the least understanding of the

184

Mlle Champmeslé. Paris, Comédie Française. This great actress (1642–98) was very close to Racine and for a short time possibly made the theatre of the *grand siècle* more rigorously classical

meaning of what he was saying. Floridor's elegance, instead, was both detached and natural: his behaviour was truly that of a gentleman.

Theatre began to hold up the mirror to its new public. The court aristocracy concealed their coarse taste for amorous intrigue behind a mask of assiduous and enthusiastic courting, and the noble ladies pretended to be broken-hearted as they rejected some lover they had already tired of, invoking loftier aspirations. The Sun King had a fine eye for the ladies, so that in Louis XIV's court affairs of state, affairs of the heart and questions of protocol were closely interwoven.

To dignify this society by expressing it in poetry was the achievement of Jean Racine (1639–99). Intense interior self-torture flows from the dilemmas of his characters, obliged to choose between the claims of love and those of honour, duty and the State. The awareness of their plight does not merely mean they express it, but it involves them in plumbing the depths of their souls to the point of despair, of which the issue is death (*Phèdre*), or the even more painful sacrifice of separation, notably in *Bérénice*, where, almost without any real action at all, we have the story of the oriental queen's parting from the Emperor Titus. Clearly, the direct expression of feeling is paramount—hence the invariably lyrical tone of these tragedies.

Favoured by a series of royal ordinances, the Hôtel de Bourgogne had succeeded in overcoming the competition offered by the Marais and in acquiring the services of its best actors. The Bourgogne company was dignified with the title 'royal', as we have said. Montfleury's school was still in the

186

ascendant there when Racine came on the scene. Coming after the elegant Bellerose, Montfleury had brought back Montdory's passionately intense approach instead, exaggerating it even more into a constant crescendo of excess. Molière took him to task for this, pointing out that a king, when conversing privately with a captain of his guard, ought to speak in an ordinary human way and '*ne prend guère ce ton démoniaque*'.

However, when Montfleury died in 1667, Racine, like his own favourite Euripides, was showing his preference for female characters, and among his interpreters it was especially the women, first Du Parc and later Champmeslé, who established as the tone appropriate to the performance of tragedy a sort of lilt that verged on singing and always followed the rhythm of the metre. Gesture, too, with ever

increasing clarity, sought to use the rituals of courtly etiquette as vehicles of emotional self-expression. The spontaneity of the performance was proportional to the degree of ease with which the complicated etiquette of social life was observed. The costume, therefore, now strove to keep abreast of court fashions with a maximum of elegance. The glad rags of the old comedians, scarcely distinguished by some accessory indicative of the particular character's rôle, were now no longer tolerated except by travelling companies. The day was coming in which the actors would, indeed, lay down the law in matters of fashion and breeding, but for the moment they simply tried to make themselves worthy of that aristocratic duckpond that wished to see itself mirrored in the heroic celebrities of antiquity. Indeed, this reflection was a close-up, because it had

187

PHEDRE

become the custom to place reserved seats on stage for the more illustrious members of the audience who, in this way, became at the same time the models for and the ornament of the performance. This, of course, had its effect on the arrangement and disposition of the scenery and reduced considerably the room for manoeuvre, so that the painted scenery was restricted to a large canvas in the background, representing the colonnade of some majestic hall.

Another theatre, besides the Hôtel de Bourgogne and the Marais, was opened in Paris, close to the royal residence of the Louvre itself. This was the Petit Bourbon. The Italian actors of the *commedia dell'arte* usually performed there, but, from 1658 on, it opened its doors to another company, back in Paris after more than fifteen years of touring the provinces. This was the group of actors whom the Duke of Orleans now permitted to carry the title of *Troupe de Monsieur*, directed by Jean Baptiste Poquelin, called on stage Molière (1622–73).

Molière, like his rivals, also performed tragedies. He was also convinced at heart that grand theatre was synonymous with noble tragedy. Yet he refused to believe that this meant the affectation of Bellerose or, worse still, Montfleury's swollen conceit. So he suggested a modest deportment which, without offending against the rules of good breeding, would restore to tragic heroes the everyday proportions of human living. He did not see that by doing this he was depriving French tragedy of its principal meaning as a dramatic sublimation of the aristocratic social ideal. The result was fiasco. His performances in tragedy were mercilessly hissed off stage. There is also evidence that Molière was a very bad tragic actor. Here is one savage caricature of his way of playing the part of Caesar in the *Mort de Pompée*: '*Il vient le nez au vent/ les pieds en parenthèse et l'épaule en avant/ . . . Les mains sur les côtés, d'un air un peu négligé/ la tête sur le dos comme un mulet chargé/ les yeux fort égarés, puis débitant son rôle/ d'un hoquet éternel il sépare les paroles.*'

Both as a writer and as an actor, however, his success in comedy was as enormous as his failure in tragedy. The modesty of his tone, together with the continual varying of the degree of dramatic emphasis, coupled with his spontaneity of expression and movement—something he is said to have learned from the Italian actor Tiberio Fiorilli who had created the masked-character Scaramouche—were heralded as the triumphant raising of comedy to new heights of self-respect. Indeed, for Molière 'truth' was not a slanted interpretation, but a detached presentation of individual situations in middle-class Paris. In the final analysis, the king's strength and the prosperity of his rule rested on these foundations. Molière, in his unassuming way, placed within this convincing setting his marvellous characters—the miser, the hypochondriac, the hypocrite—characters in the root sense of the word, unambiguous embodiments, that is, of some single abstract psychological trait, reified into an absolute. However, when his main characters were placed next to the others, whose psychological constitution was compounded of qualities brought together in normal, human and quite small doses, they did not stand out immediately on stage. Tartuffe in one of Molière's productions was not the smooth, obscene, old man Emil Jannings' expressionist screen interpretation has accustomed us to, but a likeable young man, played by an actor who normally featured as a man in love and had evident gallantry and good-breeding. After all, this is precisely what hypocrisy is about. Nor must it be forgotten that Elmire distrusts the sham display of devotion right from the start and that it is only Orgon's blindness that postpones the villain's unmasking. Even when a character could be described as abstract or distorted, he is still presented quietly, leaving the audience to work out for itself the absolute behind the mask. Obviously, this applies to the great comedies. In the *Les précieuses ridicules* and *Le bourgeois gentilhomme* there was also an aspect of caricature about the actual staging of the character.

The Petit Bourbon theatre was demolished in 1660 and the King made available to Molière the splendid hall in the Richelieu palace, the Palais Royal, where the great Cardinal had had a tragedy produced, probably one of his own, *Mirame*. After Molière's death in 1673 his troupe absorbed the remaining actors of the Marais company: in 1680, this enlarged troupe merged, by royal command, with the company of the Hôtel de Bourgogne. Thus was born the Comédie Française.

The Confraternity of the Passion had been suppressed a few years prior to the founding of the Comédie Française. The former's privileged monopoly of the Paris theatre in prose was re-assigned to the 'royal' actors. These also enjoyed a considerable subsidy and their activities were subject to the scrutiny of one of his majesty's chamberlains. It was the first and most illustrious example of a 'public' theatre, brought into being with the declared aim of preserving a specific cultural heritage which was automatically taken to be synonymous with culture as such.

From the very beginning of the 18th century the Comédie Française found itself obliged to fight very hard for its privilege, which was under particularly

191

strong attack from the little theatres which had been established in the neighbourhood of the Foire Saint-Germain and the Foire Saint-Laurent. A few troupes of real actors hired in the provinces performed in these, as well as self-styled actors from the lower-classes: shop-keepers, painters, washerwomen, who, perhaps unwittingly, found in theatre the joy of creativity and a way of swelling their slender purse, albeit to a very limited degree. Of these companies the ones which had some notable success were those of the Alard brothers and of Bertrand, Dolet and Delaplace. These staged short, extremely comic sketches about topical events, as well as genuine comedies, often using the costumes of Italian masked-players, after Madame de Maintenon had forced the Italian Company to leave in 1697.

In certain instances the Comédie Française took the extreme course of having the theatres pulled down, but they were immediately rebuilt by the fair-folk. The most that proved possible was to restrict the area of competition by means of court-injunctions first against their acting of comedy, and later against dialogues and monologues. However, the fairground theatres paid them back in their own coin, not by recourse to legal violence, but by their own spirit of theatrical inventiveness, stimulated by the very restrictions themselves. For instance, while the performers mimed the actions, huge placards bearing the words would be held up and the audience, happy to share in the conflict, would join in singing

these. Alternatively, the words were replaced by meaningless vocables which could, however, be recited in alexandrines in the accents of the great actors, whom they mockingly referred to as 'the Romans'. It was a most effective skit on tragedy. As for the great actors themselves, all they did for tragedy was to develop the approach of their predecessors in the preceding century and identify their ancient heroes with the courtiers of Versailles. In comedy, however, they occasionally struck a richer vein, largely due to the contributions of Marivaux in the first and Beaumarchais in the second half of the 18th century. Both had broken away from Molière's method of composition and the latter created the magnificent character of Figaro, the average Frenchman, brilliant, ironic and self-aware.

Gesture was by now clearer about its limits. It no longer fluctuated between inflated, violent display and punctilious courtesy. Instead, the objective was fine gesture, imparting to the feelings an elevated, deliberate, even and, of course, always controlled form of expression. This was a gesture that was full and rounded off, so that one could follow, as it were, the whole course of its development, while the character never for a moment lost his composure or self-control. The number of such gestures was obviously extremely limited—to stretch out a hand, though not too far, keeping it open, while turning one's head round, but not the shoulders, to indicate a refusal; to bring the back of one's hand to rest on

GENGISKAN
dans l'Orphelin de la Chine.

La Clairon in Corneille's *Heraclius*. Water-colour, Paris, Comédie Française

one's forehead after a wide sweep of the arm to indicate despair, and the like.

Naturally, there were distinct differences between actor and actor. Duclos, eager to exploit to the full the incomparable sweetness of his voice, was almost motionless on stage and attempted to underline all the musical features of the metre. On the other hand, Adrienne Lecouvreur, whose movements had a natural elegance, concentrated not so much on metric quantities as on the feelings being expressed. Quinault-Dufrêsne, whom the ladies adored as the most handsome of men, invariably presented himself as a French lover and a perfect gentleman. The greater interpreter of Voltaire, Lekain, was admired throughout France for having broken through the conventional barrier of reserve and managed to express his characters' feelings directly, but Madame de Staël felt his magnificently fulsome gestures lacked authenticity. In the 18th century the greatest exponents of acting were Jean Louis Lekain, La Clairon and Adrienne Lecouvreur. They introduced innovations in tragic costume with the seemingly absurd but, considering the meaning tragic then had, entirely logical intention of fusing into some sort of synthesis the prevailing court fashion and the main features of ancient or oriental styles of dress. In 18th century tragedy the taste for the exotic, already evident in Racine's *Bajazet*, although adjusted to suit French requirements, was increasingly coming to the surface.

La Clairon was the model chosen by Diderot for his definition of the ideal tragic actress. She owed her reputation among her contemporaries to her skill in modulating the finest shades of feeling in her self-expression, allowing the spectator to have as it were a foretaste of the culminating moment of her performance, while holding him in suspense until the actual outcome. Her great opposite was Marie Françoise Dumesnil, an emotional actress who gave uneven but at times very powerful performances.

It was probably *c* 1773 that Denis Diderot, the mind behind the great *Encyclopédie*, wrote an essay in dialogue form entitled *Le paradoxe du comédien* ('The Paradox of the Actor'). Curiously enough this masterpiece of neo-classical aesthetic philosophy of the Enlightenment was only published in 1830, the very year of the *Hernani* battle of Romanticism. The work is a highly significant source of evidence with which to complete and enrich our reconstruction of 18th-century, tragic stage-production, but its major importance consists in its having clarified the poles of the dialectic within which the question of the actor-character relationship works itself out. Both from a methodological point of view and at the level of straight speculation the theorists of our

Lekain and Brizard in *Iphigénie en Aulide*. Water-colour. Paris, Comédie Française

The Comédie Francaise in the 18th century. Engraving. Paris, Bibliothèque de l'Arsenal. Probably the hall in the Rue des Fossés Saint-Germain, which housed the Comédie Française from 1687 to 1770

own century who have tackled this problem should have considered what Diderot had to say—and here I am not only speaking of the theatrical ideas of Brecht and Stanislavsky, but of Pudovkin's discussion of the film-star.

Diderot takes French neo-classical theatre as unconditionally the model for theatre in general and maintains that the illustrations of human emotion which the stage sets before us are large-scale portraits created on the basis of standards generally accepted, but reproduced in a way that magnifies the proportions they have in real life. Everything in theatre has to be enlarged if it is not to appear trivial, while, on the other hand, it needs to be freed of the dross of commonplace vulgarity. The actor portraying the death of a character he is playing, should take as his model 'the gladiator of old' who knew how to die 'gracefully, nobly, elegantly and in a way that was picturesque'. His use of gesture must be more ample and less hurried, so as to create the illusion of a person whose stature has grown larger, even in a physical sense. In all this Diderot is doing no more than pinpoint accurately the 18th-century approach to tragic acting and make his own contribution to the clarification of the aesthetic ideal of beauty, which was to be defined definitively by the German archeologist, John Winckelmann in his study of classical art.

The actor, in fact, must form for himself a mental image of the character he represents, a lofty and great ideal providing a paradigm of absolute beauty. To this he must proportion his gesture and diction, striving with all his ingenuity to reproduce his model with a maximum of accuracy. In creating his image of perfection the great actor, like the great poet, will base himself on meditation, on the assiduous study of human nature; his principal attribute is not sensitivity, but discernment and taste. The age of enlightenment created the myth of the sensitive person almost to provide a counterbalance to its own image, and such an ideal person is not the actor, but his exemplar. The actor does not experience the feelings he displays, nor, to use Stanislavsky's terminology, does he relive them; rather, by accurately following the internal pattern that he has built up, he reproduces the external manifestations of such feelings. These then are not indications of his real feelings, since genuine emotion is still and unexpressed, but they are theatrically conventional pointers to the various emotions, suitably enlarged and ennobled. It is precisely because he is without feeling, that the actor can display them all, playing a scale of difficult intervals on the keyboard of his own body. Versatility is his best endowment and is synonymous with the dispassionate ability to control his own limbs and his own voice. His greatest gift is his power of observation which allows him to build up an armoury of memories such as to include the whole range of human emotions.

To complete the picture in Diderot's mind as he composed this essay, we must remember that prior to its final move to a new building in the Faubourg St Germain, the Comédie Française had in 1770 been given house room in the *Salle des machines* of the Tuileries, where it had access to a large stage, like that of the Opéra. Moreover, in 1759 the stage-seating for privileged members of the audience had been done away with. This led to two results. First, the performances began to be produced with scenery on a lavish scale in a way previously reserved for opera or productions in the court of Versailles. Second, the actor, freed from immediate contact with his public, was inclined to hold their attention with a more generous and extensive use of movement, still in keeping with his aristocratic rôle, but no longer confined to what was compatible with a drawing-room atmosphere. There was also more room for extras and the use of scenery, and this raised the problem of a proper and qualified direction of the overall movement on stage, which was the context of the principals' interpretation of their rôles. The first director of the Comédie Française in this sense was Lekain, who paid great attention to the production on stage of Voltaire's tragedies, which afforded particular possibilities for development in theatrical terms.

Chapter 16

THEATRE ON WHEELS AND IN COURTYARDS IN THE GOLDEN AGE

In the days when 'el ingenioso Hidalgo' Don Quixote was travelling the world, defending the weak and the helpless, he sometimes chanced upon a wagon '... *cargada de los más diversos y extraños personajes y figuras que pudieron imaginarse. El que guiaba las mulas y servia de carretero era un feo demonio. Venia la carreta descubierta al cielo abierto, sin toldo ni zarzo, la primera figura que se ofreció a los ojos de don Quijote fué la de la misma Muerte, con rostro humano; junto a ella venia un ángel con unas grandes y pintadas alas; al un lado estaba un emperador con una corona, al parecer de oro, en la cabeza; a los pies de la Muerte estaba el dios qui llaman Cupido, sin venda en los ojos, pero con su arco, carcax y saetas; venia también un caballero armado de punta en blanco ...'* ('... filled with the most varied and curious personages and figures imaginable. An ugly devil was driving the mules and acting as carter. The first figure to catch Don Quixote's attention was Death itself, which had a human face; next to him was an angel with a pair of large painted wings; to one side there was an emperor with a crown on his head, seemingly of gold; at the feet of Death sat the god they call Cupid, without any bandage over his eyes, but carrying his trusty bow, quiver and arrows; then there came a knight armed to the teeth ...').

Thus, as in Italy and France, so too in Spain there were to be found in the 17th century companies of strolling players, travelling from end to end of the peninsula and also successfully passing beyond the border, who performed the plays of the Golden Age of Spanish drama and never worried about the allegedly Aristotelian rules of the three unities. The plays were those of Lope de Vega (1562–1635), Tirso de Molina (1584–1648), and Pedro Calderón de la Barca (1600–81), all of them extremely talented and productive writers, accepting commissions not merely from the court and from public theatres, but also for religious productions to be performed at the public expense on certain festivals, in order to keep alive the faith which was considered to be both the moral strength and the political force which united the Spanish people. It was also always the same troupes of comedians who acted in the various productions sacred and profane.

The *comedia de santos* and the *auto sacramental* were performed respectively on the anniversary feasts of the most popular saints or during a beatification process and on the feast of Corpus Christi.

The *comedia de santos* is a dramatised life of the saint, in which his life is transfigured into a mystical exemplar, apt to express in a tangible form what is ineffable, to disclose to untutored souls the visible reality of the divine message. Hence, simply to read it through does not make it intelligible, but for it to have any impact, its flesh-and-blood realisation on stage is a prerequisite. Here everything becomes a symbol, whether it be the scenery or the accessories, a change of costume or the lighting-system. The dramatic production is at one and the same time realistic, since it makes use of the most everyday objects, and symbolic, because these very objects

Velasquez, *The actor*. Madrid, Museo del Prado. This is Philip II's court jester

199

are transmuted into so many signs of the world beyond.

In staging the *comedias de santos* the company used the very garments that served for profane productions: the luxurious costumes of the lady and the gallant, the main characters in the cloak and dagger comedies. This fine apparel was donned by those saints who had spent their early years in the world, such as Saint Francis and Saint Clare. However, at the very moment in which, moved by grace, the hero renounced the world, his costume changed as well as his life-style. This metamorphosis took place before the public's very eyes, as evidence of his conversion.

This continual, symbolic changing of costume is an almost invariable feature of the *comedia de santos*. In Lope de Vega's *El Serafín humano* the gradually increasing exterior poverty of Saint Francis is used to symbolise his corresponding interior enrichment. Tirso de Molina's *La Santa Juana*, Lope de Vega's *Los locos por el cielo* and countless others use the same device.

The choice of scenery also pivots on the twin ideas of ascension and revelation which are central to mystical experience. The saint does not take the deceptive apparent realities at face value, but uncovers their true, hidden meaning: he perceives the moral bankruptcy that luxury conceals, the disintegration in store for beauty. He also discovers a reflection of God's own grandeur in the poor soul beloved of God, in animals and in the vegetable and mineral kingdoms. From this true appreciation of reality he mounts up to the apex of human potentiality and lifts himself irresistibly towards the godhead. The stage-setting is far from secondary, no mere backdrop for the drama; it enters directly into the development of the plot and, on an equal footing with man, forms an integral part of the production. Its importance derives from accepting the Franciscan view of the cosmos as a harmonious whole in which man discovers his brotherhood and co-involvement with the forces of nature and with all things: the mountain will open to reveal truth to the saint, or to protect the life of a saint being persecuted; the sea will carry to shore the bodies of the martyrs so that they can be given Christian burial. Like the costumes, the stage-settings are full of meaning and keep on changing and every aspect of stage-craft is exploited.

The back of the stage is separated from the front half by hangings to hide a scene which is waiting to be revealed at the right moment. There is also a gallery or balcony with a twin purpose: it raises one part of the stage above the other, and yet another part of the stage above the other, and yet another scene appears inside it when the curtains are drawn back. All this opening of curtains symbolises the reality behind the idea of revelation, which is also brought out by means of machinery carrying heavenly visions down from on high or up out of the open trap-door in the stage-floor from the kingdom of Satan. This way of using stage-settings arranged on different vertical levels, hell, earth and heaven, makes the idea of ascension real. Devils emerge from beneath the stage and mingle with human beings whose appearance they assume, whilst divine beings appear on high, on the balcony in token of mystic contemplation.

These apparitions actually are complete scenes played by living characters: Christ, the Virgin Mary, allegorical presentations of the three divine Persons, etc. Unlike the *auto sacramental*, the *comedia de santos* shows a preference for real scenes, rather than paintings or statues. However, there is no need for the apparition of heavenly personalities to come after the scene on earth; the playwright is free to have heaven, earth and hell represented simultaneously. Furthermore, from the time when the future saint commences to rise above the human condition, it becomes necessary to provide him with a position different from that of his followers, yet still not on a level with divinity. Accordingly, there are certain variations in the way in which the framework of the stage is put to work. In these dramas the principal setting is not the district where the saint lived on earth nor his home; it is some location outside space, the point of contact between the godhead and that mankind which is striving to rise to meet it.

For all these plays machinery is the secret, indispensable actor, enabling a character to make his appearance by coming down from above and to stay suspended in mid-air—this is how the angel arrives to help a saint in danger. The machinery also allows actors to perform the miracle of rising above the stage, and in the same way the play can end with the saint going up to heaven.

The hanging separating the rear portion of the stage from the front part can be drawn back to disclose an apparition, in which case its location is somewhere outside space. Alternatively, it can be an extension of the scenic area, representing a place that is real, though with respect to the location presented on the front of the stage it may be dramatically close or far removed. The curtain can similarly be used to represent displacement in time. For instance, in one of Ricardo de Turia's dramas, when heaven reveals to Vincent the virtues of the future Saint Vincent Ferrer, 'a great curtain opens

Richard Southern, Reconstructed stage-setting for the 1608 Madrid production of Lope de Vega's *The Adultress Forgiven*. This reconstruction relies on Professor J E Varey's research. There is hardly any extant visual evidence relating to either the *autos sacramentales* or the profane productions. University of Bristol, Richard Southern Accession, Theatre Collection

and discloses the scene of Saint Vincent preaching to many listeners, both men and women'.

In these plays, then, the physical reality of the symbol is accompanied by extremely versatile stage-settings, allowing for continuous movement in space and time, and even outside space and time. The flexibility is much greater than that achieved by the multiple scene-settings of the mystery-plays and it would be hard to decide whether the idea is one of simultaneous or of consecutive staging—possibly a synthesis of the two, worked out with complete freedom from preconceptions. Everything becomes the instrument of mystical symbolisation and the attempt to make completely real the ecstasy of the imitation of Christ.

The *comedia de santos* is a drama with real characters. In the *auto sacramental* both allegorical and real characters meet each other in the context of a metaphysical and moral dimension, in which the mystery of the Holy Eucharist is portrayed under a variety of aspects.

The *auto sacramental* was staged in Madrid every year during the 17th century for the feast of Corpus Christi. The same was true of all the Spanish cities, but the productions in the capital were the most interesting, while in the provinces the same companies gave an identical performance, but with less elaborate settings and costumes. There were two important innovations during this period in the arrangement and number of the waggons used to stage the productions of the *autos*. Dances and interludes were featured along with the *autos sacramentales* from the 15th century onwards; before their expulsion from Spain, Jews and Moors were sometimes required to dance on these occasions, as a document dated 1481 indicates. The number of *autos* to be staged fluctuated during the 16th century; in 1592 it was apparently fixed at four.

The *comedia de santos* could be staged on waggons, but more often took place on a fixed stage. During the 17th century, by contrast, the *auto* was always played on waggons rather like the triumphal floats of the secular festivities of the Renaissance. The play

could be carried about on top of these and repeated in different parts of the city. The first showing was in the presence of the King, the second was for the City Council who looked on from the windows of the City-Hall, and the last two were for the citizens, one in the Plaza Mayor and the other in the Puerta de Guadalajara.

Initially two waggons were used, the *medios carros*, connected by a stage or third waggon, the *carrillo*, on which most of the action took place. The biblical and allegorical composition of the plays did not vary very much, and to meet its requirements there was prepared behind the *medios carros* either a wooden structure or a painted cloth, the *caja* or *casa*, a housing for the stage-machinery into which the actors could retire. The waggons had two floors, often connected by a stairway, and were distinguished as the good waggon and the bad waggon, since contrasting scenes were characteristic of plays of this sort. The audience was all round the waggons, so that each spectator, depending on his position, had a different point of view. Later on, tiers of steps were erected on three sides for those who had been invited, and the two *medios carros* were arranged behind the *carrillo*, so that the public could watch the performance from three directions.

Starting from 1647 the number of waggons on which the *autos* were produced was increased to four, while at the same time the number of plays to be performed was cut from four to two. Calderón's unquestioned supremacy in this genre dates more or less from this time and it may have been he who called for this technical innovation, which gave the dramatist eight focuses for the action and so made possible heightened theatrical effects and more complex uses of allegory.

In order to appreciate the dramatic and theatrical substance of this sort of *auto*, we can consider the text of Calderón's *Sueños hay que verdad son*, the stage-production of which was described by the author himself in his *Memoria de apariencias*. It is an allegory about Joseph's stay in Egypt and his prophetic dreams. The dreams Joseph interprets are presented in pairs on the two opposite waggons, thanks to machinery which, at the right moment, makes both persons and things appear and disappear before the public's very eyes. In the following scene Joseph is alone, wondering what has happened to his father, Jacob, who appears to him preceded by Chastity and other allegorical characters. This vision took place on another waggon, while on the fourth, after Joseph had revealed his true identity to his brothers, there is shown Joseph's final dream, in which 'three persons rise on high, where the middle one is still as his companions move to either side into the distance, until a canvas spins open like a fan and forms a sort of iris, it spins again, and everything disappears'. (One might conclude from this that painted figures, rather than actors were being used). There next appear personifications of the eucharistic species of bread and wine and, in between these, as a finale, Faith. Thus each waggon is the setting for a particular happening on stage, the location depending on allegorical rather than spatial considerations, and there does not seem to be any action so involved as to require the whole area of the four waggons.

Beginning in 1682 the waggons actually became eight and the theatrical effects reached gigantic proportions. The main person behind this final stage in the development of the *auto* was the scene-designer and architect José Caudí, who suggested sturdier and richer waggons with fixed decorations and especially statues, and these were to be kept for next year's performances. The new idea was accepted, but not for long because the waggons were very unwieldy. The architects for the waggons between 1693 and 1699 were Isidro González de Arévalo and Roque Francisco de Tapia, who were commissioned to 'paint the façade of the aforesaid theatre'. These words make one think of a proscenium arch erected with the waggons serving as floor, so that the resulting stage would be like that in a real theatre, that is, in the theatre at court.

Thus, the *auto sacramental*, fruit of the resolve to renew Catholicism from within and aiming to rekindle people's faith by celebrating the mystery of the Holy Eucharist, eventually followed lines similar to those of profane theatre among the nobility. The mobile units that had been devised to meet the needs of a travelling theatre ended up as supplementary features in a theatre on a fixed site.

It was in an *auto sacramental* that Pedro Calderón de la Barca, the greatest Spanish playwright, with the clarity that is peculiar to allegory, provided a definition of the main theme of his work: life is like a theatre and lacks real substance; each one has his part to play, as Shakespeare had already pointed out, whether it be gay or sad. In *El gran teatro del mundo* the Rich Man, the King, the Peasant, the Beggar, Beauty, Discretion (Religion) and the Child are given their rôles by the Divine Author (or Manager); but they are able to act according to their free will and receive their final reward or punishment accordingly. Predestination is likewise eliminated from his profane plays on the same theme in favour of the free election of the moral man, a man who is, indeed, certain he is living an illusion, but believes

he should live it in accord with the unconditional criteria of good and evil. This forms the subject of the third act of *La vida es sueño*. This is Calderón's profane masterpiece. He imagines that King Basil of Poland, having read in the stars his son Sigismund's evil destiny, has had him locked up in solitary confinement, but then, in order to test the truth of the prophecy, has him return to court. The prince immediately provides evidence of his natural propensity for violence and so the king has a sleeping potion administered. When Sigismund awakes he finds himself back in prison and the preceding episode seems like a dream. However, if dreams are so real that they become indistinguishable from life, life itself is a dream '*y los sueños son*', while dreams themselves are dreams indeed. An uprising in the third act restores to the prince his freedom and authority, but he now carefully refrains from doing evil, since 'reality or dream, what counts is to do good; if it is real, because it is real, and if not, so as to win friends when the awakening comes'. This twin theme runs through many of Calderón's major works. Thus, the notion of moral involvement is dominant in *El príncipe constante*, in which Don Fernando, when he is taken prisoner by the Moors, meets death rather than accept the compromise of bribery or escape. Again, in *El mágico prodigioso*, Cyprian, Faust's brother in spirit, manages by martyrdom and the strength of his faith to redeem his soul which he had sold to the devil. The idea of the world as a dream and an illusion is also at the basis of lighter plays such as *Gusto y disgusto non so más que imaginación*.

If these are the themes in depth of Calderón's dramatic output, the motive forces activating his characters are those of love and honour. In some instances the code of honour takes on the stamp of the tragic law of destiny. Loyalty towards the king and towards women is another main motive. These, of course, were the traditional mainsprings of Spanish theatre in the 16th and 17th centuries from Lope de Rueda and Juan de la Cueva to Lope de Vega and Tirso de Molina. The latter invented the character of Don Juan and in the original version he was far from being good or attractive. Before Calderón's time, movement and adventure had counted most and had determined the character of a play and of the way of producing it. The hero was impelled to travel the world by his appetite for adventure or by the need to satisfy his honour or to win his heart's desire. The main character in such plays was the gallant, who was almost always in love, although the lover could also be a separate character. It was characteristic of Spanish theatre to give the gallant

J Comba, the old *Corral del Príncipe*. Madrid, Museo Municipal de la Pacheca. This is a 19th-century reconstruction, but the artist probably had access to earlier documents

a foil, the *gracioso*, his comic servant, whose buffoonery alternated with the serious or tragic scenes in a sort of counterpoint as violent as it was irrevocable. This counterpoint serves to show that love and honour are the prerogatives of those chosen souls, the Spanish nobility, but in some places, it seems rather to indicate that from those very risks and endeavours which bring glory and love to a nobleman, a servant can only hope for a thrashing. Was this a sop offered to the lower orders in the audience watching the *corrales*, an acceptance of their way of thinking, or did it represent a profound intuition into the real basis of upper-class morality, namely the oppression of the lower orders and the destruction of their moral being? Whatever the truth of the matter, in at least one instance lower-class attitudes dominate the stage and solidarity in revolt takes the place of honour and loyalty: in Lope de Vega's masterpiece, *Fuenteovejuna*, the entire village accepts responsibility for slaying the savage Lord of the Manor who has trampled their rights under foot and wounded their feelings of self-respect.

Popular audiences made Lope de Vega their favourite, while Calderón was adored at court. Nevertheless, Calderón's major works were also performed in public theatres, while his allegorical and mythological texts and his pastoral romances, with stage-settings by Italians, Cosimo Lotti, Baccio del Bianco and Francesco Ricci, were favourite features in the court theatre of Buen Retiro.

From about 1570 onwards, public theatres flourished not only in Madrid but throughout Spain. At the end of the 16th century there were already in operation in Madrid the *Corral del Príncipe* and the *Corral de la Cruz*; in Seville the *Corral de Doña Elvira*, and others elsewhere. The old *corrales* were extended and brought up to date in the main Spanish cities during the 17th century and others were set up. In the 17th century the term *corral* becomes almost synonymous with theatre and is a courtyard surrounded by private houses with a stage built at one end. Facing this was the space reserved for the ladies, the *cazuela*, while near the stage was a place for the council of elders with, higher up, a sort of

203

The series of engravings reproduced here records a court production staged in 1652 in the Buen Retiro Palace with Italian-style settings by an Italian scene-painter, probably Baccio del Bianco. The rather naïve drawings show very clearly the flats, a series of painted scene-features. As Italian skill in scene-painting was made use of for this production, so Italian opera in the second half of the century was greatly influenced in both subject and treatment by the half-phantasies of such plays as this minor work of Calderón, *La Fiera, el Rayo y la Piedra*. It relates the loves and adventures of Iriphile, living almost like a savage in the Sicilian mountains, and of Anaxarete, a dethroned princess supplanted by Zephyr. The arrival of two pilgrims, Iphis and Pygmalion, both complicates and resolves their situation. Madrid, Biblioteca Nacional, ms 14614

1. Prologue of Iriphile as a savage. Sirens' song. Iphis's boat arrives
2. Iriphile, Pygmalion, Zephyr and Iphis with their servants. The setting should change after this scene from rocks to trees; in the engraving the change has already been made in the background, while the flats remain the same through the first 'day'
3. Zephyr, Pygmalion and Iphis in front of the Three Fates' grotto. These prophesy that Trinacria's future depends on a ray, a stone and a wild beast
4. Clash between Eros and Anteros
5. Anteros escapes from Eros by flying
6. Anaxarete (*extreme right*) calls together her maidens to go hunting and tells them how she was dispossessed of her kingdom. Then enter Iriphile (*centre*) whom Anaxarete attacks, taking her for a beast

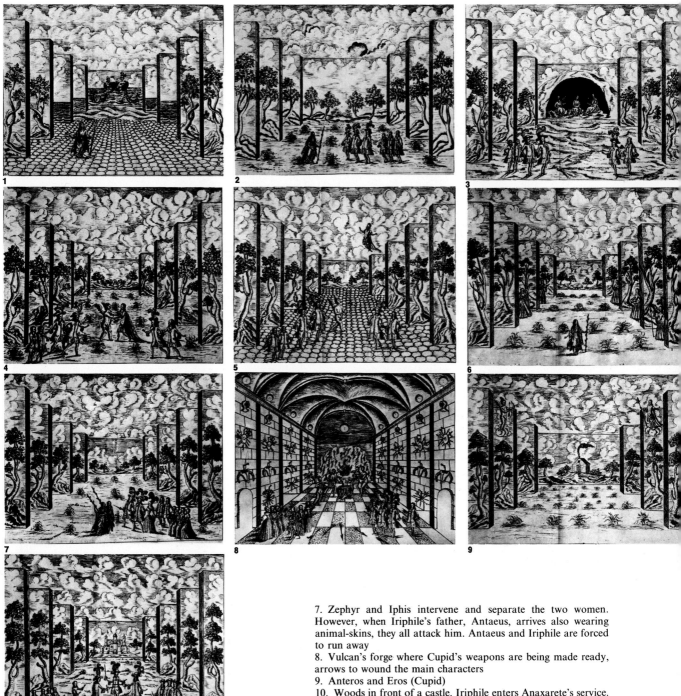

7. Zephyr and Iphis intervene and separate the two women. However, when Iriphile's father, Antaeus, arrives also wearing animal-skins, they all attack him. Antaeus and Iriphile are forced to run away
8. Vulcan's forge where Cupid's weapons are being made ready, arrows to wound the main characters
9. Anteros and Eros (Cupid)
10. Woods in front of a castle. Iriphile enters Anaxarete's service. Iphis and Zephyr fight a duel
11. A garden. Eros appears in the sky

12. Iphis, Pygmalion and Zephyr reveal their love and future plans. Then enter Anaxarete and Iriphile with the maidens. The three knights watch them from hiding. All think they love Anaxarete but Pygmalion addresses himself to a statue, and Zephyr to Iriphile

13. As Antaeus appears, looking for Iriphile, the three knights come out to defend Anaxarete, who dismisses them

14. Anteros in the sky

15. Antaeus reveals to Iphis how he fled into the lonely wilds so as not to betray his queen when she was dispossessed of her kingdom

16. A wood. Iriphile tells Zephyr of her love. Antaeus intervenes and arrests him. Iriphile sets him free once more

17. Eros, Anteros and Venus in the sky

18. Enter some villagers dragging a cart with the statue with which Pygmalion is in love. Zephyr comes up with Iriphile; he has for the time being overcome Anaxarete's supporters

19. Enter Antaeus and everyone else. Anaxarete's supporters are now strongest. Anaxarete becomes queen and marries Iphis; Zephyrs marries Iriphile and Pygmalion the statue which has come to life; the three women are three aspects of love: the ray, the wild beast, the stone

20. Eros, Venus and Anteros descend in a group

sun-lounge for the clergy, who came along in large numbers to watch the profane performances as well. Finally, at either side of the courtyard there were tiers of steps for the use of the general public. The houses around the courtyard had balconies or verandahs, of which their owners took advantage either to watch the performances themselves with their relatives and friends or to rent out to persons of quality—they were the only places where a man and woman could watch the show together. Down in the courtyard, the *mosqueteros* of the Spanish infantry stood in the audience, forming perhaps the readiest and most competent critics of the performance, considering, that is, the plots' associations with chivalry.

The stage arrangements were very simple to begin with. They merely consisted of large curtains which could be opened or closed and which let one see interior scenes or, more rarely, scenes far removed from the principal scene. Also in profane theatre, then, there were possibilities for simultaneous settings, but they were quite limited. From the second half of the 17th century on, some use was also made of scene-painting in order to make the transfer-rence of the action from one location to another more evident to the eye. We do not know if flats were used, or if the backdrop only was painted. On the other hand, there was one invariable feature, two balconies one above the other, on a level with the galleries and balconies around the other three sides of the courtyard in which the spectators of rank had their place. These galleries above the stage were the *lo altro del teatro* (upper stage) often referred to in contemporary stage-directions, and they naturally were used in those scenes which were supposed to take place in high locations: balconies, city-walls, mountain-tops and the like, or else they provided a second floor, as it were, for divine manifestations. They likewise housed the machinery that made miracles possible, these, as we have seen, being particularly common in the *comedias de santos*, but not altogether excluded from the profane performances in the *corral*.

At all events it seems likely that the pageantry of the production depended not so much on the stage-settings as on the costumes of the actors, the luxury of which provided one motive for the Church's attack on actors. In Spain this attack was not so furious as in other countries, possibly because a religious use was always being found for the professional theatre. There are no records in Spain of cases like that of Adrienne Lecouvreur, denied Christian burial by the French clergy because she had been a professional actress.

The names of many famous Spanish actors have come down to us: Alonso de Olmedo, who was more of a stage-manager and, if one can put it that way, a producer; Juan de Morales Medrano and Roque Figeroa, among the best known interpreters of the masterpieces of Lope de Vega, who, by the way, especially liked Arias de Peñafiel, of whom it was said: 'he possesses a pure, clear voice, excellent memory and perfect manners; every movement he makes expresses elegance and good-breeding. The best orators run to listen to him in the hope of acquiring the perfection of his speech and gesture.' Franzisca Bezon excelled in breeches parts and so did the famous Francisca Baltasara who was later to exchange her profession for a life of contemplation. Cosme Pérez proved a first rate *gracioso*. Unfortunately, we have very little information about how they actually behaved on stage. In Spanish theatre the hero is not a courtier, though, perhaps, he embodies the aristocratic moral ideal, which is taken as the national ideal. His characteristic features are courage and jealousy, rather than politeness. Because of this there was no theatrical equivalent in the action on stage of the typically Spanish punctiliousness. Instead the action was noted for the unusual liveliness of the development and the abrupt, immediate switches from one sort of emotional expression to its opposite. For us it would be particularly fascinating to know how the *gracioso* played his part. He may have given the audience merely some sense of a simple contrast, or may have projected a caricature, an exaggerated reflection of a reality whose virtue was only apparent. In Calderón's *El mágico prodigioso* Cyprian's possessive love and aristocratic jealousy contrasts sharply with his servant's accommodating and vulgar readiness to share a woman, or so it seems. However, the spectator knows the former love is the Devil's doing, so that, if an actor later presents a caricature or parody of the gallant's straight-faced protestations, the audience will be led to identify in both situations sinfulness and a common denial of true humanity.

This limiting case has been made too explicit, but the complexities and ambiguities of Calderón's work may have all become clear, thanks to the interpretation they were given on stage. Such a key would definitely and unconditionally open up their meaning, not, of course, at a rational level, but with the dynamic permanency of imagination. It would also have uncovered the roots of contemporary Spanish ways of thinking and judging. It is a fact of history that we have lost this key, but the very possibility of these mutually opposed interpretations testifies to the ever present vitality of this sort of theatre.

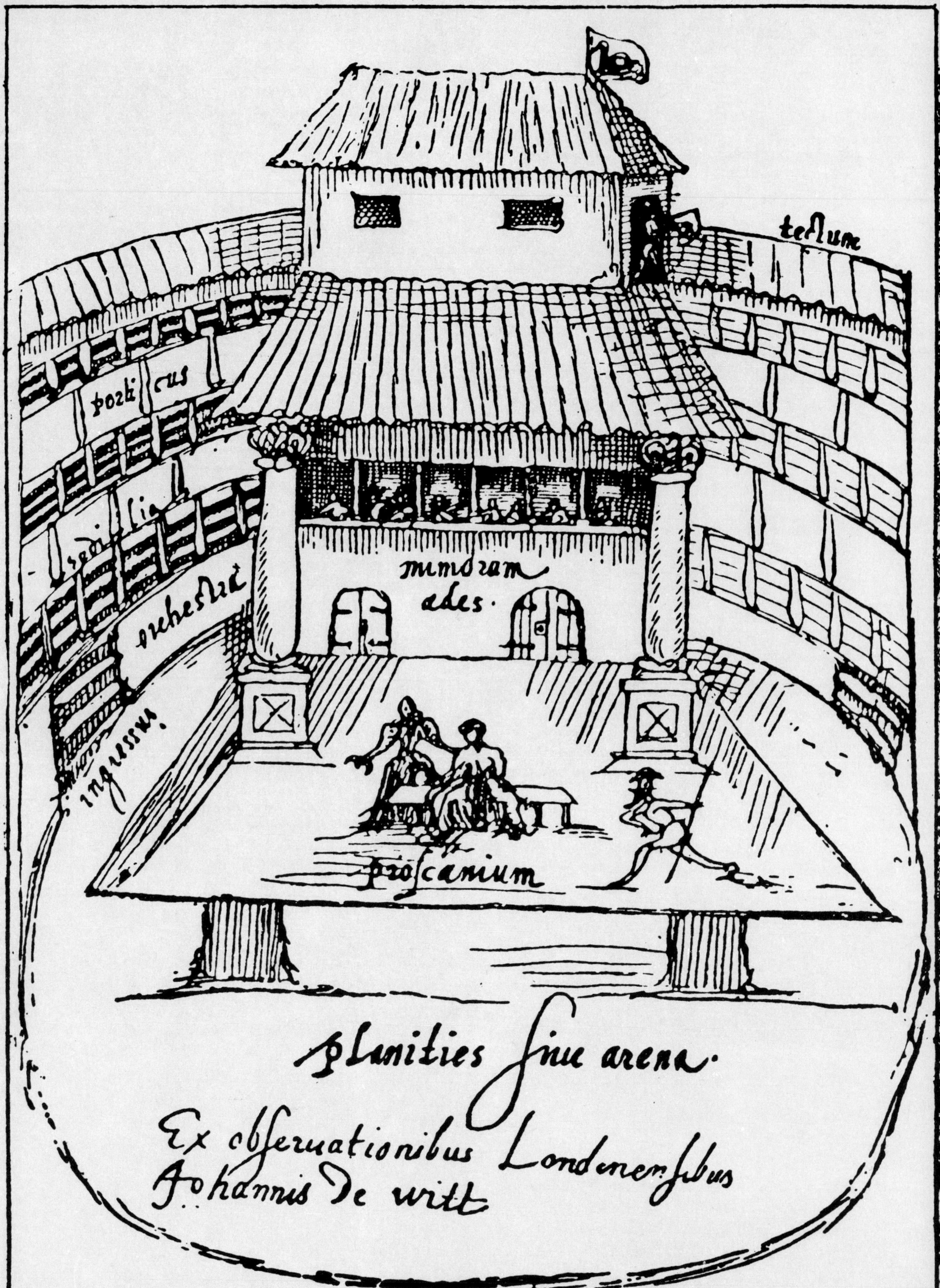

tectum

porticus

sedilia

orchestra

ingressus

mimorum
ædes.

proscænium

planities sive arena.

Ex observationibus Londenensibus
Johannis de witt

FOR THE KINGS OF ENGLAND—FOUR OR FIVE FENCING-FOILS—AND ONE WOODEN HOOP

In England the type of architectural setting chosen for dramatic productions was the same as that used in Spain for profane theatricals. Round about 1550 there were a hundred or more companies acting, and when they were not engaged in the castles of their noble protectors they displayed their skill before the public in return for payment, in the courtyards of public-houses both in London and other centres both large and small. The choice, moreover, had been almost automatic. The need was for a place openly available for public use and yet not in public ownership. In their own heroic period the French *jongleurs*, too, had used the courtyards of inns, later expressing a preference for private halls which they could rent. The Italian actors had done the same, though they frequently continued to produce their plays in public squares and market-places, arrogating to themselves that stamp of official standing which religious theatre in Italy had never had.

After undergoing certain practical modifications, the Spanish *corrales* remained the only locations available for public theatre. In England, however, after 1575, the inn-yard theatres were increasingly abandoned by the players, also as a result of legal prohibitions. Nevertheless, they served as models for the Elizabethan theatre-buildings.

The model was not conceived or put on paper by an architect, but by an actor, who was naturally inclined to reconstruct what had been his own working conditions to date, and he mixed together the lay-out of the inn-yards with that of the rings reserved for bull-baiting, the only existing buildings then expressly constructed for public performances.

This actor was James Burbage, father of Richard Burbage, who was to be the leading interpreter of the great characters of Shakespeare. James Burbage designed and supervised the construction of the first purpose-built English edifice for dramatic performances and he called it quite simply 'The Theatre'. This happened in 1576, but by the following year London already had a second theatre, in which Burbage also held interests, and it was called 'The Curtain'. Later, in 1599, he was to construct Shakespeare's theatre, 'The Globe', while in 1587 Philip Henslowe, a celebrated impresario whose private papers from one of the principal sources of our knowledge of Elizabethan theatre, opened 'The Rose', and later 'The Fortune', modelled on 'The Globe', but with a square instead of a polygonal ground-plan. In 1596 'The Swan' was opened and finally, in 1613, 'The Hope'. Thus, London had seven theatres in all based on Burbage's model. There were also a few playhouses which combined aspects of the public theatres with borrowings from the practice of halls at court where the interludes were staged—these were called private theatres: 'St Paul's, 'Blackfriars' and 'Whitefriars'. The companies of boy-actors whose success is born out by *Hamlet* were the main ones to perform in the private theatres. These private playhouses, and the adjective 'private' served merely to distinguish them from those that were 'public', were completely enclosed, so that

De Witt, Interior of the Swan theatre, 1596. Sketch. Utrecht, Bibliotheek der Centraal Museum. This is the only direct evidence relating to Elizabethan public theatre

View of London in the 16th century. London, British Museum. South of the Thames can be seen two theatres probably still used for bull-baiting

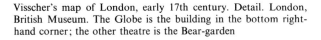

Visscher's map of London, early 17th century. Detail. London, British Museum. The Globe is the building in the bottom right-hand corner; the other theatre is the Bear-garden

artificial light was used for the performance. Instead, in the 'public' theatres, buildings inspired by courtyards and bull-rings, there was no roof over the central area, so that natural daylight was used for the performance.

Unfortunately, not a single example of an Elizabethan theatre building has been preserved. Those that did exist were demolished, first as a result of the Puritan diatribes and their closing of all theatres in 1642, and then because of the trend to imitate Italian or French playhouses. Just a few drawings and a little indirect evidence make possible a tentative reconstruction.

Each theatre, of course, had its own characteristics, both as regards the ground-plan, the proportions and the lay-out of the theatre-building. However, if we pick out the common features, it should be possible to form a fairly clear picture of a typical Elizabethan theatre. The building, at any rate, was planned around a central focus, with a diameter of between 80 and 100 feet, which would be the length along one side if the construction was square, like 'The Fortune'. The surrounding structure consisted of three galleries, one above the other, opening like balconies onto the empty space they enclosed. This enclosure could be called a courtyard because of its historical antecedents, but its diameter was somewhere between 50 and 65 feet, and its function corresponded to that of the stalls in a modern theatre. An Elizabethan theatre could accommodate between 1,600 and 2,300 spectators,

either sitting in the three galleries, of which the second was the most expensive, or remaining standing in the enclosure or pit.

Although there was, as we have seen, no roof over the enclosure, a double sloping roof surmounted the galleries, and resting against these, or better, built into them in such a way as to stand out from them, was the stage-house or tiring-house. The front of this rested on a roughly rectangular, large stage, jutting out considerably into the enclosure, so that it was surrounded on three sides by spectators. Its normal size was from somewhere between 35 and 50 feet in width, and between 24 and 32 feet in depth. This had no necessary bearing on the size of the theatre, since a large theatre could have a small stage, and vice versa. Obviously, the small stage made it possible to provide accommodation for a larger audience, while a larger one gave the actors greater freedom of movement. Two pillars about 25 feet high rested on the stage to support a sort of canopy, called the cover, the shadow or even the heavens, which surmounted the main part of the stage and sloped upwards towards the back, where it was secured to the tiring-house. Alternatively, it might also offer shade round three sides of this, like the roof of a pagoda, and then there may have been pillars at the back. In comparison with the inner line traced by the galleries, the stage-house or tiring-house jutted out a little over the stage. It comprised three floors or storeys. At the bottom and level with the stage was a wall with one or two inset doors for

210

Four outside views of The Swan. *Top left*: London from the south west, detail from Inigo Jones's 1638 drawing for Davenant's *Britannia Triumphans*. Chatsworth, Duke of Devonshire Collection. *Top right*: Panoramic view, *Civitas Londini*, 1600. London, private collection. *Bottom left*: Visscher View, 1616. London, private collection. *Bottom right*: Paris Garden Manor Map, 1627. London, private collection

the actors to make their entrance. However, a single, large opening covered over with a curtain often replaced the doors. When this was open, an inside area became visible, the rear-stage, a sort of interior scene, or den. There was a balcony on top of this ground storey and in the inn-yard theatres this had been no more than the continuation of the second gallery, a function it retained for the earlier performances in the public theatres when it accommodated spectators of distinction. The top-floor, finally, was a sort of attic, called the hut, which might stand out above the level of the roof of the main building. In this case, it was the place for the flagpole with the symbolic standard of the particular theatre: the

swan, the globe, fortune, or a theatre as such. The hut housed the machinery for descents from out of the skies, though these were none too common in Elizabethan theatre, together with equipment for making thunder and other sound effects. The stage was similarly provided with trap-doors for apparitions from below stage, sudden disappearances and, of course, the speedy arrangement of stage-props.

Our information about the private theatres is much less detailed. They were probably large halls with two galleries or balconies running all the way round. The stage would have to face the audience and not wedge itself among them, and so much more of the gallery could be used for the acting, while the

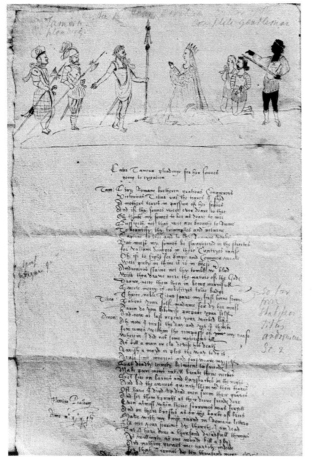

rear of the stage would have a door at either side,
with a hanging running between them. Obviously,
there was no cover and no hut.

In any case, the typically Elizabethan theatre
was the stage for the masterpieces of Kyd, Marlowe
and Shakespeare. This was the stage of the public

theatre, such as we have described it. Now let us
try and see what use was made of it.

Scenery in the Elizabethan theatre was not
representational, in other words it did not directly
resemble the particular setting of the play nor portray it by means of painted scenes. The supposed
location of the action might instead by indicated by
some suitable stage property of the sort mentioned
by Philip Henslowe, the impresario, owner of 'The
Rose', 'The Hope' and 'The Fortune', in his diary,
or else it might be suggested by painted features of
the hanging that covered the entrance to the rear
stage. However, it was never actually reconstructed,
not even in a general or summary manner. Such
brief indications aside, it was left to the audience to
guess or deduce either from the action itself or from
the words of the script in which place the scene was
set. Indeed, this was most likely the general rule,
because furniture was probably only used when it
contributed to the course of the action and never
merely to indicate the setting for it. So that, if we
recall the composition of Elizabethan plays, and
their very frequent displacement of the action from
one place to another, we have to ask ourselves how
the audience could ever manage, without definite
guide-lines, to follow this movement through space
and time. The erudite poet, Sir Philip Sydney,
author of a remarkable novel called *Arcadia*, in his
markedly aristocratic and classically inspired *The
Defence of Poesie* (written 1581: published 1595)
wrote: 'Now ye shal haue three Ladies, walke to
gather flowers, and then we must beleeue the stage
to be a Garden. By and by, we heare newes of ship-
wracke in the same place, and then wee are to blame,
if we accept it not for a Rock. Vpon the backe of that
comes out a hidious Monster, with fire and smoke,
and then the miserable beholders, are bounde to
take it for a Caue. VVhile in the mean-time, two
Armies fly in, represented with foure swords and
bucklers, and then what harde heart will not receive
it for a pitched fielde?'

Sir Philip's criticism, made in the name of realistic
representation, helps us very considerably to appreciate the peculiarity of Elizabethan theatre, in
which imaginery space and time were regulated only
in function of the action on stage, whenever this
called for it, and in terms of the action itself.

In other words, it was the actor, who, by both
word and gesture, lent reality to the setting for the
scene, which the audience had not to focus on all the
time, but only when to do so was useful for the
development of the plot, and to this end the stage-
properties were also used to extend and support the
actor's indications. Hence, the actors' miming had a

Masquers at the wedding banquet of Sir Henry Unton. 16th century oil painting. London, National Gallery. Shakespeare's *A Midsummer Night's Dream* was probably first performed during similar festivities

peculiar power, not because it was exaggerated or forced, but because it had to depict not only the characters' psychological reactions, but their physical surroundings as well. Take the opening scene of *Hamlet*: the changing of the guard on the ramparts of Elsinore castle and the tension surrounding the strange apparition of the ghost of the king so recently dead. The actor was not merely called upon to represent the usual motions of the changing of the guard and the restless anticipation of the repetition of an untoward occurrence, but even the bitter cold and the inky darkness of night. And all this without descending to superflous, exaggerated or prolonged gestures or moments of deliberate suspense; the action was always tight-knit and even precipitate, if, as seems true, a play never lasted more than two hours. Many more examples could be given. An even more obvious one is supplied by the fourth act of *Arden of Feversham*, a middle-class tragedy by an unknown dramatist about the diabolical plot by wife and lover to bring about the death of the husband. The action is set on the Kentish coast, blanketed by thick fog in which Arden is pursued by his assassins. In calling out and trying to find each other the characters had not only to convey a convincing impression of the weather conditions referred to in their lines, but to bring out the fog's moral or symbolic meaning. The complexity of this requirement is obvious. A symbol is usually the tangible aspect of a meaningful whole, with a meaning of its own that is not arbitrary although it is figurative. In this instance, however, the symbol had no reality of its own to carry such a figurative meaning, but had, in its turn, to be signified indirectly by the actors' gestures.

Now, if time and place were conveyed by the actors' words and gestures and not by the stage-setting, what function did this fulfil? Why was it not reduced to a simple ornamental backcloth and why, instead, maintain such a highly organised and complex structure? Some have seen in the Elizabethan stage-house an elaborate cosmological symbol and from it have drawn conclusions as to the ritual character of the performance, but of this there is little real evidence, and the whole is based on an old-fashioned notion of theatre in general being a part of ritual. Instead, the stage-house strikes one in the public theatres as a complex machine designed to serve the action on stage and its various features lend themselves to the representation of quite distinct things, one might almost say lend themselves to the assumption of different rôles, which can also have symbolic value if this is required, but for that very reason are not symbols as such.

We have seen already that the features that together make up the Elizabethan stage-house are the stage, the cover, the stage in front of a background with two doors or a hanging, the rear stage hidden by this hanging, the balcony above. What purpose does each part have to fulfil? The cover, rising up towards the rear of the stage, suggests the possibility of dividing it into two parts, without however indicating any line of demarcation. This does not only mean that the two areas can be regarded as separate although adjoining locations, but it allows the imaginary physical distance between two characters to be increased, so that the asides become credible, as well as the idea of a character coming on stage without immediately noticing someone else who is already there, or being noticed by him and, most of all, it makes moral separateness a possibility. Hamlet is in spirit far away from the court, even when he is conversing with the King and the Queen who has remarried scarcely a month after the death of Hamlet's father, her first husband. Hence his position will be towards the front of the stage, while the royal throne is further back, under the cover. This area is used in the main for scenes of an intimate nature, such as Hamlet's encounter with the Queen accusing her of adultery and disclosing her new husband's crime of assassination—meanwhile, Polonius will be hidden in the rear-stage alcove behind the curtain. This recess will also have been used to represent places apart, hiding-holes or the innermost rooms of a house, although only rarely for the obvious reason that it was out of sight of many in the audience. There, perhaps, was placed the bed on which Othello, once Iago has persuaded him of his wife's infidelity, kills Desdemona. It may also have provided the right location for the final scene in *Romeo and Juliet*, supposedly the crypt in which Juliet has been buried because of her apparent death. It is possible, too, that the frequent apparitions of ghosts occurred thanks to the pulling aside of the curtain over the rear stage, for instance, Julius Caesar's ghost appearing to Brutus, Banquo's apparition to Macbeth during a banquet, the ghost of Hamlet's father. It may have been the case, too, that the witches in *Macbeth* occupied the rear stage. Indeed, all these apparitions would have been most incredible if they had taken place on stage in the full light of day, although, of course, it is a fact that Shakespearian theatre was compelling enough not to have to worry about the physical feasibility of the details of its performance.

Finally all the scenes supposed to take place above ground-level will have been performed on the balcony—which became the city ramparts, a natural prominence, or the upper storey of a house. However, often, and indeed more often than not, those scenes which call for the use of some elevated location are so arranged that there is an exchange between persons standing below on the stage and others higher up on the balcony. The most convincing illustration of this is the celebrated balcony-scene in *Romeo and Juliet*. However, the same procedure was used for siege scenes, quite frequent in Shakespeare's historical plays, and we can mention the scene in *King John* in which, from the top of the city walls, the citizens of Angers refuse to acknowledge their king.

Nevertheless, since the balcony had, so to speak, some architectural history of its own, various personages could also occupy it. It was still thought of as a continuation of the central gallery of the theatre and so, to begin with, it provided room for privileged spectators, without this preventing its being used for the actual production. Later these spectators were replaced by imaginary spectators who, in certain tragedies, had the task of commenting on what was happening and were a sort of chorus. In this case, moreover, Schlegel's definition of the chorus would seem to apply. The best known instance is in Kyd's *Spanish Tragedy*. In the prologue to this, Vengeance invites Don Andrea's ghost to sit down and act as chorus in the tragedy of the revenge old Hieronimo will take on those who have murdered his sons. The *Spanish Tragedy* belongs to 1592. In the years that followed, the balcony was often used to provide seating for the musicians.

In other words, the Elizabethan stage-setting was an extremely versatile instrument in the service of a dramatic action capable of absorbing the whole meaning of the performance. Many scholars have claimed that the absence of definite scenery was atoned for by the lively imagination of the Elizabethan audiences and they base this theory on a well-known passage in *Henry V*: 'And so our scene must to the battle fly;/Where—O for pity!—we shall much disgrace/ With four or five most vile and ragged foils,/Right ill-disposed in brawl ridiculous,/The name of Agincourt. Yet sit and see;/Minding true things by what their mockeries be.'

However, the Shakespearian production probably did not need to be completed or enriched by the audience's powers of imagination: if anything, it lay open to many different renderings and interpretations, not because of its poverty, but as a result of the richness and complexity of its treatment.

It may, nevertheless, remain necessary to explain how the ordinary people who crowded into the public theatres could have been drawn towards

productions of such sophistication and complexity. For it was for such an audience that the companies performed in the main, even if they enjoyed the patronage and protection of the court and the aristocracy whose name and livery they assumed—the King's Men, the Admiral's Men, and the Lord Chamberlain's Men were the main companies in Shakespeare's own day—however much their numbers had declined by comparison with those of the strolling players of the mid-16th century. Many factors contribute to explain this: first and foremost the structure of the theatrical performance, which was poor in terms of the scenery, of the materials and of the costumes employed; and it was this external poverty that troubled Sir Philip Sidney. On the other hand it was extremely rich in mime, in movement and in the forceful use of gesture. The action, in the sense of a succession of concrete happenings on stage, came to a pause only for a battle of words or a soliloquy, in which the character took stock of himself, obliging the actor to go out to meet himself, almost to see himself reflected in the audience hanging on his words. The very poverty of the setting enabled the audience to follow without boredom, and even quite closely the rich feast of verbal somersaults and puns.

Elizabethan theatre satisfied the popular taste for bloody and violent subjects, an extreme case being that of the amputated hands in *Titus Andronicus*. The subjects of the plays also fitted well into the cultural traditions of the English people, who had been taught by the morality-plays to face up to the great themes of morals and politics. The Elizabethan playwrights knew how to strip these themes bare of their medieval abstractions and to enliven them with romantic stories, culled from antiquity or the contemporary scene. This pleased popular imagination. They were ready to take subjects from any source and so were all the time bringing their repertory up to date and so continually stimulating popular curiosity. One result of this was the rich vein of tragedies of revenge: Kyd's *Spanish Tragedy*, Tourneur's *Revenger's Tragedy*, Shakespeare's *Hamlet*. Another result was the cruel dramas of love and death, usually set in Italy, the mythical focus of evil and corruption: Webster's *The Duchess of Malfi*, Shakespeare's *Romeo and Juliet*. There were also plays in which common folk became the main characters in tales of dark passion, in which the audience could recognise their own anguish and bloodlust: the anonymously written *Arden of Feversham* is one masterpiece

already mentioned, and there was also Thomas Heywood's *A Woman Killed with Kindness*.

Besides this, England herself is quite often the real leading character in Elizabethan tragedy: it is obvious that Hamlet's famous line: 'There's something rotten in the state of Denmark' refers to a political and moral situation much closer home. Yet it is in a long series of historical plays, Shakespeare's histories and those of Marlowe and other contemporary authors, that the English nation expressly becomes the protagonist, with the problems of its policies and its dynasty. Here the history of England is seen as the story of its kings, certainly, but this is no apotheosis, both because the country's military and political achievements had no need of patriotic rhetoric and because the chronicles of the English dynasty told a tale of internecine conflict and civil wars, which did, indeed, belong to the past, but were not on that account any less savage and cruel. Those who had paid the price of that bloody sport of kings, now sought to understand its inner dynamics and its rationale.

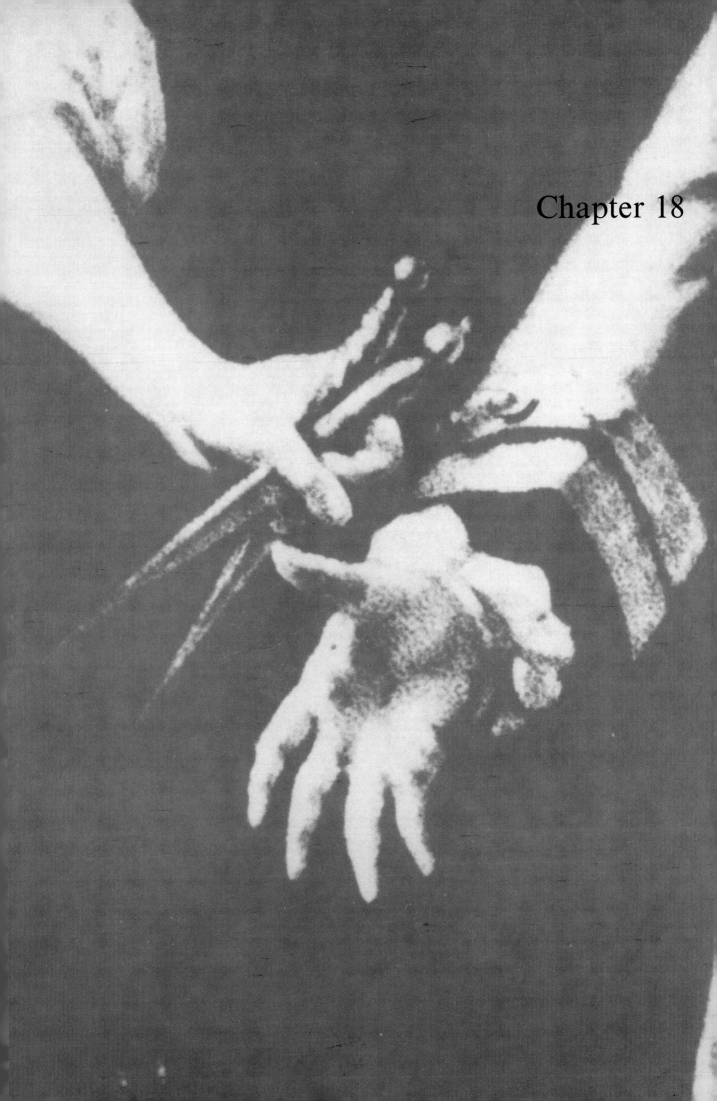

Chapter 18

Fuseli, *The Merry Wives of Windsor*. London, Victoria and Albert Museum. This painting is in no sense direct evidence of 18th-century trends in English theatrical productions. However, it does indicate a certain leaning towards the grotesque

ENGLISH THEATRE DURING THE RESTORATION—GARRICK AND SHAKESPEARIAN INTERPRETATION

During the period of the Restoration, from Charles II's return to the English throne in 1660 until the close of the 17th century, 'she-tragedies' with a woman playing the leading rôle established themselves as a distinct theatrical genre. Perhaps the most successful example in literature is *The Orphan, or the Unhappy Marriage* by Thomas Otway (1652–85). This tells the sad story of Monimia, a girl with two brothers as rivals for her hand. She marries secretly the one she loves, but the other worms his way into her bed, and this incident brings about the death of all three. However, truth to tell, the adjective 'feminine' applies equally well to many other tragedies from this period in British theatre and especially to the very ones which are still worth producing today. Otway—not for nothing did he rework Racine's most heart-rending tale of love, the play *Bérénice*—also created Jaffeir, the main character in *Venice Preserved*. Jaffeir is party to a conspiracy to bring down the Doge's Senate, but allows his wife to persuade him to betray his friends. Later he repents bitterly of what he has done, begs for their forgiveness, and kills himself like a wife, who has been unfaithful yet truly in love. Jaffeir is matched by John Dryden's Anthony. In *All for Love*, Dryden (1631–1700) very successfully reworks Shakespeare's tragedy, *Anthony and Cleopatra*, but his own Anthony is markedly different from Shakespeare's. In Shakespeare the Roman leader makes his own decisions with courage and resolve: when affairs of state call him elsewhere he abandons Cleopatra and fearlessly confronts Octavian, as cruel and treacherous as the rival kings in the Wars of the Roses. Later, with just as much courage, he abandons the battle to follow Cleopatra, for no other motive than that of his burning passion. On his lips, the well-known words 'Give me a kiss; even this repays me' are not a cry of sorrow, but a manly affirmation of his own commitment: Cleopatra's kiss is worth a world empire. Dryden's Anthony, instead, possesses a heart torn by feelings he cannot control, nor even understand; he is in no condition to evaluate, let alone choose. Ventidius and Cleopatra experience no difficulty in persuading him to accept contradictory plans of action: his mind is ruled by whoever has last spoken to him, whether to remind him of his honour or to play on his love. Thus, his character is typically female.

The male characters in Restoration tragedy are by contrast models of unambiguous and incredible heroism, to a degree that compels one to conclude their stature has been ironically exaggerated, so that they portray an excellence that is empty, inflated, inhuman, false and non-existent. Dryden's and Elkanah Settle's heroic plays are sometimes on a grand scale even independently of their subject—*The Conquest of Granada* runs to ten acts. The tone of the heroic plays is grotesque, as that of the comedy of manners is one of cold caricature. These contemporary genres run parallel in their witness to the lack of moral standards in society at the time. Restoration theatre is not much known outside England, but may very well merit a renewed acquaintance, which might also make it possible to understand why Ben Jonson and not Shakespeare was its true prophet. The learned Jonson composed one of the most extraordinary comedies of the Elizabethan and Jacobean period, *Volpone*, in which all the characters can be classed as villains, carrion crows scavenging on the patrimony of someone merely thought to be dead. Shakespeare's own success at the time was only possible because his plays were construed in a way we would see as infinitely removed from their original spirit. Anthony, for instance, had to be interpreted in a feminine way: references to court intrigues had to be added to the text of *King Lear*; *A Midsummer Night's Dream* had to be treated as a mere excuse for a ballet.

However, it would be only by a reconstruction of actual theatrical productions during this period that we could hope to verify the extent to which people actually living at the time might have accepted as valid our theory, already mentioned, about the dimension of irony in the heroic plays, about the degree of deliberate cynicism and social caricature in the comedies of William Congreve (1670–1729), William Wycherley (1640–1716) and George Farquhar (1677–1707), and about the meaning of the revival of interest in Shakespeare. This enterprise is unusually fraught with difficulty.

It must above all be born in mind that Restoration theatre is itself a theatre that has been resurrected: in other words, it is not a theatre whose structure and intent stem from an evolving tradition, but reflects at best the recovery of some elements from a tradition that had been forgotten, and the vital issues it is called upon to support or to justify are in fact new. William Davenant (1606–68) had his reasons for cheerfully allowing rumours to circulate of an affair between Shakespeare and his own mother, since this would have made him the missing-link required to cover the twenty years' hiatus between Elizabethan and Jacobean theatre and that of Charles II's reign. It was by invoking this sort of natural descent that Davenant could claim to teach his actors 'the true Shakespearian tradition'. In reality he was without the stature needed to bridge the twenty years (1642–61) in which the theatres had been closed by order of Parliament under which Oliver Cromwell, the Lord Protector who had had King Charles I beheaded, had inaugurated his own bourgeois–Puritan dictatorship. In England, as throughout the rest of Europe, many moralisers had thundered against the theatre, notably in the 16th century John Northbrooke, who wrote a pamphlet against plays and interludes which obviously referred to the performances at court, John Stockwood, a famous preacher who inveighed against theatre in his sermons, Stephen Gosson and others. Then, only ten years before the Puritan revolution, a pamphlet with the title *Histrio-Mastix*, which criticised the theatre and its actors, resulted in its author, William Prynne, being pilloried. Consequently in England alone political events resulted in radical legislation which closed the theatres and destroyed such marvellous buildings as 'The Globe', 'The Theatre' and 'The Curtain'.

In a mere twenty years the theatres vanished and with them Elizabethan stage tradition, leaving behind at best a very dim recollection of itself. Shakespeare's rumoured natural son, William Davenant, as an active royalist, was eager to meet the wishes of king and court; but whatever part he played in the revival of theatre-life in London, he definitely did not bring about any renewal of the Elizabethan traditions. Still, his name figured on one of the first two royal letters patent licensing the holders to monopolise the London theatre; the other bore the name of Thomas Killigrew. Davenant's troupe was called the Duke's Men, after the Duke of York; Killigrew's company was that of the King's Men.

Initially these companies performed in halls converted into theatres: in Lincoln's Fields and Vere Street respectively. However, in 1682 after each had opened theatres in Dorset Gardens (1671) and Drury Lane (1663) they joined forces in a common venture centred in the new Drury Lane theatre built in 1674 by Sir Christopher Wren to replace the original destroyed by fire in 1672. The same architect had also adapted Whitehall as a court theatre, working along characteristically Italian lines, with a stage running from wall to wall, 35 feet in depth, and framed by a proscenium arch. The scenery and stage-settings were also clearly inspired by those of Inigo Jones in his Italian period. The repertory was, in fact, made up principally of masques and ballets, more lyrical works being excluded for lack of stage machinery. On the other hand, the results of Wren's efforts in theatrical architecture at Drury Lane were most interesting and original—a sort of piquant mixture of the Elizabethan tradition with abundant touches of Italian and French.

The Drury Lane Theatre was almost round: three ranges of boxes set one above the other at the sides, with three galleries opening along the back. The front edge of the stage followed the arc of a circle, and jutted out about 17 feet into the pit, where the seats had, therefore, to be set along a curve. Further back than this front apron, framed by a proscenium arch more like those in modern theatres than any used in Italian theatres in the first half of the 17th

Mr and Mrs Barry in a scene from Otway's *Venice Preserved*. Drawing. London, Victoria and Albert Museum

A scene from Goldsmith's *She Stoops to Conquer*. Painting. London, Victoria and Albert Museum

A scene from Congreve's *The Way of the World*. Engraving. London, Victoria and Albert Museum

century, one which was not a real proscenium arch but merely a structural feature separating the stage from the rest of the theatre, was the main stage itself, where there were arranged the stage-settings typical of Italian theatre, in other words, painted flats and backdrops. Two doors opened one in each side of the proscenium arch, and the actors made their way on and off through these. Two balconies above these doors were used for scenes set above ground level, so that they served the same function as the gallery of the Elizabethan stage. Indeed, save for the cover, all the typical features of the Elizabethan stage can be found in this new arrangement, although their relationships had been considerably modified.

The apron or front-stage was merely an atrophied form of the Elizabethan stage which had extended right out into the pit and had been surrounded by the audience on three sides. By contrast the inner-stage had become enormous in comparison with the Elizabethan rear-stage. It was no longer used as an alcove or recess, as need required; nor, again, was it much used for the dramatic action, which took place principally on the apron, that is, forward of the imaginary line running across the stage between the two stage-doors. In this way, the inner-stage became something of a peep-show, with plenty of space and room to arrange all the flats and backdrops so as to give them the necessary realism and depth and yet far enough back to ensure that the stage-setting, while promoting the appreciation and development of the dramatic action, did not actually influence its course, this being entirely centred round the actors. The actors, for their part, were no longer obliged, as their Elizabethan counterparts had been, to use mime to convey the appropriate local colour. Furthermore, although they were still in close con-

221

tact with the audience and occupied a space within that reserved for the spectators, their relationship was now with a public which faced them and did not surround them as it had in the Elizabethan theatre. True, as in France, so in England spectators often encumbered the stage, a more or less tolerated nuisance. The inner-stage may have been used for the acting of the extras, for part of the frequent ballet-scenes and also for the tableaux in which the main characters in a tragedy arranged themselves before the final death-scene—a typical instance being that of Dryden's Cleopatra surrounded by her maids. On the other hand, the songs definitely established an even more direct link with the audience and were sung on the front edge of the apron.

Such, then, were the stage arrangements, but it would be more valuable to know in specific instances what was the atmosphere of the production and along what lines the actors interpreted their parts. The answer can be given only in general terms.

A few preliminary remarks are in order.

As already mentioned, the King's Men and the Duke's Men amalgamated in 1682. Even if this was the result of a directive from someone in authority, it goes to show that two theatres were by that time too many for a city the size of London, which had accommodated five or six only fifty years earlier. The audiences were too small to cover expenses, despite court subsidies and the king's own frequent visits to the public theatres. The fact that Samuel Pepys, as he records in his diary, found they were 'sold out' does little to disprove this theory. The popular audiences had given up going to the theatre, partly because they had lost the habit, partly because the new subjects and the new manner of treatment were little to their taste; even if the new theatre was not precisely a court theatre, it was certainly one that was class-conscious.

Nevertheless, it must be admitted that the English nobility and the upper middle-classes could observe themselves portrayed on stage with eyes that were cynical and disenchanted. The absence of moral principles was not only meant to allow for a gay and liberated display of vitality and wit, as was the case with Italian 14th-century romantic tales and the later 16th-century comedies. In English comedy the absence of morality is just a fact that is noted and pointed out—with cheerful cynicism by Congreve in *The Way of the World*, with bitterness by Wycherley, with detached objectivity by Etherege in his lifeless comedies, such as *The Man of Mode*. Yet, how did this avowal come across on stage?

The space within which Elizabethan plays were produced and staged always preserved its character of an unconditionally contemporary, concretely real, material world, fashioned on a human scale, though the dramatic action lent it its specific meaning and qualities. In Restoration theatre, by contrast, the action took place *in front of* scenery representing in more or less conventional terms a real and definite place, and yet *outside* it. There were no concrete features on which the action depended, but only a painted scene to which it could be referred. Hence, if the schemings of young beaux to secure a dowry or of some old woman to acquire a lover were detailed in the accents of contemporary society, they might come across only as elegant manoeuvres devoid of substance. If an actor simply gave an emphatic and exaggerated turn of phrase to his delivery, these schemings became disturbingly real and almost tangible. It was not that a humorous or artificial tone deprived the words of their meaning, but nevertheless it changed from 'this is our own coarseness in Restoration England, a bestiality resulting from our moral bankruptcy', to 'the game of life has always been played like this, and it is an idle pastime to look for some moralising theory to make it excusable'.

English Restoration comedy teams with characters that lend themselves to distortion and caricature, notably sexually frustrated old women, like Lady Wishfort in *The Way of the World*. On the other hand, to make too clear a distinction between the gulls or caricatures, and the wits or straight characters, would bring this type of comedy down to the level of a mere parlour game and deprive it of much of its originality, as the most amoral theatrical genre. Again, to take the example of Congreve's comedy already mentioned, this would make it well nigh impossible to show on stage the bitter hatred between the Fainall couple, each of whom has committed adultery and each of whom only waits for the other's death.

All the same, each of the three approaches offers a possible solution, and the acting of a comedy on stage in one of these ways rather than another would certainly make a whole world of difference. This goes to prove the wealth of meaning contained in the text.

We have, unfortunately, no clear information from contemporary sources. As usual, the actors, and in particular Thomas Betterton who set the tone for this period, are praised for their realism, but this tells us nothing. Right up to our own day actors have always been praised for their realism, but we should need to know what the term meant to successive generations. However, it was also said of Betterton that he got on quite well in comedies, 'despite' the dignity of his bearing; and of Nell Gwynn, who from selling oranges in the pit at Drury Lane grew into the leading actress in that theatre, becoming subsequently the King's mistress, we know she was particularly fond of the rôle of devil-may-care girl without a scrap of modesty and played such parts with a vitality that defies description.

A proper understanding of the comedies might yield the key to the question raised at the start of this chapter and suggest, if only as a hypothesis, how the heroic plays may have been handled on stage, even if it left us in the dark with regard to the languishing 'she-tragedies' themselves. Obviously, a society which was ready to see itself represented as devoid of any of the hitherto generally accepted moral values—conjugal love, sincerity and affection—was clear-headed enough to be able to laugh with gentle irony at the false virtues of heroic love and unyielding honour which Charles II had brought over from France as part of the vogue for Racine. After the middle-class revolution, England was in any case well aware of its own strength and felt no need to play the hero. So, if the vein of subtle irony that modern critics have discerned in the heroic plays was also noticed by Betterton and his fellow actors, they may have played the parts of Dryden's heroes (of whom Almanzor in *The Conquest of Granada* is the most typical representative) by filling out and enlarging their use of gesture to the point at which the sublime borders on the ridiculous, hammering out the metre of their lines so clearly as to reduce them to meaningless sound-patterns. The dimensions of the heroic would then have been attained only by the scenery, while the dramatic message would either simply evaporate or become absurdly amusing.

Naturally, this could have happened quite against Dryden's intention, but his assertion that in heroic plays we should not 'weigh love and honour by drams and scruples' strikes one already as at least ambiguous. On the other hand, not everyone can have appreciated the irony, because some of Dryden's productions were parodied, precisely because of their exaggerated proportions, in an amusing comedy by the Duke of Buckingham, *The Rehearsal*, in which Dryden himself is portrayed as the producer of his own plays, doing his utmost to deck out his characters as magnificently as he possibly can. In the original, this very excess of display may have concealed an inner irony.

The English theatrical repertory widened its scope and underwent substantial modifications in the course of the 18th century. Comedy shed its most harshly cynical characteristics and increasingly addressed itself to a level-headed portrayal of moral behaviour. Oliver Goldsmith and Richard Brinsley Sheridan made it their business to present characters and life-styles in which the contrast no longer lay between the wits and the gulls, but the good and the wicked. Human behaviour was assessed on a basis of definite moral standards and virtue was generally shown to triumph in the end. As well as this comedy of manners, increasing attention was paid to subsidiary genres—the sheer horse-play of farce on stage, represented principally by Henry Carey and Samuel Foote, and the personal satire as well as burlesque. Besides this, Shakespeare's works were performed again with increasing frequency, although the choice was restricted to the usual favourites: *Macbeth, Hamlet, King Lear, Julius Caesar, Henry IV*, and *Richard III*. Rowe's sentimental tragedies followed in the footsteps of Otway in a sense and Dryden's sort of heroic play gave way to classically inspired tragedies, such as Addison's *Cato*, Whitehead's *Merope*, and Ambrose Philips' *The Distressed Mother*. For the most part these were re-elaborations of French scripts, or modelled on work inspired by Racine. It seems likely that the style of acting similarly changed. Comedy became increasingly realistic in tone, until it stabilised round about 1750, which may have been the result of the influence of David Garrick, the greatest English actor of the century. Meanwhile, personal satire emphasised those notes of caricature which may not have been entirely absent from the Restoration productions of comedies of manners. Both from the literary point of view and from that of actual stage-production John Gay's *Beggars' Opera*, produced in Lincoln's Inn Field by John Rich in 1728, with epoch-making success, was the most striking example of this strong note of caricature. Statesmen and leading society-figures were portrayed as thieves, sharks and prostitutes,

Garrick and Mrs Bellamy in *Romeo and Juliet*, 1753. Engraving.
London, Victoria and Albert Museum

Garrick and Mrs Pritchard in *Macbeth* at the Drury Lane Theatre.
Engraving. London, Victoria and Albert Museum. Note Garrick's
middle-class dress

whose manners were accommodating and whose speech was correct, while they completely lacked the moral principles of Congreve's and Etherege's heroes, and appeared on stage as clearly recognisable personalities with their fads and foibles emphasised to the point of caricature, though they never lacked that impeccable elegance of bearing which contrasted so sharply (Brecht would say, to the point of alienation) with the coarse ostentation or else the bedraggled condition of their underworld garb. More subtle but no less biting tones characterised the literary satire, from Fielding's *Tragedy of Tragedies, or the Life and Death of Tom Thumb*, to Sheridan's *The Critic*.

Tragic productions seem to have been based on the structure of French classical tragedy, interpreted with a glance backwards to the tradition of Dryden's heroic plays. As in France, the tragic heroes wore the costumes of the court nobility, but there was also a touch of exaggeration, a certain bombast. Certain features of Shakesperian costume, such as the whole forest of feathers set on the heads of the more heroic figures, served, as they did in productions of Dryden's works, to add a certain grotesque element to characters supposed to have a classical dignity. This concept of dignity, decorum and grandeur tended, on the other hand, to bring to an end something that had been a distinguishing mark of Elizabethan theatre: the continuous vitality and forceful use of mime. The characters came on through the side-doors, advanced deliberately towards the rim of the apron and remained there throughout their performance. Here their action developed in a series of poses, which they held while they said their lines and then abandoned for a while to take a little walk while their partner went through his lines. The lines themselves, however dramatic, were recited with slow solemnity and interspersed with long oratorical pauses, in which James Quin was a past master.

The architectural lay-out of the theatres contributed considerably to this result. Substantially it remained much the same as in the preceding period. If the apron was noticeably smaller, this was with an eye to the box-office and an increase in the accommodation available for spectators, rather than the outcome of aesthetic choice. The same holds true for the substitution of proscenium boxes for the former balconies over the stage-doors.

There were two dramatic theatres in London: old Drury Lane, and the Covent Garden theatre, which replaced Lincoln's Inn Field and was inaugurated in 1732. There was also a sort of clandestine theatre, Goodman's Fields, where straight plays were ostensibly free extras, interludes during a short orchestral concert for which one had to buy a ticket. This anomalous situation became a permanency when, in 1737, by Act of Parliament only official companies could produce comedies or tragedies, while operatic works were assigned the King's Theatre (the old Haymarket Theatre). The example of Goodman's Fields soon caught on and by the end of the century London had numerous small theatres destined to have a glorious future: the Lyceum, Sadler's Wells and many more. We cannot say there was any difference in approach or style between Drury Lane and Covent Garden and actors moved more or less frequently from one to the other. Covent Garden possibly had a more stable management, since John Rich, the son of Christopher, a former manager of Drury Lane, was in charge of the former until his death in 1761, making it famous not

James Wright, *A Provincial Theatrical Performance in England*,
1788. Coloured engraving. London, Victoria and Albert Museum.
The painter's irony does not detract from the fascination of the
innocent exuberance of this production—probably the opening
scene from *Macbeth*

only for the success of the *Beggars' Opera*, but also
for pantomime in which he himself played Harlequin.

David Garrick (1717–79) made his official début
at Goodman's Fields in 1741, but when he took over
the management of Drury Lane in 1747, the old
theatre became the shrine of a new school. Garrick
received the customary praise for the naturalness and
authenticity of his performance, but other tributes to
his abilities allow us to give a more precise meaning
to this open-ended praise. Thus, it was remarked that
while other actors of the day were admired for their
skill in adapting various characters to their own
personalities, Garrick as an actor tended instead to
become unrecognisable, being successively transmuted into the different characters he played. He was
also a most able mimic and a clever imitator—
hence, his realism first of all consisted in his versatile
ability to create characters distinguishable one from

another and all individualised in their detailed
features. There was also, perhaps, the accuracy with
which he portrayed reality as he observed it to be.
One story to bear this out tells how, when Garrick
was preparing himself to play King Lear, he used to
visit a poor old man who had gone mad after killing
his own daughter by accident. This is even more
significant than Fielding's tale about the servant
Partridge claiming Garrick was not a good actor in
his portrayal of Hamlet's terror at seeing a ghost:
Partridge is made to say, 'I am sure if I had seen a
ghost, I should have looked in the very same manner
and done just as he did.' The sort of authenticity
Garrick communicated to his contemporaries must
have derived in large part from his opposition to the
sublime and static recitals of actors like James
Quin. Anyone watching Garrick and Quin act
together in 1746, might have compared Quin to a

huge, three-masted galleon, heavy and slow to manoeuvre, and he could have likened Garrick to a small frigate. Leaving aside the difference in age between the two men, not to mention their obvious and undeniable difference in weight, this means that, even when playing tragedy, Garrick had thrown aside all pose, in order to recover, although in a new and different form, the plasticity of the Elizabethan actor. Similarly, he followed the Elizabethans in making himself contemporary, adopting, at least in playing certain characters, the refined and middle-class manners of the society of his day. His suggestion, too, that the pit should be further enlarged at the expense of the apron must have contributed to the transfer of the dramatic action to the inner-stage, where it could be backed up by more properties and integrated into the stage-setting.

In what sense was this new sort of stage-production influential in promotiong the renewed interest in Shakespeare? There are phases in the history of

Hogarth, a scene from *Henry IV*: Falstaff inspects the recruits. Painting. Lord Elveden Collection

theatre in which the dramatic output dwindles away or stops altogether and in its absence people turn again to more or less antiquated plays to bridge the gap. This happened during the Hellenistic period in Greece and during the humanist period in Italy. However, from the 18th century onwards, and especially in France and England, there began a sort of alternate staging of new works and of 'classical' productions. In France, this means Racine, Corneille and Molière; in England, it means Shakespeare. This formula for the repertory has lasted right up to our own times, although the idea of what is a 'classic' has been enlarged and internationalised. Still, while in France the three classical playwrights provided the model for 18th-century stage-productions, in England, for all his influence on the writers of the time, Shakespeare found no imitators and none to continue his work. His plays have been produced more often than those of any other in modern times, but he has never been, in that sense, a 'classic'. Because

of this, and as a result of the twenty-year break in theatrical activity, the Shakespeare revival had no choice but to be an attempt to put forward his works as corresponding to contemporary interests and taste. Davenant's and Dryden's heavy-handed cuts and changes and those of Garrick himself cannot, therefore, be condemned as havoc perpetrated on a sacred text in order to destroy it, but as an attempt to make it relevant, to allow its content to be understood and to render it more acceptable to contemporary forms of sensibility. It was precisely this open-minded approach that preserved the 18th-century cult of Shakespeare from a barren, cultural narcissism.

It is significant that the characters closest to the people retained their traditional characteristics even in their style of dress. Sir John Falstaff, madcap Prince Hal's old drinking-companion, found an excellent interpreter of his rôle in James Quin, one of the greatest exponents of the classical school, and

Zoffany, *A performance by Garrick*. Oil on canvas. Birmingham, City Museum and Art Gallery

always kept his floppy, high boots, his embroidered jacket, his round, feathered hat and his large horseman's gloves. Richard III and Henry VIII, too, never followed the fashion, but wore more or less authentically Elizabethan costume. On the whole, however, from the close of the Restoration period until 1740, Shakespeare's works were treated like tragedies in the French style and Garrick, who approached them in a way that really gave life and variety to the texts, tried to supersede the monolithic heroic type by putting a stamp of individuality on each main character and also, unless there were traditions that justified retaining some special costume, took to wearing on stage clothing in keeping with the current fashion of his day. He challenged the stock interpretation of each individual character, as Charles Macklin had also done, though without departing from a stock interpretation of specific rôles. Thus, Macklin had played Shylock, the Jew in *The Merchant of Venice*, as a villain instead of as a comic character. In like manner, Garrick, beginning with his first interpretation of Richard III at Goodman's Fields Theatre, portrayed that character as a warrior-hero rather than as a political hypocrite, while still accepting the traditional characterisation. This meant the creation of a complex personality, a wicked warrior, a treacherous hero. This feel for the individuality of each character, for his inalienable and detailed personal qualities, seems to emerge from a few verses contrasting Spranger Barry's playing of Lear in Covent Garden with that of Garrick in Drury Lane: 'A King, nay, every inch a king:/Such Barry doth appear./But Garrick's quite a different thing:/He's every inch King Lear'.

In Garrick's day the audience was certainly larger and of more varied composition that it had been at the time of the Restoration and many of his modifications of Shakespeare's text were aimed at meeting very superficial requirements. An Italian singer was even added to *A Midsummer Night's Dream* and people began to talk of 'Signor Shakespeare' in consequence. The productions of many of the histories were enlivened by frequent parades and processions. On the other hand, Garrick insisted that the main characters should occupy the centre of the stage and eliminated the scenes in which they did not appear. Even in England neo-classicism had made its demands felt and there was a tendency to make the dramatic action as integrated and compact as possible. The comedies of manners may have provided an overall view of contemporary society, but people turned to Shakespeare for a true account of man's individuality and soul, naturally re-expressed in the language of contemporary sensitivity. Juliet, for instance, watched Romeo die and then followed him to his eternal rest after a prolonged, tear-filled farewell, in which her delicate soul gave full vent to all its sensitivity and sweetness.

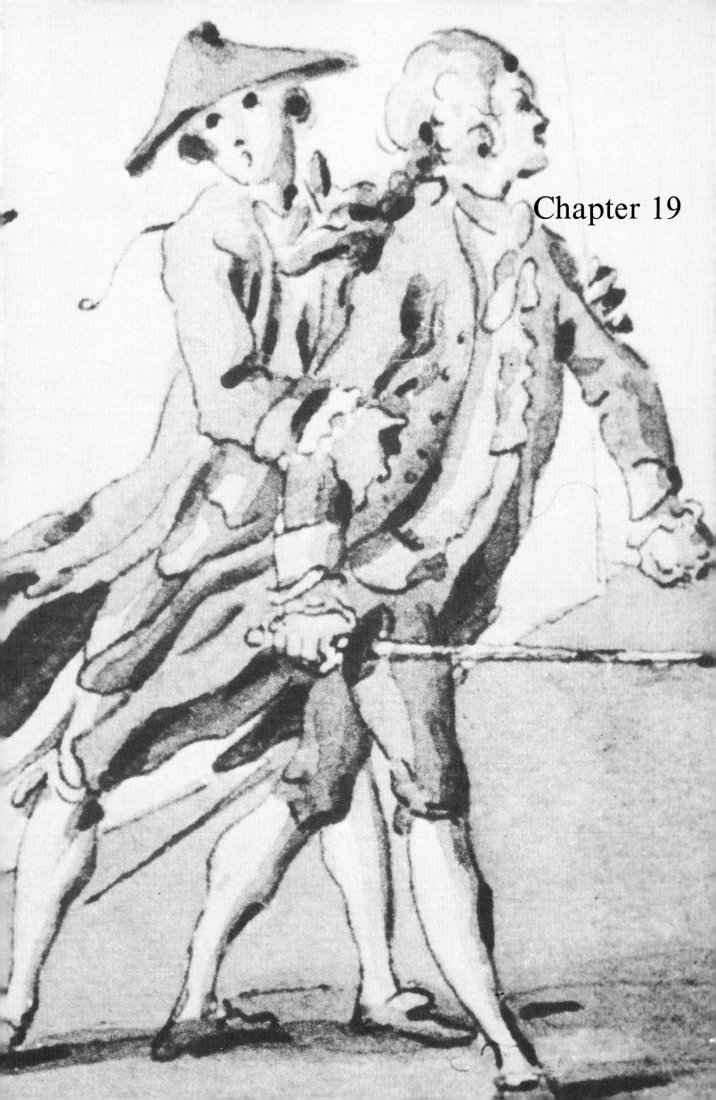

Chapter 19

M Garnier, *The Dragoon takes his Leave*. Oil on canvas. Paris, Musée Carnavalet. In French *comédie larmoyante* the classical derivation of the great, sentimental gesture was never concealed

LESSING AND MIDDLE-CLASS THEATRE

Today George Lillo's *The London Merchant* has been almost entirely forgotten, but when it was first produced in London in 1731 it was destined for tremendous success throughout the whole of Europe.

The success of this work and its importance in the history of theatre spring from the fact that, well over a century after *Arden of Feversham* and other Elizabethan domestic tragedies, it was the first example of middle-class tragedy in the new circumstances of the 18th century. At that time the very terms of such a classification would have presented a paradox and the playwright was well aware of this when he wrote in the Dedication: '. . . Tragedy is so far from losing its dignity by being accommodated to the circumstances of the generality of mankind, that is is more truly august in proportion to the extent of its influence, and the numbers that are properly affected by it.' He added in his Prologue that the need was no longer 'to show unfortunate princes and scenes of royal woe' but 'scenes of private woe'.

The plot is straightforward: Barnwell, who is in the employ of a rich and generous merchant, falls in love with Millwood, a woman quite devoid of scruples. In order to satisfy her greed he wanders from the straight and narrow path and ends by murdering a rich uncle of his. He is hanged, but before his death repents of what he has done and obtains forgiveness. Thus, the story has no references to the heroic figures of mythology and none of that concern for political questions and 'historical' events that characterised even the most 'individual' of Shakespeare's tragedies: *Othello, Romeo and Juliet* and *Hamlet*. For all that, it is a tragedy in the true sense of the word and in line with literary tradition. There are obvious Shakespearian touches. The discourse is for the most part noble and self-conscious. The characters are also 'heroic', the good because of their unconditional generosity, but especially the villain of the piece. Millwood the prostitute resembles Medea in the all-destroying fury of her consuming passion and has a savage, primitive awareness of her own predestination to eternal damnation. As a Christian tragic heroine she is unique and possibly could never have issued from a Catholic religion of hope, but needed Luther's readiness to accept providential decrees of destiny of which the binding force was eternal. But this is not the whole story: Thorowgood's personal history, to take one more character, is given an international slant: he gives the play its title, despite young Barnwell being the chief character in it, and along with the other London merchants, he brings to light the economic manoeuvres of Spain and so makes possible her military defeat. The story is set in 1587 and Elizabeth owes her victory to him, just as Venice was indebted to Othello! Tragedy does not descend to a middle-class level, but the middle-class's most typical representatives, the merchants, rise with heroism to the sublime heights of tragedy, for better or for worse—for Millwood, too, belongs to the middle-class and understands that money rules the world.

Probably Garrick proved to be an excellent Barnwell, but James Quin, the champion of the old-style tragedy, must have been ideal as Thorowgood.

The British middle-class's confident self-esteem did not succeed in finding any great following in other European countries, although there was both in France and Italy a calm and complacent, though moderate exaltation of the middle-class virtues of honesty, far-sightedness and thrift. From a strictly theatrical point of view this was quite a paradoxical situation. Goldoni's work in a commercial centre like Venice belonged directly and unreservedly to comedy rather than tragedy, and since he disapproved of the clowning of the *commedia dell'arte*, the Venetian playwright's problem in production was not how to restrain the tragic, but rather to attenuate the comic.

In France, by contrast, a new genre emerged, based initially on a sort of compromise. This was the *comédie larmoyante* of Nivelle de la Chaussée, whose activities date from about 1732. Later the name became even more decisive, 'drama', though such a term is ambiguous in its own way, especially in Italy. There is no Italian equivalent of *play*, *pièce*, *Stück* and so *dramma* can refer either to any text designed to be produced on stage, or to a specific type of theatrical script in which unfortunate mishaps and moments of suspense hold a prominent place, usually in the private lives of rather nondescript personalities.

The theoretical foundations of this genre were laid by Diderot, its greatest exponent, who, obviously wishing to score a point against the use of the expression *comédia larmoyante*, defined it as *tragédie domestique* or *genre sérieux*. What he wanted from it was 'the portrayal of the mishaps that encompass us' staged in an 'authentic setting' with 'the correct clothing' and 'dialogues in keeping with the action'. In *Paradoxe sur le comédien* he had seen theatre as the place where the thoughts of great characters were embodied in conventionally exaggerated gesture, but in *Entretien sur le fils naturel* and *De la poésie dramatique* he pleaded for the abolition of that '*bienséance cruelle*' which, at the very moment of the greatest turmoil when passions were at their highest and the dramatic action was particularly stormy, required the actors to group themselves in a circle. Diderot was only partly eating his own words, since he placed 'grandeur' before convention and refused to allow works that were 'slight' or 'modest'. Nevertheless, by demanding everyday language and a portrayal of social conditions rather than of individual characters, Diderot effectively severed his links with tragedy in the traditions of Racine.

French actors were slow in accepting Diderot's proposals and then developed those aspects of it which were more in keeping with the twin traditions of tragic style and of the *comédie larmoyante*. Diderot's disciples also did the same, notably Louis Sébastian Mercier (1740–1814), who was called by his contemporaries quite simply 'the dramatist'. Among other things, he produced his own version of *The London Merchant*. Mercier's heroes are highly susceptible and so, albeit with a certain artistry, contrive, as Hamlet might say, to 'tear a passion to tatters', which is what restores to them the missing tragic dimension. The characters on stage still deliberately grouped themselves in a circle, but for the great tragic finale formed a clear tableau which was not meant to be the statuesque freezing into inertia, but rather the immobilisation of characters whose overwhelming emotions had deprived them of the use of their limbs.

Mercier's main works, *L'Indigent* and *L'habitant de la Guadaloupe* already bring us up to about 1780, but it seems likely that the more cautious productions of Diderot and Beaumarchais (*Eugénie*; 1767) were interpreted along similar lines.

The most perfect theoretical definition of 'drama' and its most authentic realisations in practical terms were the achievement in Germany of Gotthold Ephraim Lessing (1721–81), a great critic and a scholar in the field of aesthetics, the author of several plays whose value is beyond question— *Miss Sara Sampson* (1756), *Minna von Barnhelm* (1767), *Emilia Galotti* (1772), *Nathan der Weise* (1783). We also owe this achievement to a great actor, Konrad Ekhof (1720–78).

From the point of view of both organisation and taste the situation facing these two men in their work for the theatre was a complex one. In Germany modern theatre can trace its history to about the middle of the 17th century, when quite a number of troupes of English actors toured the country to stage revised versions and adaptations of the Elizabethan tragedies. These were very soon joined and later replaced by the German *Wandertruppen*. Of these companies that of Johannes Velten (1640–92) was outstanding. He seems to have been the first to produce Molière in German and in his repertory 'standard' plays alternated with historical and political dramas featuring the bizarre character of Hanswurst, a sort of diabolical peasant with a little yellow jacket. These dramas were half improvised (*halb-studierte*), so the courts and townships had them performed at reduced prices.

For about two hundred years strolling players were a typical feature of the theatre throughout most of Europe, but more especially in Germany and Italy, which lacked such cultural metropolitan centres as London and Paris. In Italy the idea of the travelling company was accepted as an obvious necessity, possibly even as a way of life naturally suited to the actors' temperament. It was only in the second half of the 19th century that people began to talk about a national theatre along the lines of the Comédie Française, but fortunately even today this sacrilegious idea has never been put into practice. However, in Germany the larger companies pined for a place to lay their heads, in other words, they sought to become permanent companies in a particular state or city, with the grant of a 'privilege' or at least of a temporary license that the actors could hope to make permanent. The battle of the theatre

ACTE II. SCENE VII.   ACTE V. SCENE XII.   ACTE V. SCENE XIII.   MINNA DE BARNHELM ACTE I. SCENE II.   ACTE I. SCENE VI   ACTE II. SCENE II.

companies went on throughout the 18th century and they succeeded in establishing themselves finally in Berlin, Gotha, Weimar, Hamburg and in many other centres. In Germany even today most cities have their tediously well-meaning permanent theatre company, commissioned to satisfy the citizens' 'need for amusement'.

It was in 1737 that one of the companies of strolling players asked the Hamburg city authorities for a financial subsidy and a permanent site, claiming the need for this in order to fulfil their noble mission of restoring German theatre which had fallen into a state of heart-rending barbarity. This company was under the direction of Carolina and Johann Neuber, two actors who had left behind their self-centred, middle-class family to dedicate their energies to the theatre. They had a certain

refinement. The programme of restoration they tried to follow, and which the Hamburg city council in refusing the help they asked for showed it did not hold in high regard, was not their own invention but had been worked out, complete in every detail, by a Leipzig university professor, Johann Christopher Gottsched (1700–66). He wanted to impart dignity to German theatre by obliging it to follow the classical norms traced out by Boileau in his *Art poétique* and modelled on the tragedies of Racine and Corneille. Gottsched was a rigid upholder of the three unities and excluded any sort of pandering to the audience—the characters' bearing on stage had always to be most dignified and their tragic lines were to be recited as the rules of poetry required. However, he also demanded that both the play and its interpretation on stage be completely true to life. In his

J G Ziesenis, Diderot's *Le Père de famille*. Watercolour. Paris, Comédie Française. French actors froze their gestures in moments of the greatest tension to form what was called a tableau

233

view, the play was true to life if it had rational self-consistency and when this was applied to the stage-production, he wanted it to be well adapted to the period of history and the particular nation that the play represented. Thus, he was the first to argue for the historical accuracy of theatrical productions, though he, nevertheless, failed to notice the blatant lack of this very quality in the French plays which he translated or used as models. The Neubers tried to fall in with his wishes, but after a period in which educated audiences gave them at any rate a *succès d'estime*, they fell out with their pedantic mentor—and the systematic attempt to foist Classicism on German theatre audiences failed.

In German theatre, then, Classicism is not simply to take a country whose culture enjoys more prestige and to follow its fashions or re-echo the themes it has treated, expressing them in the same forms; it is a calculated cultural operation, based, no doubt, on results obtained abroad, but developed in accordance with certain rigorous principles, although their validity was impugned by a fundamental contradiction that the argument about costumes brought to light.

At all events, the Neubers' and Gottsched's considerable success allowed Lessing to turn his back on earlier popular traditions and to make Classicism the clear and easy target of his attack. Where the Neubers' company had failed, that of actor-manager (*Prinzipal*) Konrad Ackermann (1712–71) succeeded, many years later, and then only for a short time. All the most celebrated actors of the day were members of his troupe—Ekhof, Sophie F Hensel and Sophie C Schröder. Lessing himself was playwright to the group.

The resident playwright is a typical figure in German theatre and still survives today. In 1922 Brecht held this position in the Munich Kammerspiele. The function involves suggesting the repertory, preparing texts for stage use, editing and revising plays and producing new ones of his own. In this rôle a strong personality can easily acquire great prestige. Thus Lessing exercised very great influence in the administration of the Hamburg National Theatre, directed by K Ackermann and subsidised by a group of wealthy citizens. The project lasted from 1767 until 1769. The members of the troupe followed conscientiously the lines Lessing suggested regarding the choice of play and the manner of its production. Many of them were, in any case, already accustomed to considerable mental and artistic discipline, having worked along with Ekhof in the Academy he had founded in 1753 when he was acting in the company of another actor-manager,

Johann F Schönemann. All the actors in this Academy discussed together the meaning and value of the play they were to perform and worked out what Ekhof called 'a grammar for actors'. They also subjected their own efforts to ruthless self-criticism. Gottsched and Neuber had, of course, prepared the way for this by doing away with improvisation on stage.

Lessing's idea of drama, domestic tragedy or serious comedy is closer to Diderot's than to Lillo's and is, in any case, highly original. It can be summed up in three points: characters rather than events constitute the centre of a work's dramatic interest—as in English, *Charakter* in German also means the person who sustains a particular rôle; it is character that reveals what in an individual is essentially and typically human, so that his social situation (*Stand*) is secondary—the opposite view to Diderot's; the tone of the dialogue should be made as natural as possible, where 'natural' means a moderate tone, avoiding both the affectation of elaborate formality and the uncontrolled, spontaneous outbursts of passion, as well as the coarse and uneducated speech of the lower classes. It is even glaringly obvious that this moderate tone 'is not an abstract

Toni Adamberger in Kotzebue's *Die Indianer in England*. Engraving. Vienna, Bildarchiv der Österreichischen Nationalbibliothek

Scenes from Sebastian Mercier's dramas. From the left: *Le Juge, L'Indigent, Jenneval, La Brouette du Vinaigrier*. Engravings from the 1778–84 edition of his works. Florence, Biblioteca Nazionale

On this page:
Attitudes in mime from the Italian translation of J Engel's *Letters on the Subject of Mime*, Milan, 1818. Engravings. Milan, Biblioteca Nazionale Braidense

average, but the speech of the middle-classes', which is why Lessing's dramas deserve more than any others to be called 'middle-class tragedies', even if his characters include Italian princes, knights of old and even Saladin. *Miss Sara Sampson* and *Minna von Barnhelm* have, however, their exclusive setting in a middle-class environment. Lessing's middle-class characters are not tragic heroes like Lillo's; they are simply authentic, although their authenticity transcends their particular historical situation to attain the absolute. This is why, in what is undoubtedly one of the finest scenes in European theatre, Emilia Galotti can confide to her father that she is not afraid of the prince who may rape her, but of the pleasures by which she may be seduced. Thus tragedy only seems to come down to a middle-class level; in reality it reveals its timeless and essential nature. It is in terms of this natural absolute—which we today can easily see to be ideologically conditioned—that it renews its own claim to be classical: the moderate tone is a true sign of decorum, midway between coarseness and ostentation, just as true classicism is in harmony with the natural rules discovered by Aristotle and later corrupted by the French, and also by Gottsched. *Die Hamburgische Dramaturgie*, a series of news-sheets in which Lessing chronicled the activities of his theatre and at the same time clarified his theoretical and critical ideas, concludes with a detailed analysis of Aristotle's *Poetics*.

The *Dramaturgie* is mainly taken up with literary matters, but Lessing also reveals a keen interest in dramas as performances and, above all, in the actor. He was not alone. In the course of the 18th century throughout most of Europe treatises on drama were being written. Apart from Diderot's, suffice it to recall Saint-Albine's *Le comédien* (1747) and Claude Joseph Dorat's *La déclamation théâtrale* (1766) in

France, Aaron Hill's *Essay of the Art of Acting* (1743) in England, and Luigi Riccoboni's *Dell'arte rappresentativa* (1728) in Italy. In Germany Johann F Löwen had written a slim volume with a significant title: *Kurzgefasste Grundsätze von der Beredsamkeit des Leibes* ('A Summary of the Essentials of Bodily Eloquence', 1755). In 1785–86 Johann J Engel followed this with *Ideen zur einer Mimik* ('Contributions towards a Science of Mime'). This elaborate, scientific survey was descriptive, rather than theoretical, but expressly adopted Lessing's point of view. Of course, Lessing applied his general theory of theatre to the particular problem of the actor's performance and held that there, too, the guiding principle must be that of moderation, 'a moderation to which their art obliges actors even in expressing the most violent of emotions'. Hence, pantomime, by which Lessing means any dramatic action occurring in the course of a performance that is not accompanied by dialogue, 'should never go so far as to be horrible or disgusting', while on the other hand those gestures that accompany one's lines should never be unduly solemn or fawning. Indeed, although the great English painter, Hogarth, paradoxically enough produced a series of paintings which are extremely rich in moral and social content (*The Harlot's Progress* and *The Rake's Progress*), and was a friend of Garrick, an actor by whom Lessing was certainly inspired, the beauty about which he theorised was purely formal and could never realise that ideal of truth and morality with which theatre is concerned.

This means that the actor should never perform with the detachment Diderot called for, but that there is an enormous difference between 'the actor who

understands the meaning of his lines and the one who can also feel it'. This 'feeling' at its best can become the actor's spontaneous and unreserved surrender to the character and to his inner life, but it can also result from a deliberate and careful imitation of those 'involuntary movements of the body which are almost the only external signs authorising us to infer to a certain interior emotion'. Any actor who has studied the more obvious ways of expressing, for instance anger, at the moment in which he imitates these to perfection 'will be infallibly siezed by a dark feeling of rage, which cannot fail to be reflected in his person, where it will give rise to those different changes which are partly independent of our will'. This extract from Lessing fully justifies the sort of theatre that Stanislavsky has made into a system and provided with a rigorously technical and theoretical formalisation—the theatre of 'empathy'.

The dramatic force of an actor's performance depends both on his capacity for empathy and his powers of observation and is in no way compromised, but rather carried to even greater heights by self-control and the choice of those gestures which can communicate in the language of theatre the patterns of a reality whose truth is greater than that of the everyday world. Particularly at times when moral opinions are being expressed, gesture should be always meaningful and, 'provided exaggerated gestures that become mere caricature are avoided, picturesque ones are quite allowable'. By picturesque (malerisch), Engel means a gesture apt to convey a palpable impression of some object one has in mind, whereas the expressive gesture conveys the stirrings of emotion.

Lessing's and Engel's ideal actor was Konrad Ekhof. His acting on stage contained 'neither slow, measured steps, nor dance-like movements, nor mechanically controlled raisings and lowerings of his arms' in the fashion favoured by Caroline Neuber's and Gottsched's classical school of drama. 'Truth came before anything else for him, and then, in dependence on it, beauty: his diction and posture were such as they might have been in a real conversation', in the sense, Engel continues, that he never sought to embody 'a general and premeditated idea of his character', or what we would today call a 'type', but rather the individual features of his subject, pruned of those contradictory elements which they have in everyday reality but which would deprive the theatrical performance of its moral or intellectual content.

Ekhof had none of the physical or vocal qualities that were regarded as indispensable for an academic actor. He slightly resembled Lekain without having any of his self-assertion, indeed, he was thoughtful and withdrawn by nature. In contrast with Garrick's, his acting was somewhat static, but his 'picturesque' gesture 'gave life and movement even to general considerations and transformed into visible realities his innermost feelings'. Thanks to this, with relatively limited external means he was able to bring into being a high level of emotional tension around the character he portrayed.

The action for the most part took place towards the front of the stage, not so much because this was narrow or because the actor unconsciously tended to come close to his audience, as in order to focus attention on the character, in his individual and yet universal reality, and on his responses instead of on the stage-setting or the mere events. The back of the stage was mainly used for actors to make their way on and off and for exchanges subsidiary to the main action. Nevertheless, Ekhof, at least in theory, gave a certain amount of attention to the scenery, which was meant to be studied by the whole company in collaboration with the scene-designer. He was, however, obviously much more interested in the costumes, which he regarded as closely related to the nature of the character being portrayed. Hence he attempted to restrict the actors' traditional freedom of the wardrobe.

Thus Ekhof was a producer as well as an actor, a forerunner, no more, of the classical interpreter-producer, whose task is not to interpret the text in his own way, but to bring to light the only way in which the play really fits together. Ekhof believed that every drama contained its own interpretation within itself. This, unfortunately, was pure theory; Engel himself criticised him for interpreting Corneille's characters with excessive spontaneity and so for going clean against the exaggeration called for by highly rhetorical lines.

After little over a year the attempt to establish a permanent 'national' theatre in Hamburg collapsed. Lessing's ideas about the repertory were only partly put into effect. French plays were always in the majority, though they were drawn mainly from the generation that featured Nivelle de la Chaussée, Voltaire and Marivaux. German productions and adaptations of English originals were of insufficient quality to have compelled their acceptance. Nevertheless, Lessing and his company gave the long-term lead for the direction European public theatre would take, both in its organisation and its cultural outlook, during the two centuries that followed.

Chapter 20

HISTORY, SHAKESPEARE AND ROMANTICISM

The German tragedies produced in the Baroque Age and also during the 18th century by the many travelling companies, who had followed the example of those English actors who had taken refuge on the continent, had kings and princes as their principal characters. This was quite in keeping with the allegedly Aristotelian rules which had provided the guide-lines for French tragedy and neither did it depart from the traditions of Italian *melodramma*, which often provided the themes of these plays. Yet there was still a fundamental difference between the works of Gryphius and Lohenstein and those of Corneille and Racine, or between the more popular *Haupt-und-Staatsaktionen* of Joseph A Stranitzky (1676–1726) who had created the character of Hanswurst, and Minato's libretti. The mainspring in the development of German drama was not the king's amours, but his royal status, the tone he gave to his administration, the answers he gave to the political questions confronting him. There was no attempt to retrace the stages of the nation's evolution, but nevertheless, as with Shakespeare in his histories, the kings and princes were true, historical figures, not figments of the imagination. History is the best source for the writer of tragedies to turn to. Indeed history and tragedy are so closely linked that one might say the tragic playwright had nothing else to do than capture the drama which lies at the core of the historical process—such, at any rate, is the notion behind 18th- and 19th-century German tragedy.

The stage-settings and particularly the costumes were obviously influenced by French and Italian theatre. However, the extravagant variations on the fashion of the court of Versailles represented a sort of personification of royalty, which contrasted sharply with the humble resignation and the sense of the ephemeral nature both of historical events and of their protagonists which runs through these dramas. Such costumes had already annoyed Gottsched, because they were used for the production of French plays or ones with a classical turn, and he tried without success to have them replaced by others that were more faithful to the facts of history. However, Gottsched did not notice that he was contradicting himself, did not notice the 17th-century reality of the great characters in French tragedy, their resemblance in attitude and behaviour to the princes and courtiers of Versailles. His attacks would have been much more consistent if he had directed them against the *Haupt-und-Staatsaktionen*, but he scorned this form of theatre too much to give it so much attention, although he was the one who invented its name, which means literally the doings of princes and states, and served to indicate its political theme and distinguish it from the farces which featured next to it on the theatre programme.

Still, the 'reform' was only delayed for a few years, though the dramas which launched it were certainly much more at home in the baroque traditions of popular theatre than they would have been in the more classical forms called for by Gottsched.

Brockmann in *Hamlet* (with the Ghost and Hamlet's Mother). Engraving by A Chodowiecki. Munich, Theatermuseum

In novels the passion, or the fashion for historical subjects found its greatest exponent in Britain in Sir Walter Scott, but in Germany it had a precocious development in the theatrical world, within the context of a literary movement that took its name from Klinger's comedy, *Sturm und Drang* ('Storm and Stress'), and ran from 1770 to 1790.

It needs to be said at once that neither *Sturm und Drang* nor the Romantic movement which followed it, limited themselves to the consideration of historical themes. Indeed, the former movement led to some of the finest specimens, after those of Lessing, of middle-class drama, with such plays as Lenz's *Der Hofmeister* ('The Private Tutor'), Heinrich Leopold Wagner's *Die Kindesmörderin* ('Infanticide'), and Schiller's *Kabale und Liebe* ('Love and Intrigue'). Undoubtedly, however, the most striking and novel feature of this period was the production on stage of plays with a historical setting.

Probably the first example was that of a production by Ludwig Schröder (1744–1816), the most typical actor of the period. After the death of his step-father, the actor-manager Konrad Ackermann, he assumed the direction of the Hamburg theatre. Later on Schröder was to show that he had no great interest in historical settings for their own sake, but in 1774, when he had to stage *Götz von Berlichingen*, Goethe's historical play, he felt it was necessary to set the mighty deeds of Emperor Maximilian's just and loyal subject in their historical context of the Reformation period, and he tried his best to re-create on stage the architecture and furnishings of the medieval castle of Götz and the magnificent court of the Bishop of Bamberg. He also attempted to produce something resembling the armour of the old knights and the rough cloth of the medieval townsfolk's clothing. It is not at all unlikely that a contemporary audience would have felt they were being brought much closer to 1100 than to 1500, but at that time 'medieval' was still something of a portmanteau word.

The stage-production in Berlin of Goethe's play for which Heinrich G Koch (1703–75) was responsible, probably followed very similar lines. At the end of his own long and brilliant career, Koch came face to face with the young poet's work, immediately appreciated its theatrical potentialities and commissioned J W Meil, the engraver, to design the costumes, asking him to give special attention to their historical accuracy.

The recovery of a sense of history is not, as we have said, the whole of Romanticism, but it is one of its principal features. Moreover, it also involved making one's reference-point something other than the hitherto traditional criteria of the cultured and the civilised—hence, the well-known weakness for medieval themes. Furthermore, at the level of pure poetry, historical romanticism became the dream of a lost world, believed in imagination actually to have been experienced in a remote past that could not be precisely dated, but which one could now attempt to reconstruct in tangible form and bring back to life.

From this point of view, even the neo-classicism of Johann J Winckelmann, the archeologist, and of Goethe, now an intimate of the court of Weimar and

director of the court theatre, could be classified as exquisitely 'romantic'. A typical illustration of this was the production in Weimar in 1779 of Goethe's *Iphigenia*, directed by the author himself. The costumes were the simple tunics and drapes Winckelmann had noted on Alexandrian statues, the scene-setting was a small round temple against a background of countryside, and Goethe himself, whose Apollonian physique and intellectual prestige easily reminded one of the Greek ideal of *kaloskagathos*, played the part of Orestes with dignity and sobriety. A modern critic would have been reminded by all this more of Poussin's *Et in Arcadia Ego* than of anywhere in Greece. Still, it cannot be denied that while subordinating historical precision to an ideal of beauty, as he himself admitted, Goethe did his best to give the kiss of life to that world of perfect harmony in which his artistic ideal was summed and strove to freshen the memory of a historical reality that represented at the same time the Golden Age. If later, in dictating his 'rules for actors', Goethe mistook the most out-of-date rules of theatrical propriety for principles of harmony and proportion, this did not matter too much. All colloquialisms were excluded from the actor's vocabulary. There was to be no getting carried away in his delivery. His tone of voice was never to change too abruptly. 'His bodily carriage was to be correct: chest out, arms by his sides from the elbows upwards, the head slightly inclined in the direction of the person to whom he was speaking, but never too much, since he must always be able to present a three-quarters view of himself to the audience.' Despite all this, Goethe's production of *Iphigenia* did provide an adequate response to the historically demanding requirements of such a great romantic play, possibly with greater success than was the case in his later productions, which were staged in collaboration with Schiller.

Theatre, therefore, demonstrated its capacity to revive the image of the past, not just with exceptional visions of heroic events, but also by a presentation of the daily round of life. Dramatic composition began to take for granted the employment of an increasing number of characters not strictly needed for the development of the plot, but it was only in actual production that the new image could become a reality, as the scenery and the extras ceased to be relegated to a purely decorative or symbolic rôle, ceased to be mere background, but, without taking over the principal actors' direct function, became, in conjunction with the costumes, of basic importance for the presentation of a particular time and place, it being admitted that the setting carried as much weight as did the action of the principal characters, since both alike made it possible for the audience to relive the past. The scenery was still painted, but no longer merely consisted of flats and a backdrop. Instead, there was a three-dimensional arrangement of various features, technically inspired by Italian Renaissance uses of perspective, but without its symmetry of arrangement. The backcloth, no longer needing to be seen in conjunction with partly-moulded flats representing things on a gradually

A Kauffmann, Scene from Goethe's *Iphigenia in Tauris*. Drawing. Weimar, Goethe Nationalmuseum. This is the première of the final version of the play in Weimar in 1802; Goethe, who played Orestes, is in the middle

diminishing scale, became larger and, especially when it represented a landscape, extended sideways into a semi-circular panorama.

The reconstitution of what is past begins as a dream in which strange forms run into each other, but little by little a precise historical picture emerges. For men of the theatre at the end of the 18th century the idea of the Middle Ages, as we have seen, was quite a vast span of time without any specific character. The scenery for a play set in the 11th century might feature Gothic cathedrals, while costumes ranged from Roman breastplates to uniforms in the style of the Thirty Years' War. The productions of August W Iffland (1759–1814) were typical of this sort of thing. He directed the Berlin theatre from 1798 to 1814. Iffland was a man of indefatigable energy, a great actor and an authority on stage-production. Like his contemporary Kotzebue, he himself mainly produced middle-class dramas with impressive qualities. However, he also produced 'historical' plays, though as a producer he could

never be accused of excessive attention to detail. It is hard to imagine how his own meticulous and rationally constructed way of acting could have been wedded to Johann F Fleck's intuitive and diabolically clever performance, yet Iffland did, in his productions, bring together actors whose styles and personalities were completely different. He also learned from the balance and symmetry of Goethe's Weimar productions, but whenever the play afforded him the opportunity he would introduce a large number of extras whose movements provided, as it were, a commentary on the main action. Finally, and especially, Iffland brought into an originally rational construction an absurdly romantic medley of historical and local styles of dress and scenery. For the production of Kotzebue's *Das Zauberschloss* ('The Enchanted Castle') ancient German and Spanish costumes were combined, knights appeared in helms and breastplates and modern-style closed carriages were there in abundance. In like manner, the women's dresses used for plays set in the Greek

J F Matthaei, *The Bride of Messina*, Act V. Oil painting. Munich, Theatermuseum. The painting is inspired by the 1808 Weimar production of this play by Schiller. Notice how the costumes are of different periods

or Roman periods resembled very closely the imperial fashions of the Napoleonic age.

Iffland gave of his very best in preparing the stage-production of Friedrich Schiller's masterpiece, *The Maid of Orleans* (1801), which recreates the Joan of Arc of history and legend. The supreme moment in the performance was the great coronation procession, featuring the participation of hundreds of persons, with another 43 extras to represent the people of Rheims watching the parade go by. The procession went on for a very long time and wound its way three times onto the stage: first it could be seen at the front of the stage, later it appeared in the middle of the stage on an elevated platform-area, and finally it passed through the porticoes leading to the great Gothic cathedral, whose façade dominated the back of the stage. Costumes ranged from armour of the high Middle Ages, to 16th-century doublet and hose, and included the white ruffs made familiar by Rembrandt's paintings. Nevertheless, no one doubted for a moment that this really was the procession which on 17 July 1429 accompanied Charles VII on his way to receive the crown of France. The picture was still out of focus, but not on that account any the less fascinating: the costumes of the leading characters were all infinitely removed from the drab fashions then current and that was enough; the delicate, aetherial quality of the painted scenery and the suggestive use of special lighting suffused the atmosphere, creating a sort of hazy veil between the spectators and the scene before their eyes—it was the veil of time.

The need for historical consistency as well as for an imaginative and plausible presentation very soon made itself felt in the actual staging of plays and was not confined to an intellectual discussion. Iffland's successor as manager of the Berlin theatre quite deliberately made archeological precision his 'theatrical mission' and even took up the cudgels in its defence. The old theatre was burned down in 1817 and Count von Brühl, therefore, had at his disposal a new building, designed by the architect Karl F Schinkel, who later proved to be the Count's ideal collaborator in scenic design. Von Brühl believed that fidelity to both history and folk-traditions must be the first objective in the preparation of any stage-production because 'our eye needs to be conducted by means of external seemings to that time and place whither the poet would transport us with his spiritual creation', and also because the public should be able to learn something from such a 'scientific presentation'. We must concede that von Brühl was quite entitled to speak about a science because his activity as theatre-manager was accompanied by unremitting research into questions of architecture and fashion, research that often entailed long and tiring journeys and the findings from these are preserved in Schinkel's stage-settings and in the costumes J H Stürmer designed under von Brühl's direction. For him the composition of a production, or in other words the recreation of a

F Beuther, Schiller's *The Maid of Orleans*. Sketch for Iffland's production. Aquatint. Munich, Theatermuseum. This Weimar presentation came fourteen years later than Iffland's much more ambitious 1801 production

picture from the past, was almost an end in itself. The audience, certainly, was in no position to appreciate the value of the materials he used, which were the real thing, even the gold and the bronze. Nor could they appreciate the way in which the costumes were made and the cloth sometimes even woven specially to reproduce the identical texture it would have had in the period concerned. This delightful attention to detail of his is what merits for Count von Brühl his title as the first archeologist in the history of the theatre. In this direction, in fact, he anticipated by almost half a century the Duke of Meiningen's company, and the 'historical' productions of Stanislavsky and Nemirovitch-Dantchenko. Moreover, his productions, considered as a whole, remained quite within the boundaries of neo-classical forms of composition and, despite everything, his Middle Ages were clearer and more polished than Goethe's ideal of Greece. The only thing that disturbed the static repose of his statuesque groupings was the agitated and unpredictable, enigmatic performance of his leading actor, Ludwig Devrient (1784–1832).

This style of stage-production, which gave most importance to the historical setting of the play being performed, to what would, in France, be called its local colour, was entirely in keeping with the style and spirit of such works as Heinrich von Kleist's *Kätchen von Heilbronn*, Goethe's *Götz von Berlichingen*, already mentioned, and Schiller's *William Tell*. However, during the years 1780 to 1850, both in Germany and England, Shakespeare was perhaps the author whose plays were most frequently performed. And this makes the whole question more complicated. The sort of stage-setting designed for a production could very well be quite different from the type of thing envisaged when the play was originally written. Moreover, in the case of plays written in the past the question of their interpretation becomes increasingly important.

In *Wilhelm Meister's Apprenticeship* Goethe makes the principal character a reflection of himself, so that the novel traces his own spiritual development. It is also the most complete expression of his personal convictions about art, especially with regard to the theatre, and there is a proposed re-adaptation for the

stage of the tragedy he most loved in his early years: *Hamlet*. Critics have attempted to suggest that Ludwig Schröder is the actor-manager whom Goethe portrays as satisfying Wilhelm Meister's desire to witness a performance of Shakespeare's masterpiece. It is undoubtedly true that Aurelia closely resembles Schröder's step-sister, Charlotte Ackermann, whose passionate life and mysterious death fired the imagination of more than one poet. However, it is hard to imagine Schröder accepting the logic of Goethe's proposed adaptation and, in consequence, like Serlo in the novel, remaining satisfied that with such an adaptation 'there is no need for the audience to imagine anything' because they see everything on the stage. For, in Hamburg in 1776, Schröder's famous production of *Hamlet*, with the great actor Johann F H Brockmann playing the title-rôle and himself cast in the part of the Ghost, demolished the basis of that way of thinking and showed the Prince of Denmark's tormented life in intermittent lightning flashes. Two years later, in Berlin, Brockmann returned as a member of Doebbelin's troupe to the interpretation he had worked out with Schröder.

Brockmann in two scenes from the 1778 Berlin production of
Hamlet. Engravings. Vienna, Bildarchiv der Österreichischen
Nationalbibliothek

There was certainly nothing precise about the historical detail of the setting: many of the characters wore powdered wigs and clothing of an 18th-century cut, while others, notably the King and Queen, were dressed instead in the German style of the preceding century; Brockmann wore a black gown, the design of which was pure fantasy. Both in Hamburg and Berlin his interpretation created a deep impression. It is hard to recapture its essentials today, but he must have given his character an air of poignancy and pathos. He built this up in mime by a series of unforeseeable and out of the way gestures and attitudes, ranging from the child-like position he took up to sit at Ophelia's feet in the scene of the play within the play, to the unnatural positioning of his arms throughout his conversation with the King. Hamlet was presented as a weather-cock creature, hard to fathom and hard to grasp, and the entire performance created the atmosphere of legend—one of those 'theatrical legends' so much loved by Tieck,

in which the time is 'long ago', and the place is 'far away'. After Brockmann had left Hamburg for Berlin, Schröder himself played Hamlet and the whole production became definite and self-consistent, the character of Hamlet being no longer elusive, but that of a man possessed, a man with a mission. When the Ghost appeared, Schröder drew back in terror, the back of his hand to his mouth, his eyes wide open, his body quivering with fear. Brockmann used to bend forward, with almost no trace of emotion. All considered, Brockmann, especially in his Berlin performances of *Hamlet*, set the fashion for a poetic reading of the play, something he did quite by instinct, but which very soon became the subject of specific theories. This was the doing of various poets and men of letters writing on behalf of romantic theatre in Germany, and some of them were great men, such as Tieck and Hoffmann, the composer and writer of supernatural stories. Schiller led the field, by demanding that the witches who

Devéria and Boulanger, English actors staging *Hamlet* in Paris. Paris, Bibliothèque de l'Arsenal. In Brockmann's rendering of the same scene there is a dreamy atmosphere. Here the tension is quite explicit, especially in Hamlet, whose uncomfortable position expresses his inner turmoil

prophesied to Macbeth his royal destiny should appear on the stage of the Weimar theatre wearing the *cothurni* of Greek tragic actors, since he regarded them as reincarnations of the ancient Fates.

Paradoxically enough, this fashion reflected the same preoccupation as did the concern for historical accuracy: the dream of a lost world. On the other hand, it made it possible to avoid the inconsistencies resulting from attempts to provide exact, historical settings for plays, and especially for those of Shakespeare. The Romantic dramatists may, indeed, have shared, at least to some extent, the dream of a lost world, but Shakespeare had certainly no part in it. Thus, the result was to superimpose on characters and speech that were Elizabethan costumes and situations that were Roman or medieval. The more accurate the reconstruction, the more obvious became the inherent contradiction. Yet it was this very contradiction, which after all only existed in the logical order, that made it possible for a romantically

inclined public to appreciate Shakespeare as theatre, because in fact it enabled them to discover in Shakespeare unexpected points of interest, such as the contrast between a character and his situation, or the fact of the hero's rising above the conditions of his social class. It need occasion no surprise that this period, which devoted so much attention to questions of local colour in stage-settings, was also noted for the rise of outstanding interpreters of Shakespeare in both England and Germany. Brockmann has been mentioned. Schröder gave a masterly interpretation of Iago, bringing out, as well as his downright wickedness, his interior torment and his fierce, burning irony. Fleck was an awe-inspiring and demonic figure as Shylock, but also gave his character a certain grandeur and nobility, which was set in high relief by Iffland's majestic stage-production which made the contrast glaringly obvious between the splendours of Venice and the impotence of the Jew in that situation. Ludwig Devrient was partic-

247

Edmund Kean as Hamlet. Engraving. London, Victoria and Albert Museum

Ludwig Devrient as King Lear. Engraving. Vienna, Bildarchiv der Österreichischen Nationalbibliothek. Devrient apparently played Lear as a sort of angry Jupiter wearing the dress of a 16th century monarch

Hinweg erborgter Plunder!
DEVRIENT
als
König Lear,

ularly fine in interpreting the plays of Schiller; the Wallenstein he played was aloof from the world, preoccupied, immersed in his private astrological and metaphysical meditations; then he was outstanding as Franz Moor—the main character in *The Robbers*, inevitably wicked, utterly devoid of scruples, impulsive, like a man possessed. It seems strange, but he was the favourite actor of Friedrich Alois von Brühl, the great archeologist of German theatre. Yet he was the brother in spirit of Edmund Kean, the greatest English romantic actor; he was Hoffmann's drinking companion—Hoffmann, who wrote the most disturbing short stories in the whole

of German literature and whose ideas about the actor as mediator of the infinite Devrient embodied to perfection.

In England Edmund Kean's son, Charles, held the same place in the theatre-world as von Brühl did in Germany. In 1843 the privileged position of those theatres that had been granted royal letters patent was abrogated and a few years later, in 1850, Charles Kean assumed the direction of the Princess Theatre and staged a long series of Shakespearian productions which made history because of the magnificence of the stage-settings and their historical exactitude. Not surprisingly, Kean was among the few who ventured to stage Lord Byron's 'impossible' dramas. He was attracted not so much by the rather dry composition of the texts, as by the difficult challenge historical works such as *Sardanapalus* represented and also, no doubt, by the ideas of Byron, who claimed to prefer historical subjects for the sake of the moral truth they contained and exemplified.

The most famous of Kean's Shakespearian productions was that of *The Merchant of Venice*, in which he was helped by Edward Godwin, the architect, father of Gordon Craig, and he designed accurate reproductions of the structures of the Venetian palaces of the late Gothic era.

Towards the close of the 19th century, the historical turn in English theatre was to find its most consummate exponent in Beerbohm Tree, but it was Charles Kean who did most of the basic work. What sort of influence German theatre had in all this remains hard to say. What is certain is that the conditions which made a development of this sort possible came into being in the course of the preceding ten years, partly as a result of certain ideas taken over from French theatre. When the old theatre-building in Drury Lane was destroyed by fire in 1809 the new building imitated the design of the theatre in Bordeaux. The balconies and doors on either side of the stage were, together with the apron,

Immermann's stage-setting for *Twelfth Night*, 1840. Engraving. Munich, Theatermuseum

Measure for Measure produced by the Elizabethan Stage Society. Photograph. London, Victoria and Albert Museum

abolished, and the inner stage was made very much bigger, effectively to accommodate scenery and to permit the large-scale use of extras. In this vast expanse Edmund Kean's cruelly subtle irony was lost, but it suited the unhurried, expansive gestures of John Kemble and his sister, Sarah Siddons who, when she played Lady Macbeth, seemed to William Hazlitt the very personification of tragedy. Later the Kembles moved to Covent Garden, where their productions were increasingly characterised by the elaborate pomp of the scenery and costume, based on relevant archeological and topographical research. Such a policy of expensive productions obliged the Kembles to increase the prices of the tickets and an unforeseen consequence of their action was a popular uprising in protest, which passed into history as 'the O.P. (Old Prices) Riot'. In those days theatre was certainly a marginal extra, but one that made life worth living!

The vestal virgins of pure poetic diction ranged themselves against Charles Kean's meticulous, archeologically based attention to the details and accessories of his stage-productions. They claimed that the excessive munificence of the scenery tended to absorb the audience's attention, and that a bombardment of visual details suffocated the sacred words of the author, which ought to be conveyed exclusively by the actual voice of the actor. This point of view was not shared by men of the theatre, but by critics and intellectuals. Nevertheless, it had a certain influence on many stage-productions and especially on those of Samuel Phelps (1804–78). As long as he was manager at Sadler's Wells, he tried to re-introduce Shakespeare's lesser known plays (such as *Timon of Athens* and *All's Well that Ends Well*), and promoted a slow, even delivery. He believed clear speech was indispensable to enable an audience of taste to appreciate the meaning of a complex and sophisticated dramatic poem. Hardly surprisingly, his productions were praised for being 'consistently beautiful, yet without ever distracting attention from the poetry, with which, indeed, the whole performance blends in perfect harmony'.

Thus Phelps' position could be described as moderate. For, his productions, which included the celebrated performance of *All's Well that Ends Well* (1852), did not lack the elements needed to situate the action within the period in which it was supposed to take place, costumes in particular, but this was never regarded as the priority question. However, the more extreme position, which aimed to do away with all use of theatrical artifice in stage-production, did

249

find an opportunity of showing how it worked out in practice here and there. Furthermore, in the specific instance of Shakespearian theatre, the idea of the stage-setting's being kept as simple as possible was deeply rooted in a historicist approach to interpretation, one that had been originally formulated and translated into practice in Germany, mainly by Ludwig Tieck and Karl Immermann.

In 1825 Tieck was responsible for the repertory of the theatre in Dresden and in 1842 he took over the direction of the Berlin theatre. Celebrated as a writer, he was the author of, among other things, dramatisations of the tales of *Bluebeard* and *Puss in Boots*. This last provides one of the earliest examples of audience participation in the dramatic action: actors seated among the audience commented on the comedy as it was being performed. Pirandello was to do something similar with *Tonight We Improvise*. Tieck considered Count von Brühl's historical display was useless and harmful. It placed restrictions on the spectator's imagination by tying it to one particular attempt to reconstruct the scene. Moreover Tieck thought that if some historical reconstruction should prove necessary, this should not concern the historical setting in which the action of the play supposedly took place, but rather the historical situation for which it had been devised and written down. The scenery for Shakespeare was, of course, abstract, a springboard the audience could use to take a daring leap into the infinite. In Berlin Tieck showed in a practical way how the conditions of Elizabethan theatre, without being actually created anew, could be interpreted within the context of the theatre of his own day. He was responsible for a much discussed production of *A Midsummer Night's Dream* (1843), for which the stage-setting comprised a framework on three levels with a connecting stairway. Painted scenery was not entirely eliminated, but was kept in the background and served to create a vague impression of being in the countryside. Dancing to music by Mendelssohn featured prominently in the performance, certainly much more so than an accurate Elizabethan interpretation would have ever allowed, but Tieck intended that this should serve to bring out the elusive, fairy-land meaning of the comedy.

Karl Immermann was more painstaking. For five years, from 1833 to 1837, he was manager of the small provincial theatre in Düsseldorf where an unpretentious company of actors performed under the direction of a certain De Rossi. Immermann profited from the absence of great actors to bring about a more integrated style of performance in which the various parts came together and balanced each other. He was a friend and admirer of Tieck and produced *Bluebeard* in Düsseldorf, but it was only later on, after resigning from his position as manager, that he followed out Tieck's ideas on Shakespearian theatre in arranging a private production. This was a performance of *As You Like It* and for it he created an entirely architectural setting which blended together all the various features of the Elizabethan stage, but arranged them quite differently.

There were also similar ventures in England. Perhaps the one that aroused most interest was a production of *The Taming of the Shrew* in the Haymarket Theatre in 1844, and again in 1847, directed by Benjamin Webster, but inspired by J R Planché, who was directly influenced by the ideas of Tieck. The production also made very generous allowances for the taste of the Victorian audience. The opening scene shows Sly being picked up drunk by the servants of some noble lord who is going to play a joke at his expense. This introduction, in fact, reminds one of Calderón's *Life is a Dream*. They will make Sly think he is rich and that his life of poverty has been all a dream. The scene was played in front of a public-house, reconstructed on stage with the typical lay-out of the real, historical 19th century. The comedy proper, the story of shrewish Kate and of Petrucchio's persevering until he succeeded in making of this untamable girl the very best of wives, took place in the lord's apartment, in Elizabethan instead of Italian costumes and with no definite scenery. Changes from one place to another were indicated by placards, in accordance with John Payne Collier's and Edmund Malone's theory of Elizabethan theatre, which they developed about that time.

Within the ongoing process of British theatre this tradition was always to remain no more than a single strand, which found its most painstaking expression in the productions of William Poel's Elizabethan Stage Society, for which the entire fabric of the Elizabethan stage-setting was reconstructed on the basis of meticulous archeological studies. Today Peter Brook and Toby Robertson are the most direct heirs of this tradition. Robertson concentrates particularly on the renewed appreciation of recitative. His actors go through their lines almost without any pause, and at break-neck speed. Both men in some of their productions rejected the use of clearly localising scenery.

Chapter 21

THE BOULEVARDS OF PARIS
AND THE STROLLING PLAYERS
OF ROMANTIC ITALY

Throughout the 19th century the preference for lavish spectacle exercised a notable influence on the details and composition of the vast majority of Shakespearian productions. All those aspects which offered scope for large-scale effects were fully exploited. This is even brought out in some of the sub-titles provided for the tragedies, for instance *Richard III, or the Battle of Bosworth Field.* The approach was not confined to Shakespeare. Historical drama flourished in England though not as much as elsewhere. The most abundant output in the genre came from Byron and Bulwer Lytton, whose works were staged with a suitable flourish.

Until 1843 when the patent law was abrogated, grand spectacle similar in kind to the Italian *melodramme* of the Baroque Age possibly found its most congenial setting in the unofficial theatres catering for the lower orders of society. In the 19th century an evening performance in an English theatre might take five hours, from seven till midnight, and after the interval more spectators were allowed in at half price. Thus even in theatres featuring full-scale plays the evening might be rounded off with some farce, pantomime, ballet or similar amusement.

A special word should be said about pantomime which was something quite peculiar to England and had a great run of success from 1800 to 1830, mainly thanks to the celebrated clown Joseph Grimaldi. Pantomime had an unvarying plot: the father (or guardian) wishes to give his daughter's (or ward's) hand in marriage to some elderly gentleman and, in order to obstruct her alternative plan to marry her young lover, threatens to murder him. At this point enter a magician who transforms the lover into Harlequin and the girl into Columbine, while the father and the elderly suitor are transformed into Pantaloon and the Clown. Then begins a long and fantastic chase, with an extensive sequence of highly theatrical shifts of scene, during which contemporary situations and topical talking-points are often brought in, such as gas-lighting or the current fashions, the progress of the war, the way justice is administered, etc. Other shows of this sort concentrated exclusively on social satire; the dramatisation of Pierce Egan's significantly entitled pot-pourri, *Life in London* was one such production that enjoyed a huge success. Naturally the dimensions of the wicked and the sensational were not neglected, but were often even the main ingredients in melodrama. The hero might be some famous outlaw, such as Robin Hood, in whom the people of England could focus and express their own impulse to rise in revolt.

Melodrama as a literary genre developed in France as middle-class drama evolved into a play with characters drawn from the lower orders, while retaining the structure Louis Sebastien Mercier had given it: a plot packed with *coups de théâtre*, a vibrant action, primitive, uncomplicated characters, a straightforward moral message and often a keen appreciation of besetting social problems. Mercier himself had already made provision for a lavishly spectacular treatment, did not neglect historical

Talma and Mlle Duchesnois in *Hamlet*. Engraving. Turin, Biblioteca Civica. This is most likely J F Ducis' adaptation, and the engraving shows the scene between Hamlet and Gertrude

themes and also took intolerable liberties in his adaptations of many of Shakespeare's plays.

The cultural, organisational, political and, especially, technical conditions which were to lead to such a rapid and large-scale development in the lavishly theatrical staging of melodramas came into being in Paris in the early years of the 19th century. For, after 1790, the rule of privilege was swept away and theatrical ventures were left free to their own devices. However, after Napoleon came to power, as a result of an edict of 1807 the number of the first-class Paris theatres was restricted to eight, of which two (the Comédie Française and the Opéra) were subsidised. Four were listed as second-class, and two of these (the Ambigu Comique and the Théâtre de la Gaieté) were described as *théâtres à spectacle*. Another theatre, the Cirque Olympique, was also allowed to remain open, but only for *pantomimes à spectacle*. In practice the number of theatres flourishing in Paris was very soon much greater. However, the Comédie Française, the Opéra and the other first-class theatres entertained the aristocracy, while the second-class theatres, which soon came to be known as 'the boulevard theatres', drew their audiences from the lower orders.

Moreover, many technical experts began to criticise more and more severely the use of Italian-style scenery: a backdrop together with painted flats arranged to create an illusion of perspective. They favoured, instead, a more elaborate arrangement of scenery with plenty of three-dimensional features, rostra and pierced flats. At the same time there was plenty of room for intensive experimentation with more traditional scene-settings, with new stage techniques and with lighting effects. All this soon had its effect on production.

As early as 1788 a Scottish painter called Barker showed a 'panorama' in an Edinburgh playhouse. An American, Robert Fulton, followed this up in Paris in 1799. At Napoleon's command, the French theatre architect Cellerier made plans in 1810 for seven panoramas to line the Champs-Élysées.

The first two panoramas had been continuous circular paintings with clever lighting arrangements which the onlooker could look at from his place in the half-light in the centre of the hall. Louis Jacques Daguerre, who had already begun his brilliant career as scene-painter for the Ambigu Comique, designed a similar panorama. However, in 1822 he was to transfer his optical show, as it was called, to the inside of a properly constructed stage-setting, with the front part rather dark, while the background, which was brilliantly illuminated, changed continuously either showing a series of different views or representing changing atmospheric conditions. The most common scenes were landscapes with all the phenomena of nature, but there were also views of cities with all the bustle of life and people and carriages in continuous movement. Daguerre christened this sort of show the 'diorama' (or see-through) and it is evident that his research in this direction was later of great value to him in his pioneering work in photography.

Pierre-Luc-Charles Cicéri was Daguerre's pupil and made a systematic application of his master's findings to the technical as well as to the purely scenic side of stage-design. He gave 19th-century stages their characteristic lay-out, which can still be seen in our own more conservative theatres. Pierced flats and rostra replaced the painted flats, and the background was consequently arranged on different levels in front of a moving panorama. The borders, a sort of series of raised flats representing the sky, were also abolished. Lighting was no longer confined to the use of footlights, but more complicated effects were aimed at and as gas-lighting replaced the oil-lamps success became easier to obtain.

Chaperon, Rubé, Rousin, Roqueplan, Delaroche and, we may say, all the great scene-painters of the 19th century who worked now in one now in another of the theatres of the capital, were pupils of Cicéri and Daguerre. We have mentioned the boulevard theatres, which got this name because most of them were in the Boulevard du Temple, popularly known as the *boulevard du crime* on account of the high number of crimes committed on stage. They were the start of the tradition of the macabre which towards the close of the century yielded the black fruit of the Grand Guignol. These second-class, more

Marie Dorval in Soulié's *Clotilde*. Engraving. Paris, Bibliothéque de l'Arsenal

Frédérick Lemaître as Figaro (*left*); and as Robert Macaire (*right*) in *L'Auberge des Adrets*. Photographs. Paris, Bibliothèque de l'Arsenal

popular theatres were the first to make use of the new techniques, which were indeed often the result of attempts to meet the special requirements of the melodramatic repertory. Changes of scenery were so frequent that the play consisted of a series of pictures rather than of acts. As well as this, there was no shortage of simulations of natural phenomena exploiting all the possibilities of optical illusion; and dream-visions, ghosts and divinities also put in an appearance. The setting was often medieval. It was on the boards of boulevard theatre that romantically styled productions, so frequently quoted as typical of the 19th century scene, assumed their final shape. Even landscapes were depicted in a 'romantic' way. The most prolific and most widely applauded exponent of the genre was Guilbert de Pixérécourt (1773–1844), whose *Coelina, ou L'enfant du mystère*, had its première in the Ambigu Comique in 1799. This already contained all the typical ingredients for

F A Arnault's *Les aventures de Mandrin* performed in 1856 in the Théâtre de la Gaieté. Paris, Bibliotheque de l'Arsenal

a romantic landscape setting: wild country with rocks to be scaled, a Devil's Bridge and a raging storm. The lighting used would make the whole atmosphere mysterious, if not terrifying. He set the scene for the appearance of Baron Frankenstein and his monster which took place at the theatre of Porte Saint-Martin in 1826 eight years after the publication of Mary Shelley's novel. Two years later the same theatre staged a much abridged adaptation of Goethe's *Faust*. Topics of current interest were not neglected, although their interpretation would be in romantic and highly imaginative terms. Indeed, around the middle of the century the social inspiration of the melodramas became more obvious. As if in anticipation of the sort of themes the naturalist movement would select by preference, the dregs of Paris were frequently shown in all their disturbing reality. Dupeuty and Cormon's *Paris la nuit* which was played at the Ambigu Comique in 1842 was certainly no guided tour of the midnight pleasures of the *ville lumière*. In 1844 at Porte Saint-Martin came Eugène Sue's adaptation of the *Mystères de Paris*, and in 1850 Paul Meurice's play with the stark title: *Paris*. The audience saw their own city depicted with fuliginous and brooding realism as an ant-heap crawling with humanity, to which they, too, belonged, but which was enveloped by an atmosphere of unnaturally cruel tensions. They felt as if they themselves were actors in these blood-curdling plays and, coming nearer home, that they were the victims of an outrageous and wicked abuse of power. The little orphan-girls in Eugène Cormon's classic melodrama (*mélo*), *The Two Orphans*, seemed their own daughters. The more conservative took affront and believed such performances constituted an

255

invitation to rebellion, but on this occasion the police had greater foresight and judged that the cathartic, and therefore soothing effect of the play outweighed its revolutionary implications.

In any case, as we have noted, melodramas were more often than not set in the past, very often in the Middle Ages, but also in Greek and Roman antiquity or in the Renaissance period. Right from the start of the century, then, the boulevard theatres competed in offering productions which, as well as being dramatically powerful, were accurate, or at least convincing in their use of local colour. The already legendary Pixérécourt's production of *La ruine de Pompéi* at the Gaieté in 1827 was outstanding from this point of view. Obviously the whole point of the play was to show Vesuvius in eruption, but no less pains were lavished on that account on the detailed reconstruction of the Roman buildings and period costumes. For *The Doge of Venice* six years before, Cicéri had reconstructed on the stage of the same theatre a marvellous synoptic view of Renaissance Venice.

We could continue indefinitely listing 'epoch-making' productions in the Paris boulevard theatres. By some miracle or other they succeeded in putting on extremely lavish performances without incurring any of the fearful debts which were contracted by the Opéra and the Comédie Française as soon as these, faced by a continually empty auditorium, tried to follow this example. It will be enough to mention once more the Cirque Olympique, the theatre which was most successful in this field, thanks to the unusual way in which it was built—a circus-ring with a stage adjoining. In such a setting the most spectacular mass-movements were quite feasible, including a ride-past of cavalry. Throughout France after the

1830 Revolution, popular enthusiasm for the Napoleonic ideal was re-inflamed and, in the Cirque Olympique, the epic story of the Emperor was evoked with magnificent pageantry. The play was Prosper Saint-Alme's *The Republic, the Empire and the Hundred Days*. The producer was M F Laloue, the first of the great stage-directors. It was said that not even David could outdo him in the composition of his scenes.

Thus, the battle for romanticism was won long before the famous première of Victor Hugo's *Hernani* at the Comédie Française in 1830. If Alexandre Dumas père (1803–70) was correct in maintaining that the first task of romantic theatre was '*ressusciter des hommes et de rebâtir un siècle*' (to restore men to life and reconstruct a world), then the second-class theatres of Paris did carry out this task. Furthermore, if historically oriented settings began to acquire free right of access to the Théâtre Français, following on from the timid attempts in this direction of Talma, Napoleon's own dear, neo-classical actor, this was certainly not due to the efforts of its members, the *sociétaires*, but to those of Baron Taylor who had been installed as its new director in 1825 and who had worked alongside Daguerre in arranging one of the first 'panoramas' of Paris.

The great romantic playwrights were Victor Hugo (1802–85), who wrote his preface to *Cromwell* as a manifesto for romantic theatre, and Alfred de Vigny (1797–1863) whose character, Chatterton, embodied the myth, which was to haunt men's minds throughout the century, of the poet banished from a materialist society by its own brutality and stupidity. Neither of these men found any actors at the Comédie Française capable of interpreting their plays in a way that was to their liking. For the opening night of *Hernani*, when the defenders of the classical tradition in French theatre sought to prevent the violation of the sacred temple of the Comédie Française by making sure Hugo's play was a flop, Mlle Mars, the stiff and formal reciter of Racine's alexandrines, surely must have been a very cold Doña Sol. The romantics' darling was a fragile creature, Marie Dorval, an extraordinarily subtle and passionate interpreter of Kitty Bell, the silent, submissive heroine in de Vigny's *Chatterton*.

Frédérick Lemaître (1800–76), the greatest and, apart from Sarah Bernhardt, perhaps the only great French actor of the century, excelled in his interpretation of the romantic repertory. He also made valuable contributions to the success of plays which differed considerably in theme and treatment: Casimir Delavigne's *Les vêpres siciliennes* which had

Hernani — Acte Premier. Plantation et mise en état

M ——————————————— M

A *Grande fenêtre à petits vitraux peints.*

B *Porte.*

C *Porte ouvrant en dehors.*

D *Porte dérobée ouvrant sur la Scène*

C   pantalon intérieur

D

H *Grande armoire*
- *la porte s'ouvre sur la Scène*
(*double porte pour Communiquer dans la coulisse*

M *. décor du fond.*
Grande Salle ou Vestibule

H

manteau d'Arlequin

souffleur

1. *petit Siège.* 2. *table avec tapis, sur laquelle une lampe allumée*
3. *Fauteuil.* 4. 5. 6. 7. 8. *Chaises,*

been first performed in 1819 (Odéon; 1830), A Dumas's *Kean* (Variété; 1836), Victor Hugo's *Lucrèce Borgia* (1833). However, his most characteristic personality as an actor came across in heavy melodrama, whether historical or contemporary, in other words, in those plays peculiar to the repertory of boulevard theatres. Dumas and Hugo, too, served their apprenticeship as dramatists by learning from these melodramas and from the plays of Schiller. Lemaître's own name remains linked in a special way with his interpretation, or better, to use the French word this once, *création* of one character, who was to remain with him for the rest of his career. He had been born in 1800 and so was a very young actor when, in 1823, the Ambigu Comique offered him the leading rôle in a melodrama written by one of those societies of authors which were so common in the Paris theatre-world. This was *L'Auberge des Adrets* by Saint-Amand, Antier and Polyanthe, turned by Lemaître into a brilliant parody of tear-jerking melodrama, which even includes the classical recognition scene! Robert Macaire, the main character, is not a young man down on his luck, but an easy-going rogue who always manages to outwit the police and the respectable citizens. Lemaître, wearing a tattered tail-coat, gave his character a carriage which was ludicrously self-contained, a hard-hitting skit on the 'good manners' of the Parisian aristocracy. Moreover, Robert Macaire's personality seemed different every evening, as Lemaître kept on improvising new lines and devising novel situations. It became necessary to write a follow-up to the *Auberge des Adrets*, and in this Lemaître finished up almost identifying himself with his hero in a success that lasted more than twenty years.

An identical demand for realism is present in both the provision of drama with an appropriately historical setting and the staging of scenes drawn from contemporary life. Despite the careful attention to detail, this demand remains unsatisfied throughout the whole first half of the century except in the restricted area of local colour and fails to find any concrete form for its expression. One reason for this is that the image of the past is perceived only through the distorting lens of a dream. On the other hand, the present is seen with its own colours and contrasts of light and shade so exaggerated as to make the picture in the final analysis unreal and far from the truth. Theatre was going to need to return to the traditions of Lessing's and Diderot's middle-class dramas in order to recover its sense of everyday reality. For once the Comédie Française pointed the way. From 1827 on, its repertory included Picard's

258

play, *Les trois quartiers*, which introduced the audience to the fashionable salons of Paris. Thanks to this production, the Comédie Française won back the sympathy of its public. Instead of consisting of a few die-hard enthusiasts for classical tragedy in alexandrines, obstinately rejecting all that contemporary theatre had to offer, including any change in the place of the action, the audience now had to come from the new ruling-class, heirs to the Napoleonic Empire, the financial circles of the upper middle-class, now well able to vie with the aristocracy of the *ancien régime* in standards of living, culture and refinement, while far outstripping them in courage, to the extent of preferring the spur of criticism to the mirror of flattery.

Seen in this way, 1852 was a landmark. The new school finally came into its own as Mme Doche played in the Comédie Française the leading part in Alexandre Dumas *fils*' *La Dame aux camélias*, he and Emile Augier being the most illustrious representatives of the movement. Got, Worms, Mlle Desclées and all the other *sociétaires* of the leading theatre in France were to find themselves quite at home in this new classicism, which like the old was full of rules and conventions. During this period, round about 1870, and under the auspices of the most listened-to critic in France, there was born a new definition of theatre inspired by the structure of the *pièces bien faites* of Dumas. François Sarcey pulverised plays he did not like, not by analysing their intrinsic claims, but by exposing their lack of fidelity to this canonical norm. '*Ce n'est pas du théâtre*'—that's not theatre—was his sentence of condemnation and many still use the phrase. The stage-setting most favoured was a salon in white and gold. The actresses' costumes were the *toilettes* of society ladies. Good acting meant to behave on stage with the same natural elegance with which the gentry moved in society. Theatre became the simple reflection of this society, not enlarged, nor idealised, nor decked out in the regalia of ancient heroes as had happened in the 17th and 18th centuries. However, the actors' conversations seemed enmeshed in a plot that held everything in suspense and left the characters facing the preliminaries to some urgent moral problem, since, as actors, they could not go beyond the clearly defined limits of good-breeding, either in society or on stage. Dumas *fils* was unsparing in his criticism of this prejudiced society to which he, too, belonged. His solution to the conflict between the moral exigences of conscience and the prejudices of society transformed brilliant talkers and refined gentlemen into tragic heroes. In Dumas the moral demand and the prejudice were always

Scene from *Francillon* by A Dumas *fils*. Paris, Bibliothèque de l'Arsenal. The salon for *Francillon* is typical of the stage-settings used in French theatre in the second half of the century

confined to relationships between members of the same social class. His criticisms never took relationships involving power into account and he also granted that the prejudice one had to fight against was entertained in good faith. It was not until 1877 when Henri Becque wrote *Les corbeaux* that the so-called values of middle-class society were shown up for the sordid and ruthless, selfish concerns they were, though even then the bonds of oppression between social classes were not examined directly. Hardly surprisingly, this play was rejected by almost all theatres in Paris and not performed at the Comédie Française until 1882. By this time the boulevard theatres were trying to be as elegant as the first-class theatres.

The tradition to which Dumas returned did not die with him, nor with Becque. Paolo Ferrari, himself a pocket-edition of Dumas, was to keep it alive in Italy by making it his business to defend the very prejudices Dumas had been wise enough to attack. Oscar Wilde maintained the same tradition in England, where he eliminated moral questions of right and wrong as fictitious or non-existent and reduced the interaction between his characters to a mere social game in which the supreme good is elegance and discretion. Later, in our own century, T S Eliot would try to discover some soul in these drawing-room puppets, some yearning for salvation and the infinite. However, it would be left to Eugène Ionesco, in his only really powerful, biting play *The Bald Soprano*, to demonstrate the extent to which middle-class, drawing-room conversations are merely a futile attempt at mutual communication, since the sounds that are used are thought to carry some meaning, but are in fact empty with nothing at all inside.

In the 19th century the touring companies, which from the middle of the 17th century onwards had spread theatre into every corner of Europe, almost completely disappeared. There were still a lot of them in Germany in Goethe's day, but they were gradually driven out of existence by the national and municipal theatres which were opening in all the large towns; in France they had to submit to the already absolute supremacy of the Paris theatres. It was only in Italy that they continued to be the main vehicles for the transmission of the theatrical tradition and were indeed the whole of theatre, since both before and after the unification of Italy the isolated attempts to set up such permanent drama-companies as for instance the Royal Sardinian troupe, and the Duke of Modena's company never lasted long. It was only in the years following the last war that permanent theatres became predominant.

Some sort of hierarchy did in practice exist between the different companies. The more important ones, which played in high-class theatres in the larger cities, such as Il Re in Milan and the Carignano in Turin, quite reasonably boasted the title of First-Class companies, but the others, which made use of arenas or very shabby theatres or even performed in village halls and public squares, were not at all sparing in their use of high-sounding titles. A few of these troupes, which in terms of their rank could be listed as second-class or third-class, managed to penetrate the most remote parts of the peninsula. Here they staged their show in the open air for the most part or else in an area closed off by blankets brought along by the peasants themselves, and they were almost always paid in kind, since extreme poverty, which has always been the legacy left to the

(*Left*): E Rossi as *Othello*; and (*right*) T Salvini as *Hamlet*. Usually these rôles were reversed. Salvini's *Othello* is carefully described by E Tuckerman Mason. Rome, Raccolta Teatrale Burcardo

Italian peasant by his ancestors, made the circulation of money extremely limited even in the 19th century.

The traces left of these companies are extremely few, mostly in the memories of people who are dying out. However, until 1950 there were still a certain number of them and even today they have not entirely disappeared. I myself managed to see in Trentino one such company performing a repertory mainly composed of the French melodramas which we mentioned in an earlier chapter (*The Two Orphans*, *The Blind Woman of Sorrento*, *The Ironmaster*), and also of Pirandello, which was regrettable, because they included him in order to appear 'up-to-date'. The D'Origlia-Palmi Company in Rome may well be the last direct and fully conscious heir to this tradition.

These Italian drama companies were, in their turn, the direct heirs of the *commedia dell'arte* and retained many of its characteristics. For them, theatre was before all else a trade to be handed down from father to son, even though from time to time some new arrivals might come on the scene, attracted by their love for the theatre or for some actress, or urged on by lust for adventure or by some quirk of chance. These 'children of the art', as they were called, learned to ply their trade when they were still in nappies; as their legitimate mothers clasped them to their bosoms they played the parts of children born in sin, and then gradually mastered all the parts in the repertory that had to be played by children or teen-agers. The masked characters of Pantaloon and Harlequin had been abandoned, though they still put in an occasional appearance for some farces or on evenings given over to an improvised revival of old-fashioned theatre; the composition of the companies was now very much governed by the lines of business. As a rule, a company comprised male and female leads, two juvenile leads, a lady to play the noble-hearted mother, a father who could be a tyrant if required (the 'heavy') and a character actor. Obviously, all the rôles could be duplicated whenever the company was powerful enough to feed fifteen or twenty mouths, instead of eight or ten.

Usually the leading actors were also the managers and the company was named after them. Each actor had to specialise in a single rôle not only because that had always been the practice, but also for very sound technical reasons. Actors, and especially those in the larger companies, always tried to exploit their 'pitch' to the greatest extent possible, in order to avoid the expense and inconvenience of always moving about, but even in the larger cities it was hard to keep a play on the boards for more than three or four evenings; more often than not the actors had to change their programme every night. Rehearsals took place in the afternoon, if at all, and that evening the play was on the boards. Obviously it was impossible to know by heart a repertory of thirty or forty plays, and so the actors had to be capable of improvising their lines whenever they did not manage to hear what the prompter was saying and without departing from a style in keeping with their character. They also had to possess a battery of miming skills sufficient to make good the lack of rehearsals. This all implied specialisation which, though no longer entirely determined by a single masked character, had to confine itself to a narrow range of rather similar characters, in other words to a particular rôle.

Only the leading actors switched from one character to another that was entirely different, thanks to their greater versatility which was a very much appreciated quality. Among those famous for it was Alamanno Morelli (1812–93). Other leading actors contrived instead to adapt any character to their own personality, to impersonate themselves in their rôle, as Stanislavsky might have said.

Naturally the repertory underwent very considerable changes in the course of the century. In the case of the First-Class companies to a greater extent than the others, it was dependent on the tear-jerking dramas of the end of the 18th century, and later on French historical and contemporary melodrama. Before the middle of the century Shakespeare made his appearance on the Italian stage, suitably adapted as a matter of course, and often improvised. Nevertheless, Italian actors managed to express their own

(*From left to right*): Gustavo Modena in Alfieri's *Saul*. Engraving. Milan, Raccolta Bertarelli. C Quirico as David in Alfieri's *Saul*; Adelaide Ristori in Schiller's *Mary Stuart*; and Adelaide Ristori as Micol and Ernesto Savini as David in a scene from Alfieri's *Saul*.

Rome, Raccolta Teatrale Burcardo. Of all Italian actors Adelaide Ristori gave most attention to the choice and cut of her costumes. Many of these are preserved in the Teatro Stabile Genoa

overwhelming personalities and love of the limelight in interpreting his great characters. Tommaso Salvini (1829–1915) excelled in parts calling for energy and exuberance, while Cesare Rossi (1829–96) had a leaning towards introverted and more finely drawn characters. In Italian criticism it became the accepted thing to regard Salvini as the ideal Othello and Rossi as the perfect Hamlet. Almanno Morelli as well as also playing Hamlet was the author of a somewhat tedious adaptation of the play, in which Hamlet does not die at the end, but is condemned to live on. Particularly after 1860, he concentrated on upper middle-class characters and for this reason became the favourite actor of Dumas' Italian imitator, Paolo Ferrari. Morelli is regarded as having enhanced the quality of the stage-settings, which certainly always remained very unpretentious in Italy, as well as lending social taste to the costumes and presence to his actors.

The history of Italian theatre in the 19th century is by any account that of its actors. To be more precise, records of productions and performances taken as a whole are only the records of worthless stage-properties and of a few extras in rags playing the parts of whole armies. Moreover, the reason for this was not, as it would have been in the Elizabethan theatre, that a symbolic token was thought to be all

that was required, but quite simply that money was short or production was slipshod. The technical innovations and changes in stage-design of the French and German theatres never penetrated the world of Italian drama. Until Morelli introduced his salons, the scenery for this invariably consisted of four flats and a roughly and vaguely painted backdrop which could be used for many different plays. There was no acknowledged approach to stage-direction such as that which had developed in Germany out of Goethe's 'read-throughs' with a view to relating the individual interpretations of the different parts to one another within the framework of a reading of the script as a whole, nor even in order to coordinate into more or less complex groupings the movements of the various characters and the extras who would be needed as was the practice of contemporary French stage-directors such as Laloue, Harel, Duponchel and others. It was taken for granted that each actor would interpret the character he represented in accordance with his own general rôle. The only work of coordination was that of making sure there was plenty of space and greater prominence given to the acting of the main character who, as we mentioned, had to be in the limelight because leading actors subordinated all other considerations to their own personal requirements and demanded the audience's undivided attention. The need for stage-direction was certainly felt and some directors did try to impose their own particular interpretation of a play or their own ideas about stage-settings, but the constant harking back to this very need, and that in its most elementary terms, shows how much it was neglected in practice.

We have, then, a history of actors, and even this must confine itself to external details and fragmentary anecdotes which at their best have some bearing on nuances of interpretations or reflect the desire to reform the theatre and create an Italian repertory. Vittorio Alfieri (1749–1803) worked hard and gave his name to various spasmodic attempts to bring back a classical sobriety of style in acting. He hailed from Asti, but his tragedies were too dry for the public's taste, which enjoyed only the lurid passions which certain actors brought out in his characters. Carlotta Marchionni, herself from 1823 to 1840 leading actress in the Royal Sardinian theatre and one of the most reserved of Italian actresses, transmuted the character of Mirra, incestuously in love with her own father, into the furiously raging passion of a bacchante interspersed with moments of surpassing sweetness.

Alfieri was always included in the repertory as a sort of alibi, and the classicism, the theory of 'ideal

E Gordigiani, *Portrait of Eleonora Duse*, 1896. Detail. Rome,
Raccolta Teatrale Burcardo

beauty' he enshrined, was for the actors an illusory ideal. How lacking in substance it was, was proved by Antonio Morrocchesi, who was himself the most prominent interpreter of Alfieri: claiming to believe that there was a mimed action corresponding to every word, he suggested he should act out eighteen lines from Alfieri's *Orestes* and assumed for the purpose no less than twenty-four different positions in quick succession. It was a bizarre frenzy of gestures, a sort of deaf-and-dumb alphabet which extended from the hands into convulsive shudderings of his whole body. Alfieri would have been horrified; he was always so concerned to reduce words, situations, characters and everything else to the bare minimum.

If Morrocchesi's lessons in declamation (1832) attributed so much importance to mime and posture, this shows what importance Italian actors gave to it. Indirectly, it also shows that highly dramatic and meaningful gestures were a great part of the secret of the success of such actors as Gustavo Modena, Adelaide Ristori and on down to the great heirs of this magnificent tradition in our own century such as Ermete Zacconi and Eleonara Duse. Zacconi never tired of research into the symptoms and pathology of his characters. Duse by long silences, by behaving as if she were in a dream and by suppressing or cutting short her use of gesture in order to intimate the presence of some repressed interior conflict, managed to impart a high degree of dramatic reality even to the characters of D'Annunzio's aestheticism at its most outmoded. In Duse the whole of the Italian tradition was, we might say, purged and made pure. Gustavo Modena and Tommaso Salvini, however, were not opposed even to the most violent gestures and never hesitated about tearing people's feelings to shreds. Nevertheless, it may have only been in the smaller companies that such uses of gesture and mime were carried to their extreme limits by actors who have remained unknown, but whom the ordinary people went along in crowds to see in open-air theatres or arenas, of which the Sun in Bologna was the best known, or in playhouses in small towns, without ever restricting their freedom to act by invoking the need for propriety. In some of these, with their complete extroversion and their total lack of inhibitions, Italian theatre may have attained its zenith, though unfortunately we cannot know this. The way in which these actors and their way of performing was violently attacked by the fanatics for classical moderation rings in our ears today as a paean of praise. They should have been proud to boast of their trade. Instead, the best known actors, victims as usual of an inferiority complex with respect to the more affluent and better equipped foreign theatres, tried to reform their own and killed it with schools and academies. Their trade, which was the special heritage of Italian actors, had given them a series of *clichés*, standardised gestures for the expression of specific interior states which were not fully concrete situations but psychological abstractions from them —jealousy, love, anger. The actors often used these gestures repeatedly and even without thinking.

When Alamanno Morelli stopped acting and started teaching, he codified this traditional patrimony of mime. He did his best to lend order and dignity to Italian theatre and, in accordance with the best academic traditions, he did this in his writings by laying down rules considered necessary for it and against which there was no appeal, rather like the 'laws' of Aristotle. However, quite contrary to his own intentions, the *Handbook of Stage Gesture* he published in 1854 ended up as a sort of codification of the use of mime traditional in Italian theatre, a sort of dictionary of gestures which were even listed in alphabetical order, without considering the difference in quality of the various gestures discussed, which might, in other words, be mere spontaneous reactions, or gestures that had become automatic as a result of social conventions, or ways of acting that were deliberately contrived. Although Morelli probably was acquainted with Engel's work, which had been translated into Italian in 1818–19, he was nowhere near so intelligent and penetrating, but thought that every gesture had some natural necessity about it. He wanted to determine what the essential features of these natural gestures were, but did no more than list the types of mime Italian actors had invented in order to lend some plastic expression to certain, abstract, psychological notions. In order to have some idea of the sort of stage jargon dominant in Italy during the last century, it may be worth reading one or two items from his dictionary:

'*Rage*: Take off your hat, put it back on, press it down into place, throw it on the ground, pick it up again, tear it to pieces; stride up and down restlessly, sometimes in a straight line, sometimes turning sharply. Sometimes run your hands through your hair, at others take off your doublet, undo the buttons, unfasten the laces: pause for a moment here and there. Bang hard with your fist on the furniture, turn chairs upside down, smash vases and crockery, bang your fist against the back of your neck, close and open doors, throw yourself down into a chair, keep banging on it, jump to your feet again.

'*Pride*: One arm set crossways over the breast, the other resting with the back of the hand on the hip and the elbow thrust forward, the head held high.'

Chapter 22

Aspect of a *kathakali* production representing episodes from the
Rāmāyaṇa

FORMS AND MOTIFS IN THE ORIENTAL TRADITION

With an inaccuracy that is widespread we spoke about 'theatre among primitive peoples' when it would have been much more objective to have referred to 'the theatre of small communities'. This phrase might perhaps enable us to appreciate why theatre in certain African or Alaskan communities bears a resemblance to that which flourishes in the European countryside in association with such festivals as Shrove Tuesday, May-day and so forth. On the other hand, it would also allow us to pick out of that most wide-embracing geographical location that we call the East a few themes which are, at least in some sense, characteristic and which sum up the main features of a theatre which, like that of the western world, is institutionalised and chiefly addressed to an urban audience frequently split up into different social classes, occasionally opposed to any sort of class privilege, but never organically related to the actors as cells in a single community. Nevertheless, this sort of theatre immediately strikes us as different from our own because of its greater ability to retain its traditional features, because of the continuing presence of religious and ritual elements, though these are sometimes obscure, and principally because of the clear-cut refusal to separate song, dance and speech. These invariably enter into an organic combination to constitute a single, integrated performance.

The Sanskrit root *nrt* from which the word for drama, *natya*, derives, is also the root for the word that has dance as its primary meaning. Similarly, the mythical origins of the Japanese *nō* are to be traced back, according to ancient tradition, to the singing and dancing of a goddess.

Indian theatre, too, according to the religious account of it, has a divine origin. Indeed, it was Brahma himself who made this gift to men, establishing rules for it in a fifth *Veda* that unfortunately was not handed down to us along with the other four sacred books of Hinduism. In fact it seems extremely unlikely that this fifth *Veda* ever existed and our only source of evidence consists of a treatise dating from about the fourth century AD, the *Nāṭyaśāstra* ('Treasury of Rules for Drama') by a probably entirely mythical author, Bharata, which is simply the word for 'author'.

Bharata states he is summarising the theatrical *Veda* which Brahma gave to all men and all castes, so that the humblest souls might be allowed to refresh their spirits and to learn the rules of right conduct by means of drama. Accordingly, the halls in which the performances took place were to be divided by four columns into four sections, one of which was to be reserved for each caste. Bharata emphasised the educational content of theatre which 'brings together all branches of learning'. Drama is 'an imitation of people's activities and behaviour. It is rich in a variety of emotions. It portrays different situations. . . . It describes the doings of the good, the bad and the indifferent, and should be a source of courage, joy and sound advice.' It is fascinating to find in this definition the 'imitation of people's activities' which is equally contained in Aristotle's *Poetics*. Compared with this the *Nāṭyaśāstra* gives the uncanny impression of an extremely sophisticated intellectual systematisation, devoid of all concrete references.

The earliest extant dramatic works date from no earlier than the 4th or 5th century AD, which was the period in which the greatest Indian dramatists flourished: Śūdraka and Kālidāsa. *The Little Clay Cart* and *Śakūntalā* are the best known of their plays, which combined prose and verse, the prose serving mainly to advance the action, while the parts in verse, which were danced and sung, were, if not lyrical interludes, at least moments of sublimity. There were several acts, from five to ten and even more, preceded by a prologue during which ritual actions were also performed. There were lots of characters whose many and varied adventures were sometimes taken from the epic poems of the heroic saga of Rāma (the *Rāmāyaṇa*), or from the *Mahābhārata*, but which were also often entirely invented. Unity of action was guaranteed by the presence of the hero, or better, by relating to him all the different threads of the plot. It is hard to find anything resembling what in Europe would be called a psychological study. Nevertheless, the Indian dramatist would focus most attention on the feelings of his characters (*bhava*), and from these he would derive the general atmosphere of the performance (*rasa*) which the actors had to mediate to their audience by whatever means of communication the stage had to offer—bodily movement, mime, intonation, costume, gesture and the like. All these were referred to in the manuals as *abhinaya*. There is an extremely delicate relationship between the *bhava* or feeling represented and the *rasa* or feeling communicated to and even lived by the audience as well as by the actor, because the *rasa* is a disembodied feeling, devoid of realities to explain it—Artaud would speak of the virtuality or latency of theatre. The means with which this sort of feeling is communicated are, therefore, numerous and complex. They do not exclude, but cannot be reduced to natural empathy and a psychological identification with a particular character. They also comprise symbolic behaviour, conventional allusions, straightforward references to a fact or an idea. Such symbolic behaviour, allusions and references are chiefly summed up in a carefully detailed system of gestures. The complexity of these is increased by the complete absence of real scenery for the performance of a play in which the scene is imagined to be changing all the time. The theme of Śūdraka's *The Little Clay Cart* is not the mighty deeds of some god or hero, but that of the love be-

tween Vasantasena, the prostitute, and Carudatta, a nobleman whose own generosity has made him destitute. Hence, there are no great shifts of location in this play. However, the action moves all the time from the home of one or other of the leading characters to the street, the park, and even, in one episode, through the eight different courtyards of the prostitute's residence, in which one character observes events that were obviously not actually shown. Thus it is clear that an actor was obliged to use mime to express his own reactions and feelings, which would vary with the different situations in which he found himself, and that he had also to give some immediate indication whenever the imaginary location changed. This was not all. He had also to use gesture to make explicit the different relationships between the characters. Thus, for instance, if an actor was speaking an aside, he would use his hands in a clearly prescribed way to indicate this and bend forward his thumb and his little finger.

Gestures of the hands were of extraordinary importance and did not merely comprise gestures normally used to indicate or express some action or feeling, but also a series of ritual rather than theatrical gestures, which were abstract in character and had been codified in the course of centuries of tradition. These gestures or *mudra* are the very ones used to accompany the celebration of the Vedic rites, though their range of meaning is shifted considerably when they are used in theatre. They might be compared to a deaf-and-dumb alphabet and can, indeed, represent individual letters, but in theatre their use is rather that of hieroglyphics and they become the signs of certain ideas of which the content remains, nevertheless, symbolic. Thus, the *mudra* of the letter *i*, which is regarded as representing the 'head of a gazelle', comes, by extension, to symbolise the god Siva-Isvara.

Even so, the extraordinary fact is not so much that there are available for use gestures of such widely different kinds as a natural stretching out of one's arms to ask for help, a conventional raising of one's hand in greeting, a token bending forward of one's fingers to show one is standing 'to one side', a symbolic arrangement of one's hands in the shape of a lily to represent purity, or the use of a *mudra* as the hieroglyphic for some idea; the amazing thing is that all these different gestures are being used simultaneously and in combination with the most varied and conflicting forms of mime. The *kathakali*, one of the four classical dances of India, offers what is possibly the most perfect illustration of this simultaneous blending process. It is not really accurate to call it a dance since, in keeping with one of the

characteristics of all oriental theatre, it combines together all sorts of display as it goes along. The *kathakali* is something like our ballet or pantomime to the extent that the characters never, or very seldom, use words. Two singers, accompanied by a small orchestra of percussion instruments, relate a story taken from the epic poem *Rāmāyana*, which, therefore, involves, as well as Rāmā, the hero, the gods of the Hindu Pantheon. As well as having this thematic link, the *kathakali* is connected with religion by the minutiae of ritual that go into its preparation. Moreover, while more prosaic productions began, as the plays in the ancient Greek theatre probably did, at dawn, the performance of the *kathakali* takes place at night and even lasts most of the night, a characteristic it has in common with many other forms of theatre, ranging from the *wayang*, or shadow-theatre of Java, to such sacred performances in small Indian communities as the *chhau* in the Kurni villages of Purulia, a district in West Bengal. With the exception of the women, whose rôles are played by male actors, and of the monks, the *kathakali* actors wear sumptuous apparel without any realistic or historical meaning whatever —a decorated bodice with full, brilliantly coloured skirts over their trousers. They also wear a dome-shaped head-dress, to which a sort of halo may be added whenever they represent some divine character. They use no masks, but their faces are so heavily made-up as to transform their appearance completely, although here, too, those playing female rôles provide an exception and are made-up barely enough

to soften their features. These actors mime the events being related by the singers, often in dialogue-form, and the result is rather like the medieval idea of Roman theatre-production. This mimed action, which might be termed an *abhinaya* (which literally means, primarily, 'illustration') of the narrative, draws upon the entire range of varied and complex gestures we have mentioned. However, the density of its dramatic impact is increased beyond measure by the absence of any verbal exchanges between the characters, though these do 'talk' by means of mime and gesture alone. When the *kathakali* actor is not 'talking', his reaction to his partner's contributions is minimal and he remains almost stationary. In contrast, the movement of the one who is 'speaking' is often quite frenzied. His hands form the shapes of the various *mudra*, or makes gestures of a spontaneous sort, or give to the emotions some plastic expression. The face, although heavily made-up, is extremely mobile and every part of it, especially the eye-brows and the mouth, has a precise part to play in the performance. The line of the body, which is often tilted forwards, follows the dancing movement of the feet, which have their own contribution to make to the expression of very clear meanings, depending on whether the soles rest completely on the ground or not, whether they are turned inwards or outwards and the like. There is nothing arbitrary nor even metaphorical about the terms 'dialogue', 'discourse', 'conversation' in this connection. For the most part the *kathakali* is not acted, but 'spoken', albeit in a non-verbal language. Real dramatic

269

action is not lacking, such as the duels the hero must fight or the trials he has to undergo, but the plot is mainly carried forward by the characters conversing with each other in a dialogue that is often broken up by and interspersed with long monologues which cannot by simply identified with the solo performances in European ballet, because a mime as powerful and complex as this is never a movement in the abstract, but always the significant vehicle of information it represents and transmits. It is, then, a concrete dialogue, for just as emotions colour and give shape to the intonation in verbal communications, so they pervade and complete the meaning of the *mudra* or gestures no matter how minutely they are codified, as well as that of the actor's only apparently more spontaneous movements. Thus the *kathakali* is a dance only in part and only then by stretching the meaning of the word; it is certainly dramatic theatre, though it is more besides; it is a dance to the extent that the actors' every use of gesture and mime is kept in time with a definite musical rhythm to which they hold.

The apprenticeship of a *kathakali* actor is not at all like the training of a European ballet-dancer. He does not need any special acrobatic skills, but rather a minute voluntary control of all the muscles in his body, so that he can execute gestures which are often imperceptible, but which are needed to impart some particular nuance to his speech. His apprenticeship is long and arduous, mainly because he must possess and be capable of carrying out the whole complex repertory of gestures that go to make up the heterogeneous vocabulary of *kathakali* language, which an actor must use to convey to his audience the *rasa*, or disembodied feeling of the tale being told. Obviously each spectator's degree of understanding is in direct proportion to his own knowledge of this vocabularly which is acquired by the actor in the process of long and arduous studies, but possessed by the audience to varying degrees and only approximately. Hence, though in India as elsewhere actors are frequently despised and shunned, they possess a language of their own that only they fully comprehend and know how to use.

This is typical of the corporate and professional nature of much of oriental theatre. Schools and academies for actors have flourished in the East from the very earliest times; the first drama-school in China seems, indeed, to have been established in the T'ang period, in other words, between the 7th and 9th centuries AD, with the aim of educating actors, musicians and dancers for the court theatre. The first great Japanese actor of whom we hear, Kan'ami Kiyotsugu (1333–84), and his son, Ze'ami Motokiyo,

The encounter of two warriors: the pheasant-feathers of the actor on the left show him to be a commander-in-chief and the four flags on the back of the actor on the right give him the rank of general. Scene from the Peking Opera

(1363–1443), mention schools in the 14th century. Ze'ami it was who gave *nō* theatre its final shape both as a style of acting and as a dramatic structure, features which he regarded as so inseparable that each actor was required to be the author of any play he interpreted. These were not schools only in the general sense of a shared tradition in matters of style, but there was a real organised curriculum of learning situations, and the apprenticeship did not consist merely of practical experience, but of a course of studies, definite stages, in each of which the future actor, who had to begin his training when he was seven, mastered specific features in the technical, linguistic, literary and cultural heritage that was the theatre. A large number of *nō* schools flourished after Ze'ami's day to satisfy the demands of the aristocratic audiences who chose to make this sort of theatrical their favourite intellectual pastime. However, round about the year 1700, their number was reduced to five officially recognised schools: Kwanze, Komparu, Kongō, Hōshō and Kita. Each of these schools had its own family tradition, with the rôle of Master being handed down from father to son, by 'son' being sometimes meant the favourite pupil who was regarded as a son. In each school the family's entire dramatic heritage was learned by

The highly stylised make-up of the Chinese actor, which he applies with a brush, is intended to be aesthetically pleasing and symbolically meaningful. Red indicates a loyal, honourable or courageous person. Character in Peking Opera

The highly stylised make-up of the Chinese actor, which he applies with a brush, is intended to be aesthetically pleasing and symbolically meaningful. Red indicates a loyal, honourable or courageous person. Character in Peking Opera

ancient Japan. The *nō* was considered indispensable in the training of the samurai, who were forbidden, on the other hand to attend the popular *kabuki* theatre.

Despite the perfection and complexity of the *nō*, perhaps it is a performance unrivalled for the clarity of its lines and the stark exclusion of external, theatrical features; there are no lights, no extras, no scenery. It probably evolved out of more popular sorts of theatre, and mainly those centred on dance (the *dengaku*, the *bugaku* and especially the *sarugaku*) by a process of successive purifications, until Kan'ami and Ze'ami finally established the noble and limpid genre of the *sarugaku no nō*, the professional *sarugaku*, in other words, *the* profession, the *nō*.

The lay-out of the theatre for *nō*, or rather of its stage, which was generally set up in a courtyard and always in the open air, was perfected by Ze'ami between 1400 and 1435: a square platform, about twenty feet each way, with four columns at the corners to support a pagoda-type roof, together with a bridge to complete the scenic area and connect it with the actors' dressing-room. A verandah on the right-hand side of the stage accommodated the chorus. A small set of steps along the front ran down from the stage into the audience. Its value was entirely symbolic, because it was never used. The only scenic or ornamental feature of the *nō* was an old, gnarled pine-tree, painted on the back-wall, in front of which sat the orchestra, on the part of the bridge that served as a back-stage (*atoza*). A small lobby was built between the bridge and the verandah for the chorus, and into this the actors occasionally withdrew when they left the stage.

There are two characters in the *nō*. The *shite* plays the lead-part, and the *waki* takes second place. A third person, the *tsure*, may be there as their companion, if required, but he never speaks. Often, and particularly in Ze'ami's plays, the *shite* is a dream or vision of the *waki*, a word which means host or spectator, but can also signify medium or charmer. The *waki* is the first to come on stage and, after a short orchestral prelude, he describes the place in which he finds himself. The *shite* at this point makes his appearance and crosses the bridge. The *waki* goes up to him and invites him to speak. While the *shite* is dancing, he tells his story in the third person and then vanishes. He is really the spirit of someone famous for their eventful life or untimely death and has not yet been entirely purged of passions or memories of his life on earth. After a short interlude involving the *waki*, the *shite* comes back differently dressed and looking just as he did when he was alive

heart, a repertory of between 150 and 250 plays, but the Master preserved the 'secret' which was handed on only to his son.

The secret of Ze'ami's school, which he called the flower of his *nō*, consisted in the actor's ability to appear to his audience always new and unexpected. If this shows, on the one hand, that the concept of artistic achievement was linked to that of success, though Ze'ami always made a distinction between the approval of people in the know and that of outsiders, on the other hand it provides evidence of the great subtlety and craftsmanship that the actors had to bring to each performance, especially considering the narrow limits within which variety was allowable. It is easy to imagine who were the people in the know: not so much, or at least not only the cultured classes, but more especially the military aristocracy. From the 15th to the 17th centuries the *nō* became increasingly subtle and refined and in the end was forced to take refuge in the feudal castles where the audience could follow the performance with the text of the play open in front of them. This tradition became continually more abstract and sophisticated, more elusive; nevertheless, it was regarded as highly important for the preservation of that right conduct which was the prerogative of

271

The Nakamura-za Theatre in 1859 during a *kabuki* production.
Coloured woodcut. Tokyo, Memorial Theatre Museum, Waseda
University

and still suffering. The *waki*, who is either dreaming
or seeing some unreal vision, asks the *shite* to speak
once more and the latter relives his own history in
dialogue with the chorus. This structure for the *nō*
changes little. Naturally the character of the *shite*
can vary: he may be a brave prince, a samurai slain
for not betraying the trust placed in him, a woman
who has lost her lover or her child. Even so, the
drama nearly always unfolds in the same way. Hence
the performance passes through much the same
stages. Costumes vary with the sort of character
portrayed, but, while the *waki* is unmasked, the
shite always wears a neutral mask with a serene
expression, very different indeed from the violently
distorted and disturbed looking masks of more
ancient theatre. As his part unfolds, each character
makes his progress through a number of definite
stages, beginning with the bridge over which he
comes on and on which he may pause once or twice,
and ending with the small door through which he
leaves and may return. On the stage itself, which is
almost devoid of anything tangible to serve as a
reference-point, there are different spots with
particular abstract connotations and there is no
denying their importance. The only physical ref-
erence-points are the columns. The front one on the
right is assigned to the *waki*, who sits in front of it
to listen the *shite* tell his story, his place being the
rear column on the left, where he comes to a halt
when he first makes his entrance.

The movements which propel the actor across the
stage and which very gradually develop out of a
simple glide into a dance, are almost always in a
straight line and devoid of any swerves other than
the dancing undulations of the body itself. This is
because motion in a straight line conveys an impression of unlimited distance, removes all possibility of
measuring space in a matter-of-fact way and helps
to carry the audience away into a dream-world of
perfection transcendent to all material conditions.
Like the gestures, this movement in one direction
only, the residue from a long process of selection
and purification, is the indispensable minimum for
perfection. In the *nō* the gestures are extremely few
and very carefully selected; a single gesture portrays
or symbolises a complete action—to weep it is
enough to carry a hand to one's eyes since the whole
action is concentrated in this gesture and one or two
steps forward symbolise a journey that has reached
its close. The value of another series of gestures is
not even representational, but purely fixed by convention—to turn up one's face means consolation,
ecstasy and also the light of the moon; to point a
fan (riding-whip) to the right means getting onto a

horse, to point it to the left means to dismount; to stamp one's foot means to demand the audience's attention.

Acting in the *no* must not dissolve into a series of gestures but rather they must flow together to form a single objective representation, and this in turn, says Ze'ami, must yield up 'a subtle magic'. The individual characters' understanding and execution of their individual gestures remains cold routine unless it is personalised by the actor's own contribution, the facility with which he makes whatever he does always new. No matter what character he portrays, the actor's expression must always be gentle and soft. On the stage the audience will see prostitutes and ladies of rank, men and women citizens, peasants and boors, even beggars and outcasts, but each must give the impression of wearing a decoration, a branch in flower. Such an effect can be obtained only by inspiring oneself constantly with the exemplary style of the court aristocracy, their distinguished way of behaving, that bearing which sets them apart from ordinary people. By imitating their refined and elegant ways one produces the 'subtle magic' which dies away no sooner than it springs to life and can never be repeated.

Thus the *no* is no more than the sophisticated and ephemeral sport of a cultivated class. Its distinct charm is that of the flower just before it starts to wither. It is an abstract, intellectual game that transcends the delicate form, attains an ineffable essence, transcends understanding itself and becomes sensitively aware of some ancient feeling that goes on renewing itself. The *no*, we can say, has been frozen for centuries so that the discerning audience has no other possibility than that of appreciating the accuracy with which each gesture is performed—a *no* company is very much like an orchestra that specialises in ancient music.

In Japan today it is not merely *no* which embodies classical theatre, but equally a sort of performance with quite low-class origins, the *kabuki*. The origins of the *no* are mythical, since it is traced back to the dancing of a goddess; those of the *kabuki* are historical, but are still connected with dancing, the dancing of a woman, probably, indeed, of a prostitute, O Kuni, who lived at the beginning of the 17th century.

The very name of this sort of theatre indicates the extent to which it was despised by the upper classes. The word probably derives from a root connected with the idea of eccentricity. The performance itself was very much connected with pleasure and amusement. Thus from the very beginning the companies comprised only women more or less openly available as prostitutes. Later on, when these were forbidden

to perform, though not of course to ply their trade, young boys took over their parts and were the object of the soldiers' homosexual lust for pleasure. This is also proved by the fact that the theatres were situated in the same district as the geisha-houses. A *kabuki* could last for as long as ten to twelve hours, although the traditional length was five or six. In the large theatres people ate, drank, chatted, amused themselves and, from time to time, watched the show—or rather, they were always watching it out of the corner of one eye and, from time to time, they gave it their undivided attention. The religious concentration with which some people watch the performance is, of course, a peculiarly European phenomenon and even in Europe there are acknowledged exceptions. In 18th-century theatres the boxes were used to receive guests and to flirt and only during the arias did the audience concentrate on the performance. In the East, also on account of the show being usually quite long, attention is always much more relaxed. The Java shadow-theatre, the *wayang*, lasts all night, and the spectators go outside, chat in small groups and then come back to their places without anyone complaining he is being disturbed. Until a decade or two ago, the same thing happened in the Peking Opera.

At the beginning of the 18th century men replaced the companies of women and children who acted the *kabuki*, and in this classical period the performance partly took place among the audience. The *kabuki* stage, like that of the *no*, is also linked to the dressing-room by a bridge, but instead of this being at the stage-end of the auditorium, it runs right across it. For the highlights of their performance actors often come back onto this bridge, also called the 'flower path', and so act in the middle of the audience, or better, right over their heads. In some theatres there are even two 'flower paths', parallel with one another, so that two people in an argument can face each other from a distance to speak their piece and the action in two different points of the room bounces from the stage to one bridge or the other and back again. Unlike the *no*, the *kabuki* is a performance full of energy and movement: a large number of characters are crowded onto a platform up to 90 feet wide and the acting is always lively and often violent, occasionally freezing into a tableau at a moment of particular significance, for instance when the hero arrives on the scene to prevent some injustice and shouts out: 'Just a moment!' Frequent changes of both scenery and costume take place, often in full view of the audience, and there are also special effects, such as apparitions, secret traps and the like. A revolving stage was already in use in the

Photograph of a scene in a *kyōgen*: the peasant and two devils

Scene from a *kabuki* in a poster. Paris, Musée des Arts Décoratifs

A performance in a People's Commune. Poster photographed in
China by Van Moppés

18th century and made quick changes of scene possible. The stage-settings and the mime were never realistic, at least not in any western sense. The conventions are many and far-fetched: a black cloth unrolled in the background indicates night, to raise one's shoulders abruptly shows hate or jealousy, to push the train of one's costume further back means anger. The style of an actor's costume and the way his face is made-up indicate the sort of character he is playing. Servants carry any properties onto the stage and help the actors to change. Thus there is no scope for illusions, even if the temples, houses and other scenic features on stage are quite accurately constructed. Nevertheless, the setting for the *kabuki* is extremely concrete and direct.

The *kabuki* began as amusement for the people and naturally developed its trend towards visual and theatrical effects. Like many forms of theatre in the Far East it is an amalgam of dance, song and drama. Indeed, it started off as a series of numbers, sketches, dances, popular songs and acrobatic acts, and even after they had been integrated as a dramatic whole these remained its indispensable ingredients, although they were never so tightly-knit as in the *nō*.

Moreover, because of its low-class appeal the *kabuki* attained that dialectical balance of progress and tradition which so often characterises theatre destined mainly for a popular audience. The people insist on recognising in the show heroes they know and, above all, familiar costumes, dance-movements and tunes, but they also like the plot to change and the situations and problems to be different each time. Hence the *kabuki* has known a continuous evolution in subject matter, in dramatic treatment and in acting techniques which, during the second half of the 17th century, had been inspired by the dry, geometrical movements of the then enormously successful puppet-theatres.

Some development in dramatic treatment is already evident in the output of the greatest Japanese playwright, Chikamatsu Monzaemon, who wrote both for the *kabuki*- and for the puppet-theatre. He worked from about 1673 to 1725 and in his early years derived his themes from history and mythology but, starting in about 1703, when he wrote his best-known play *The Lovers' Double Suicide at Sonezaki*, which was based on a topical news item, he turned increasingly to contemporary topics. Thus Japanese

277

theatre did not reject historical and mythological themes, provided the criteria with which they were selected was always new, but it now opened itself to the contemporary world and to its various situations, including in the 19th century even those of the thief and the prostitute. This implied a continual renewal of the style of acting, which was already differentiated into various schools and movements. It became less rigid, more forceful and dramatic, or seemed the acting of a romantic dreamer, or else was exaggerated and became rhetorical—some gestures are said to have lasted several seconds.

Precisely because of this special characteristic of being a traditional form of theatre yet open to new ideas, the *kabuki* suffered a crisis with the westernisation of Japan. The *nō* is a museum-piece and so immune from crises, but the *kabuki*, now that it has been deprived of the traditional foundations of both its classical form and its adaptability, will find the difficult and uncertain choice between stagnation in a form now regarded as antique and radical and total transformation, one between two sorts of suicide.

Confronted by a similar impasse, the Peking Opera has opted for the second alternative. The Peking Opera was, perhaps, more static than the *kabuki*, despite its large number of acrobats, and concentrated more on song and on theatre as a pure art-form. It is a theatrical genre, not a company with a permanent location, and was a central cultural feature in the national life of China. Very often during a festival or at the end of a banquet people might sing the better known arias or quote the lines that all the playwrights tended to use in such situations. Mainly as a result of the activities of Chiang Ching, the wife of Chairman Mao, the Cultural Revolution of 1966 took only a few years to effect a complete change in the form and content of this theatre. Everything was new. The legendary tales of the King of the Monkeys and the girl who wanted to reach the other side of the river were replaced by triumphant accounts of heroic deeds during the Civil War or of the formation of the Socialist Republic. The actors had to wear Red Army uniform or factory-workers' overalls with, quite often, European-style ballet-shoes as well, instead of their traditional, brilliant and magnificent costumes. Only the old music survived as an accompaniment to new words. Still, the actors were the same, a professional body, the owners of a technically perfect style of theatre, something they had made their own by years of hard work. Their acrobatic dancing and subtly symbolic gestures give the lie to the new costumes and the new words. The actors are being paid to spread a political message that their audience can only respond to in a passive way and that is imparted to them by persons whose life-style quite contradicts it.

However, since the Long March began, groups of Red Army soldiers have improvised plays for their comrades and, in the People's Communes, as the peasants gather the rice harvest to the ancient rhythms of the *yangko* dance, they renew the strength and meaning of their own cultural traditions. During the Civil War, in the zones where there was intense guerrilla warfare, companies travelling round the countryside were already staging this sort of play, gradually adding words and actions to the dancing, working out a precise theme in which traditional forms were used to explore not only new problems but the immediately practical problems facing those who were taking part in the performance. Since the Communes have autonomy of administration, they naturally have their own policy regarding culture and on every festive occasion more or less stable 'theatrical' companies made up of peasants and factory-workers stage their plays; they also act during break-time at work. In 1960 there were about 244,000 amateur companies active in China, but the number of those improvising some drama to the dance-rhythm as they gathered in the rice must have been incalculably greater. The problem is that of knowing if and how this cultural experience of peasant communities can be transferred to the towns, whose cultural tradition has been to accept only what the professional stage has to offer. To reform this profession, which may in the past have lived too exclusively on the basis of its own excessively rigid traditions to be able to open itself to new themes and fresh forms without a moral shock, is certainly a very big problem indeed. The choice lies between a theatre bereft of the exceptional technical resources of the Opera actors, but rich in its own, ancient and yet always adaptable qualities and, on the other hand, a theatre that is still technically perfect, but has been made the toy of a political propaganda machine which merely sings its own praises with unvarying monotony. Upon this choice will depend whether China can serve as model for some new form of theatre or whether it will join in reducing it to just one more among so many ways of conditioning the masses.

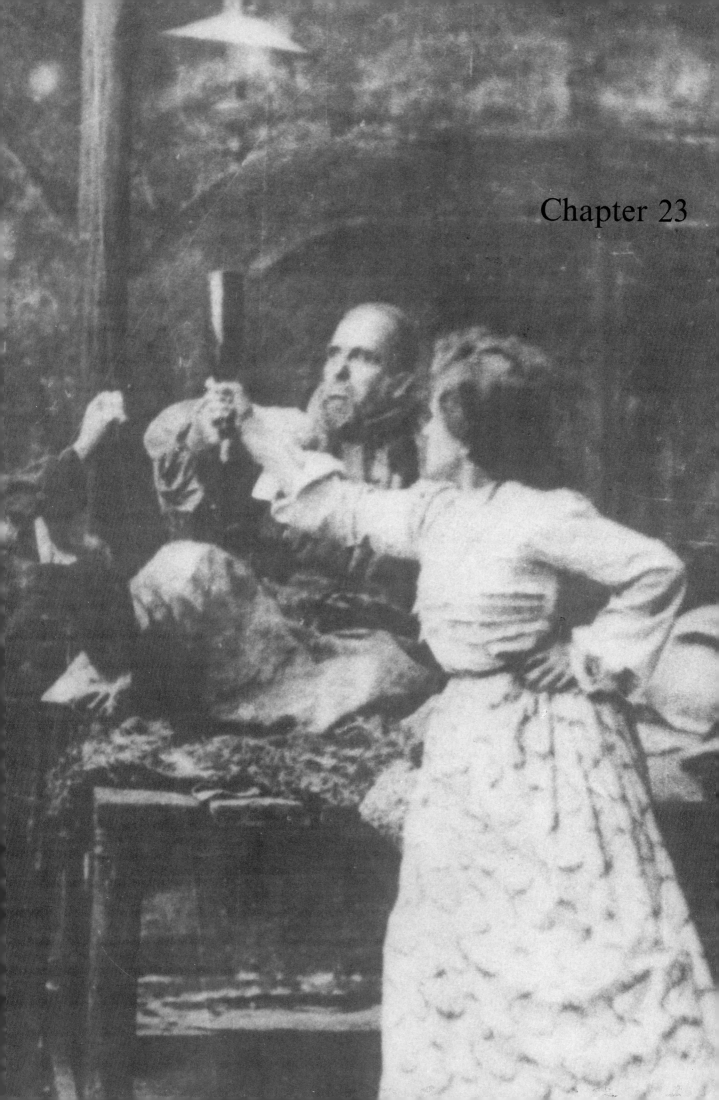

Chapter 23

280   Photographs of two scenes from one of the first performances in
Antoine's Théâtre Libre: Méténier's *En Famille*. Paris, Biblio-
thèque de la Comédie Française

NATURALISM AND PSYCHO-LOGICAL REALISM: ANTOINE AND STANISLAVSKY

In the western world the 20th century belongs to the avant-garde. The avant-garde is not a movement, nor a school, nor does it entail acceptance of any particular articles of artistic faith. Indeed, from a historical standpoint, the avant-garde comprises a number of considerably different movements: Symbolism, Cubism, Surrealism, Pop Art—these share neither a language, nor a theory of art, nor an ideology. The avant-garde is rather more of a psychological climate, a specific sensitivity; it seems to be characterised by a tendency to approve of rebellion and to reject whatever has been generally taken for granted, a tendency to work towards a future that is only vaguely in view and also a certain sense of emptiness and solitude that we have come to describe as alienation. In addition to this general psychological stance, the avant-garde movements share at least the attempt or the hope of integrating their theory with concrete results, and so of recent years there has been in all branches of the arts a quite incredible spate of manuals and treatises. Indeed the theory often anticipates the actual practice, so that an experimental approach is equally a characteristic of avant-garde movements and writers. This experimentalism is linguistic, inasmuch as artists try certain combinations to see what sort of product results from a specific approach, and educational, to the extent that they try to manipulate the reactions of the audience or people's tastes. To experiment could mean to strive to discover the necessary laws behind the creation of a work, such as Mallarmé's 'Grand Œuvre' which would be by nature not merely feasible nor effective as a matter of fact, but unconditionally good. However, it can also mean to persist in one's efforts to work out new subjects and fresh questions; in this sense, the notion of experimentalism does imply a rejection of tradition. More precisely, as Romanticism rejected the classical tradition in order to find an alternative tradition in the neglected riches of the Middle Ages, so the avant-garde rejects the European tradition so as to explore the riches of primitive peoples and Asiatic civilisations. The main cultural achievement of the avant-garde is their rejection of the value of European history as an absolute, their questioning of its superiority to that of other peoples. The black statuette may be more beautiful than the Venus de Milo. It is, in fact, only at the intellectual level that the European tradition is ruled out of court, but this is bound to have its practical repercussions in the history of contemporary art. Hence the avant-garde is obliged to come to terms with three cultural heritages: the development of one is known and can be retraced, the other two are characterised more intuitively, as huge monoliths—'primitive' culture, and Eastern culture.

The history of the avant-garde may be regarded as starting with the movement to which all subsequent ones intended to be quite clearly opposed, in other words, Naturalism. The emergence of this movement was certainly not unconnected with the demand for historical truth that had made itself so strongly

Three scenes from Alexey Tolstoy's *Tsar Fyodor* in the 1889
Moscow Art Theatre production directed by Stanislavsky.
Photographs. Moscow, Bakhrushin Theatre Museum

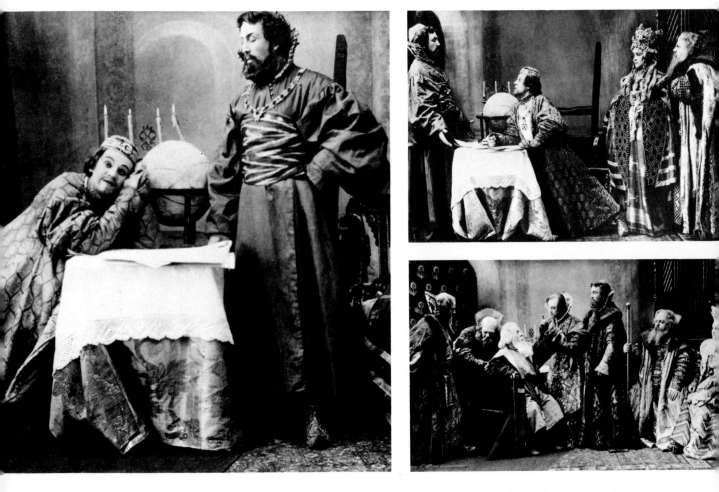

felt in the first half of the 19th century. Indeed, even
from the most exactingly technical and structural
point of view, a physical reference-point is provided
by the supreme example of this sort of 'truth'
being actually achieved on stage. When the Duke of
Meiningen's company was directed by Ludwig
Kronegk, he, unlike Count von Brühl, was not
content to reconstruct on stage historical environ-
ments that looked realistic. In addition, he as far
as possible refused to use painted scenery and
brought real objects onto the stage instead. During
their numerous tours, the Meiningen company
caused quite a stir also on account of their perfect
discipline as a team, and this was a considerable
contribution towards a clearer definition of the
producer's rôle.

In his second period of activity André Antoine
(1858–1943) was also to devote himself to historically
accurate reconstructions, quite explicitly inspired by
the Meiningen theatre. This, however, is not the
reason for including him in the history of theatre.

In literary work, in the figurative arts and in
theatre, Naturalism does not simply mean closely
adhering to empirical reality as it manifests itself;
it is much more the struggle to capture this reality,
in its everyday crudity of course, but at those very
moments when this is all there is. Hence, Jean
Jullien, who together with Émile Zola was the
theoretician of Naturalist theatre, maintained that
the actors ought to move about and speak as if they
were still at home, without ever giving any attention
to the audience, and so he wanted the front-view of
the stage (*l'emplacement du rideau*) to be a sort of
fourth wall, which the actors could not see through,
although the audience could—in this way their
situation became that of chance witnesses of a
happening, *une tranche de vie*.

Beginning with the first production with which he
inaugurated his own theatre, after a few amateurish
efforts at the Cercle Gaulois, Antoine remained
faithful to this theory of art, perhaps without
thinking, but certainly because he felt it was right.

282

The *Théâtre Libre* opened on the evening of 30 March 1887 in a cramped building, and its dirty and dusty atmosphere was to be for many years almost the emblem of avant-garde theatre. The play was an abridgement of Zola's short story, *Jacques Damour*; there was no scenery, but just a few sticks of furniture from Antoine's mother's dining-room, real things, indeed, which could not help but stimulate the naturalness of what was happening. The Théâtre Libre became acknowledged from that day forward as the centre for Naturalist theatre, and it inspired other ventures, of which the most notorious was the Freie Bühne in Berlin.

In reality, however, the repertory of the Théâtre Libre was quite a mixed bag: plays by Curel and dramatisations of novels by Zola, the Goncourt brothers and Daudet to represent Naturalism just as frequently as productions of such 'poets' as Catulle Mendès. Nevertheless, only the former performances helped to give shape to Antoine's experience. What we remember of the Théâtre Libre, what carried weight and had influence in France and abroad, were the plays which presented the dark, pathological or violent side of the social situation. The characters who shook to their roots those who went to see the Théâtre Libre were certainly not the Duc d'Enghien or Queen Fiammette in the plays of the same name by Léon Hennique and Catulle Mendès, but a wretched servant-girl, Germinie Lacerteux, old and ugly, but still racked by insatiable desires. She was played by Réjane, an actress from the boulevard theatre (which was then synonymous with a theatre of upper-class brilliance), whom Antoine had managed to transform. One particularly striking scene was that of the well-fed children having their tea, abjectly waited on by this half-starved wretch. There was also the character of Jacques Bouchard in Pierre Wolff's play. Antoine himself played the part of the almost dumb bartender, busy rinsing out the glasses behind the bar.

Antoine built up his character by a series of small, markedly idiosyncratic gestures and rejected stereo-

283

Three aspects of Act IV of the 1902 Moscow Art Theatre production of Gorky's *Lower Depths* directed by Stanislavsky. Photographs. Moscow, Bakhrushin Theatre Museum

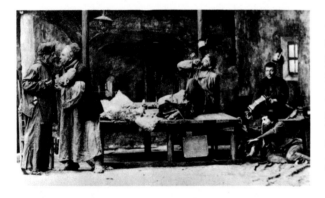

types of any kind, concentrating instead on the symptoms of that pathology which had become his character's life-style. An Italian disciple of his, Ermete Zacconi, would fail to appreciate the underlying meaning of this procedure of Antoine's and would try instead to portray in scientific terms the symptoms of characters who were ill, playing these by preference. His interpretation of the part of Oswald in Ibsen's *Ghosts*, when he tried to show the progress of congenital syphilis, was to be remembered as outstanding.

After making his point successfully in his own small avant-garde theatre, Antoine was to receive the honours of the official theatre. However, he never forgot his own origins and the representation of daily life was to remain a frequent theme in his productions. On the other hand he tried his lot with the classics with ever increasing frequency and, especially when he was stage-manager at the Odéon, interpreted these with insight and scholarship. His *Tartuffe* was worth remembering. He stripped away all the superficial coarseness and unction, so as to make him appear the perfect gentleman. Then, of course, he followed in the Meiningen company's footsteps and staged any plays on historical subjects with minute attention to the archeological detail, as he had already done in the Théâtre Libre, but now with many more resources to call upon.

From the time when he devoted himself to theatre and undertook personally a considerable part of the expenses for the productions staged at the Moscow Society of Art and Literature, Constantin Alexeyev, known by his stage-name of Stanislavsky (1863–1938), had been deeply impressed by the Meiningen company's impeccable *mises en scène*. In 1898 he and a writer, Vladimir Nemirovitch-Dantchenko, founded the Moscow Art Theatre and it was natural their first productions should concentrate on the same qualities of archeologically researched reconstructions and complex ensemble movements which seemed casual enough but were really planned out in detail. Every production was prepared for by a long and painstaking study of the period in which the action was set, whether this was Boyar Russia, as in the case of Alexey Tolstoy's *Tsar Fyodor*, or Republican Rome for Shakespeare's *Julius Caesar*.

When it was a question of representing contemporary settings on stage, Stanislavsky brought this same commitment to truth into play. In order to find out about the day-to-day life of the outcasts of Moscow, the company organised an 'expedition' into the doss-house and brothels of the city with the same enthusiasm as they had visited Rome before staging *Julius Caesar*. The outcome was the production of Gorky's *Lower Depths*. Those bits and pieces of life which had been portrayed with microscopic attention to detail, but only as a background in previous productions, now occupied the front of the stage. Every line was related to and directly expressed some trivial daily occurrence—card-playing, sewing, preparing a meal—of the sort that gnawed the heart out of the unhappy lives of Gorky's characters. Such ventures were not isolated incidents, but lines of development in Stanislavsky's artistic career. Nevertheless, the most decisive event in his life as an artist was his meeting Anton Chekhov. The experience with Chekhov meant for Stanislavsky clearing up

once and for all his fundamental ideas and options about theatre (in fact, about his own theatre): the microscopic realism of the scenery and the settings remained, but their object was different—they now served to express the character's inner world.

In December 1898 the Art Theatre put on with tremendous success *The Seagull*, which had already been howled off stage in St Petersburg. In October 1899 they turned to *Uncle Vanya*. Nothing happens in this play. Vanya has discovered right from the start that Professor Serebyakov, to promote whose genius he has sacrificed his entire life, is a downright imbecile. Stanislavsky plunges the characters into an atmosphere of depression. In Act I they fight like demons against the heat and mosquitoes, going through a continuous sequence of abrupt, nervous movements that keep their tensions barely within limits they can tolerate. Objects, always scrupulously real, and particularly noises off stage—the barking of a dog, a song in the distance—make the place where this is going on believable, first of all to the actor, and also to the audience. These effects taken one by one are also highly significant. The toys which, from Act II onwards, begin to invade the house of *The Three Sisters* (1901) indicate that Natasha, their sister-in-law is gradually taking it over, and she finishes by sending them away with their dream of a return to Moscow still unrealised. In *The Cherry Orchard* (1904) the almost uninterrupted shrill theme-song of the birds and cicadas brings into being an atmosphere of rural melancholy, the setting for the characters' farewell to their home, the ever-recurring Chekhovian motif of regret sublimated in a tragic elegy.

Stanislavsky never departed from this detailed reconstruction of the setting for a play, not even after the considerable failure of his experiments in Symbolism; and when he produced Turgenev's *A Month in the Country* (1909) he kept the characters motionless for almost the entire length of the play, almost buried in a large divan, their eyes staring into space, trying to lay bare the very dregs of their souls, phlegmatically, yet with hesitation in their voices.

The scenery, the properties, the sound effects, the noises off stage and the costumes are not just features in a picture placed before the audience; they are also, and even primarily, for the actor's benefit, to enable him to 'relive' the character he represents. The art of theatre and that of the actor are indivisible.

Stanislavsky's life as an artist was an indefatigable search for a science of the art of acting. With his dogged determination to go on trying, he sought to resolve this paradox, which can also be formulated as a question: how can one gain admittance to the artists' paradise by free choice, instead of by chance? How can inspiration be wooed by artifice?

Such romantic questions demand a down-to-earth response, and this is what Stanislavsky gives us in his vast theoretical work, that summarises his system in two volumes entitled, *An Actor Prepares* (1936) and the posthumously published *Building a Character* (1950).

The actor's art is that of re-living (*perêzivanje*); he must live again his character's emotions, sufferings, sensations even, so as to bring to life the personage the author has traced out only in skeleton form. He cannot just re-live him once and then go on repeating indefinitely the image thereby brought into being, but every single time he is called upon to represent that character he must live him. Hence there are not really any repetitions, but every night, even when the hundredth time comes round, the actor must experience Othello's jealousy, Hamlet's self-questioning. If, then, sensations and feelings are spontaneous occurrences springing up from the depths of the psyche, if they are facts of the subconscious, how can they be aroused whenever they are needed? Stanislavsky's answer is: by means of well-adapted, externally controllable stimuli. His system offers no more than a battery of psychological techniques that make it possible to stimulate and control subconscious, psychic events. Just as Proust was able to recapture the lost feelings of his childhood by tasting the flavour of *madeleines* once more, so Stanislavsky's actor can, by performing a particular gesture or taking up a specific stance re-evoke mentally some emotion he has previously experienced, a feeling that has already been his, sufferings now in the past, and this enables him to behave spontaneously like someone actually involved with that emotion, that feeling, those sufferings. The actor is not re-living someone else's feelings and sufferings, but his own, thanks to what Stanislavsky calls 'emotional memory'. Obviously it will be a question of feelings, emotions and sufferings analogous to those of the character he represents. Hence the actor must know his character not only in those moments in which he has a part to play on stage, but he must know his entire life. The actor ought to know the social circles in which his character moved, his home, his town, his friends, his past life. In other words, he must make an inventory of the complete history of his life and on this basis find the justification for the acts he performs on stage. The director, the scene-artist, the light and sound technicians must surround him with all those things with which the character himself may be supposed to have been surrounded. Stanislavsky's realistic settings are aids towards psychological realism, which can be defined as the process of becoming acquainted with emotional realities. After an actor has ascertained in all its detailed circumstances, including dates, the life his character has led and has satisfactorily pieced all this together as a consistently developing process in his imagination, that character, previously known in analytical and external terms, becomes someone the actor knows intimately from the inside, so that, in his character the actor now lives himself.

Chapter 24

THE THEATRE ARTIST AND HIS SYMBOLS

It is in Stanislavsky's theoretical writings and in those of Antoine, which happen to be few and are anything but systematic, that we find the beginnings of a definition of the director's rôle. This is not to deny that some similar function had existed in the theatre in the past. Indeed, there has often been someone charged to coordinate the various components of the production, from the *meneur du jeu* of the medieval mystery-plays to the actor-manager in Italian touring companies, from the choregus of Greek tragedy to the one idealised by Leone de' Sommi and right down to the stage-managers who in French theatres of the last century had to think first of all about organising the ensemble movements of the extras and giving some definite shape to the tableaux. However, this person's duties were as a rule unspecified and secondary. He certainly did not influence the style of acting, the costumes themselves were in most cases chosen by the actors, while lighting, scenery and special effects were left to the experts.

Antoine, who was naturally an actor before all else, did not trust actors at all. He regarded them as ignorant people, incapable of understanding the value and meaning of any literary work. In his view actors at best were no more than 'puppets, marionnettes, dressed up and manipulated by the author's caprice'. Hence, although he never explicitly mentions the director, his words make it clear enough that someone is needed to tell the actors how to move and act in order to realise the author's aims, in other words, an interpreter capable of grasping the real meaning of the play.

Stanislavsky sees the director as a transitional figure. Once the actors have thoroughly mastered the psychological techniques they need, a director is no longer necessary and in the meanwhile his function is mainly educational. However, this educational task is, in fact, creative. For the director as he orientates the actor in this psychological and technical direction finds himself in a much more effective position to influence him than would be the case if he confined his attention to external suggestions, no matter how detailed these might be. Furthermore, it is the director who furnishes the actors with the more significant portions of the prevailing situation, by suggesting to them how the narrative might proceed beyond the point where the dramatic action breaks off: imagining, for instance, what happens in the pauses between one act and the next, what the characters are up to when off stage, how the play fits into its historical and social context. He often replaces the actor's phantasy by his own, imagining for him his character's previous life and specifying his personal qualities.

This does not alter the fact that, in theory at least, the director is a secondary figure for both Stanislavsky and Antoine. The former's approach to theatre is summed up in the actor, to whom he did his best to impart social and professional prestige; for the latter the director is basically a rather poor substitute for the author.

The cultural climate in which the figure of the director was to be more sharply defined and allowed his properly independent function was far removed

Gordon Craig, Sketch for Ibsen's *The Vikings at Helgeland* Act IV, which he staged in London in the Imperial Theatre in 1903. Ellen Terry played the female lead. Paris, Bibliothèque de l'Arsenal. The illustration on the preceding page is another sketch for the same production

Adolphe Appia, Sketch for *Tristan und Isolde* Act II, 1896. Berne, A Appia Foundation. Appia had very few opportunities to utilise his own drawings in actual production. However, he wrote detailed schemes for the staging of Wagner's *Tristan und Isolde* and for his trilogy *The Ring*

Adolphe Appia, Sketch for Gluck's *Orfeo*, showing the descent into the underworld (rhythmic space). Berne, A Appia Foundation

renounce trivial episodes and psychological musings, in order to rise up into the higher realm of pure forms. For the Parnassians the ideal of art had been embodied in sculpture. In a similar way, music meant everything to the Symbolists—'music above all', Verlaine wrote. It is obvious that it was harder for drama than for other art forms to adapt itself to the requirements of such a philosophy of art. The actor by the impact of his own physical presence cannot help but bring us back to the empirical world and its daily concerns. Hence almost all those theoretical writers who expounded Symbolism and gave some attention to theatre, from Mallarmé to Albert Mockel, and Maeterlinck himself, criticised heavily the actor's being actually present on stage. Mallarmé finds the stage fascinating, but prefers it empty, though he will allow a ballerina on it because, by dancing, she can abolish the physical aspect of her own body. Baudelaire and Maeterlinck can tolerate the actor only if he succeeds in making himself seem like a statue or a puppet, only if he divests himself of his living body and makes us forget him. Theatre must be just a harmony of movement, gesture, colour and sound that point towards a symbol. Gordon Craig was to argue that, if such really is the case, this harmony can only issue from the intuition of its unique creator, the director, the theatre artist *par excellence*, who is neither painter nor musician nor even the interpreter of a play, but the minister of an art with its own laws and values: theatre itself.

Symbolism had direct repercussions on the practical work for the stage of Paul Fort, who in 1891 established the Théâtre d'Art, and Aurélien Lugné-Poë, who in 1893 opened another called the Théâtre de l'Œuvre.

Being a poet, Paul Fort thought theatre should be mainly a matter of speech. As he envisaged it, the theatre for art was to be a theatre for poetry. Nevertheless, although his productions were very rough-and-ready and sometimes in downright bad taste, they are remembered particularly for the way in which they were staged as theatre and for the intrinsically meaningful and ingenious stage-settings. In *La jeune fille aux mains coupées* ('The Girl with the Severed Hands')—a poetic play by Pierre Quillard about the incestuous love between father and daughter—the actors recited their lines in a slow and monotonous voice behind a muslin curtain and against the background of a gold backdrop framed in red hangings; meanwhile on the main stage a girl actress, dressed in a long blue tunic, read the characters' lines once more and explained their feelings.

from and even quite explicitly opposed to the ideals of Naturalism and Psychological Realism. It was only as a result of the actual practice as well as of the considered opinion of such theatre people as Adolphe Appia, Gordon Craig, and Vsevolod Emilievich Meyerhold, all of them more or less closely wedded to the aesthetic ideals of the Symbolist Movement, that the director began to be regarded as the central figure in theatre, the only one able to impart substance and shape to any self-contained art form, the one who created the performance.

The re-evaluation of the status of art as compared with that of science, with the appeal to a higher knowledge than that of the empirical world, that is, an appreciation of spiritual realities attained solely through some poetic intuition, also serves as an attack on the values of the consumer society which is threatening to eliminate whatever man has that is free and noble. In practical terms, any art that claims to perform this service must renounce whatever is connected with the earthly reality of things, must

290

Until that performance it had invariably been the practice in dramatic theatre either to insert a play into some traditional stage-setting, or to provide it with a setting based on the actual evidence of the play itself. From that time onwards anyone producing a play has felt free to do so in ways which are no longer governed by any such evident necessity. A poetic text may suggest a vision and one may try to reproduce this. This procedure can even be justified by maintaining that the vision expresses the atmosphere of the play, but this is an obvious tautology: 'the atmosphere' is merely an individual vision evoked by the play itself.

Relatively few productions were staged at the Théâtre d'Art and the Théâtre de l'Œuvre, but in these there recur with some frequency certain features which together make up what can be called the character of Symbolist theatre. For instance, the idea of having the actors recite their lines behind a veil returns in the production of Henri de Régnier's *La gardienne* (Œuvre; 1894), and the intention behind it is clearly to deprive the actors of their physical impact and reduce them to shadows and figments of the imagination. In most cases the lines were recited in a tone of ecstasy, in a singsong, as if the characters were immersed in some distant world from which their voices came back like echoes. Referring to the production of *'Tis Pity She's a Whore*, Sarcey wrote: 'Lugné-Poë and Berthe Bady have had the unusual idea of acting these outrageous scenes with their hands joined, their eyes turned heavenwards, carrying themselves like mystics, walking slowly, using a colourless, monotonous voice like some saint out of one of Giotto's frescoes.' However, the other characters said their lines in a natural tone of voice, to typify the dimension of the empirical world, while the main characters, the incestuous couple, urged on by fate rather than passion, which John Ford had had in mind, act out their parts in a world of absolutes.

Edward Gordon Craig (1872–1958) and the Swiss Adolphe Appia (1862–1928), the two major representatives of the first avant-garde movement in theatre, are for different reasons both connected

E Munch, Sketch for Ibsen's *Ghosts*. Basle, Öffentliche Kunstsammlung

with the cultural tradition of Symbolism, though they were active when this no longer existed as an organised movement with set limits and a fixed aim.

Gordon Craig, the son of the greatest Victorian actress, Ellen Terry, occasionally acted as a young man, but later sought to realise his artistic ambitions as a director and stage-designer. His main pre-occupations were the autonomy of theatre as an art-form with its own status and position and the definition of the rôle of the theatre-artist. His cultural diet was Nietzsche and Carlyle and he proclaimed in prophetic tones that if theatre was to live, it would have to die. The true theatre-artist, he who could produce theatrical works out of his own mind and partly with his own hands, would alone be able to restore it to life. In order to promote the production of a theatrical work of art, it is necessary to outlaw from the theatre anything that obstructs the unconditional affirmation of unconditional values, that is to say, on the one hand anything trivial or empirical, and on the other hand anything that is fortuitous. Especially what is fortuitous—like Mallarmé, Craig is convinced that artistic creativity is a constant struggle against chance, against whatever is not unconditionally necessary. Mallarmé had understood the struggle was doomed to failure: '*un coup de dés jamais n'abolira l'hasard*' ('a throw of the dice will never do away with chance'). The trivial, the empirical and the fortuitous are, for Craig, embodied in the person of the actor; like Mallarmé and Maeterlinck (the most interesting of the Symbolist playwrights) and Albert Mockel, he would like him replaced by a marionette. Indeed by a super-marionette, defined by Craig in his more temperate writings as an actor with more fire and less selfishness, a robot in the true and proper original meaning of the term and so not subject to changes of mood, nor possessed of any of his own ideas which would be bound to clash with those of the director, but entirely submissive and obedient to him. Moreover the marionette has idols for its ancestors and so is in a unique position to be the central character in the theatrical ritual.

Craig is again repeating, perhaps unwittingly, ideas expressed by the French Symbolist school: theatre is ritual. This idea later became a common-place and many historians have taken it as axiomatic. However, to François de Nion's way of thinking, and to Craig's, it is a question of a self-contained ritual, a vision in which the audience is forbidden to participate and can only observe in reverent silence. Never was there a sharper break than this between stage and auditorium; the theatrical ritual in the very instant of its performance is a self-contained work of art, an absolute, that one can only admire from far off. Theatre is, indeed, a vision. In fact, it would be better defined by the Greek concept of *theoria*, which contains the ideas of vision, contemplation and knowledge. It is a vision of movement without noise, a celebration of the mystery of movement. In his longing for discipline and purity Craig reaches the point of eliminating from theatre not merely the author's script, but all use of speech, all sound. Hence the theatre artist, and in this context it would be quite inappropriate to call him a director, is someone who creates a pure vision of movement and celebrates its rites as the rites of life itself.

Craig's major effort to translate his theatrical ideal into practice was his production of *Hamlet* in the Moscow Art Theatre and so in collaboration with Stanislavsky. He had already directed a certain number of productions in England and abroad (Ibsen's *The Vikings at Helgeland* in London in 1903, Otway's *Venice Preserved* in Berlin in 1905, etc.), but it was only in this 1912 production that he attained full maturity, although false notes and compromises were not lacking, partly because of disagreements with Stanislavsky, partly because of Craig's character and his basic inability to complete any undertaking which demanded great effort and considerable sacrifice. The scenery Craig devised for *Hamlet* consisted of very high screens set on runners which were supposed to move throughout the performance in keeping with each slight change in the situation or, more precisely, in the idea that this embodied. However, for technical reasons this was not feasible and the position of the screens had to be changed with the curtain closed. For scenes of court life the screens were gold, a colour which symbolised the corrupt splendours of the court itself; when Hamlet was alone they became grey instead, the greyness of the sadness in his soul. The main characters also wore gilded costumes and the scene in which the King and Queen appeared together for the first time seemed a veritable sea of gold. However, to show up the falsehood of such luxury, even the gold seemed dull, as if it were seen through a pall of smoke. The only explosion of colours was in the play within the play: theatre is Hamlet's only memento of the happy life.

Thus the stage was ritually clean in the extreme, devoid of all descriptive features: just a series of perfectly smooth screens, so arranged as to create a geometrical rhythm in space rather than a specific location, while their strong, vertical lines gave the impression of a different world from that of empirical reality, a world with which one could not possibly communicate.

We find the same simplification of the scenic features and an identical geometrically rigid structure of design in Adolphe Appia's stage projects. Like Craig, he was a first-class draftsman. However, Appia's way of dividing space is more complex and this is because he has a different approach to theatre.

Appia's ruminations on the problems of theatre start out from one problem in particular: how to produce Wagner's dramas in words and music (*Worttondrama*). His first monograph about theatre bore precisely this title: *La mise en scène du drame*

wagnérien (1895). It was followed by *La musique et la mise en scène* (1897) and *L'œuvre d'art vivant* (1921). It must be remembered that Wagner was very highly appreciated in Symbolist circles, not just for the quality of his music, but also, and perhaps predominantly, because of his aesthetic principles. If, on the one hand, his theory of the complete work of art, that is the *Worttondrama*, delighted theatre people, it could, on the other hand, be integrated perfectly into the theory of 'correspondences', which was a cardinal feature of the Symbolist aesthetic and which maintains that the essence of reality is arrived at by bringing together colours, sounds and words. This is so far true that the *Revue wagnérienne* became the organ more of the Symbolists than of Wagner's own followers.

Because of this link it is logical enough that, after a first period in which it is clear from his drawings that Appia regarded the stage as a mysterious world of half-shadows in which lighting effects were predominantly used to produce symbols, he should finally think of space as a direct function of the music, as something precipitated out of musical time. The earlier idea is fascinatingly illustrated by his project for a production of *Tristan und Isolde* in which the normal light-darkness relationship is reversed, so that the latter becomes an emblem of life and joy. The later idea is exemplified particularly in a series of drawings with the title: 'Rhythmic Spaces'.

For Appia music is the supreme art-form. It is pure expression or, as Schopenhauer maintained, a revelation of the essential. Yet it needs the intellectual support of speech. In achieving a synthesis of music and words Wagner gave proof of his perfect understanding of art, but even he did not succeed in extending the poetry of the music and the words into the poetry of spatial relationships and so fulfil the dream of the total work of art. Yet to Appia's way of thinking, this transition is no more than a necessary, logical step to take. For music is the origin of movement which it stimulates and controls by setting it in regular time. Thus the actor mediates between the arts of time (music and poetry) and those of space, because his movements impart the final form to the structure of the scenery, which cannot be something painted in two dimensions, but has to be a three-dimensional ongoing process, not simply an empty space, but something that offers resistance to the moving body, something, therefore, made up of levels, ramps and steps. Painting is either to be totally excluded, or used only as a sign to indicate the empirical meaning of some specific scene, whenever this proves necessary.

What about the director? His rôle is a passing one in Appia's estimation. In Wagner's operas his task will be to bring out explicitly the lines of movement which they contain implicitly. The true director remains the author, and the author of the future will need to set out his *Worttondrama* following a division into three staves, the third being the notation for the movement and, therefore, for the space. As soon as authors wake up to this requirement, the director will become just a teacher of gymnastics. Or else he will continue to fulfil his function for works which

I Nivinsky, Calaf's costume for Vakhtangov's 1922 production of Carlo Gozzi's *Princess Turandot* in the Third Studio of the Moscow Art Theatre. Moscow, Bakhrushin Theatre Museum

are less than perfect and are not complete works of art, in other words for straightforward drama, which being without any music to specify the timing of its movements can leave these to follow their own course in the loose framework of intelligible speech and empirical experience. However, Appia does not give much attention to this inferior sort of theatre.

The outlook of Georg Fuchs was different in some ways from that of Appia and Craig. He was manager and director of the Künstlertheater in Munich. Here, together with the scene-designer Fritz Erler, he was responsible for a series of productions which utilised a stage-setting comprising two horizontal features, rather like towers, linked by a vertical feature. These elements could be very rapidly re-arranged in different ways and so provided the main setting, which was then specified further by means of a few suitable properties. The first production in the series was Goethe's *Faust* which was staged in 1908.

The concept of artistic activity with which Fuchs begins is considerably removed from that of Symbolist and aestheticist mysticism. It derives instead from the attitude of craftsmanship common to workers in the applied arts whose activities featured in the 'secessionist' movement. Fuchs sees art with a supremely practical purpose, that of meeting the

psychological need for a 'higher quality of life'. The rhythmical movements of the actor's body at stage-level is experienced as an emotion and brings about an increase in the onlooker's vital rhythms. Hence, it is not the director, but the actor who creates the specifically theatrical emotion and 'drama is possible without words or sounds, but as a simple, rhythmic movement of the human body'. All the rest is embellishment. The director's task is to embellish the action, but in the first place he must acknowledge its value. Hence he must agree not to use the back of the stage, but encourage the actor's inclination to reduce as much as possible the distance between himself and his audience, since art is nothing objective, not a thing in itself, but a relationship: in the case of theatre a relationship between the actor and the audience from which there springs up a collective emotion that builds up society.

Thus the pre-eminence of the director, which Craig's view vigorously and unconditionally affirmed, very soon begins to be called in question at the theoretical level. At the practical level, however, his view, though much less imperious, was destined to establish itself and become widespread, so that it is only in very recent years that the notion of 'collective creativity' has secured a footing in actual theatrical production. The more significant personalities in the history of theatre throughout this period are almost all directors. Even the authors lose much of their prestige.

The Vieux Colombier, a small theatre on the Left Bank caused a stir throughout Europe between 1912 and 1924. Some of the greatest actors in French theatre between the two wars, such as Charles Dullin and Louis Jouvet, were formed in this school. Its founder, Jacques Copeau, denied out of hand the value of contemporary drama production, although Pirandello, Crommelynck, Yeats, Shaw, Eliot and Claudel were active during these years. He formed the idea of making something positive out of it by creating a permanent stage-setting to provide writers with a fixed reference-point. Shakespeare, for instance, in composing his tragedies, had had in mind the Elizabethan stage-complex. Copeau was director, promoter, educator; educating the audience no less than his actors. He strove to make theatre a cultural nucleus irradiating uplift and spiritual values, giving fresh impetus to the classic qualities of simplicity and moderation. Two centuries previously Ekhof had assigned to the actor the task of bringing to light the *mise en scène* implicit in the play, and at the start of his own career Copeau presented himself as a director-interpreter in this sense. However, whether or not he had done so

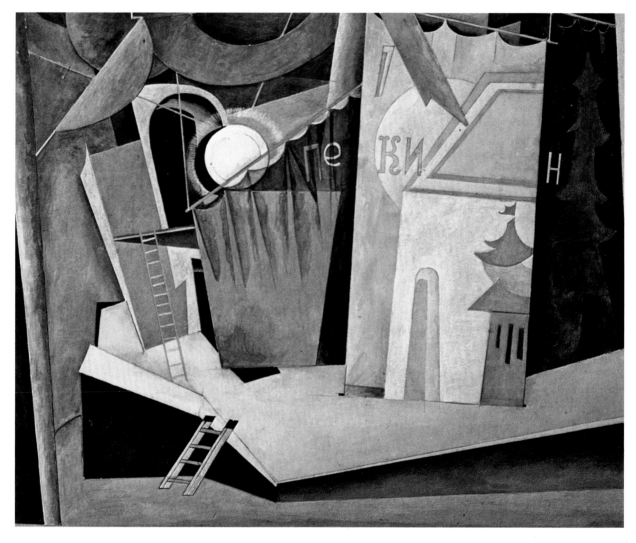

before, he finished up superimposing his own vision
onto the play.

In any case, the analysis of the theoretical problems
of theatre no longer focussed mainly on the area of
the mutual relationships between author, director
and actor, but on that of the very meaning of theatrical production as such, on the qualities to be
looked for in the content and structure of drama
itself. Because those doing the theorising were almost
always directors, their reflexions often provided the
foundations or served as justification for their
practical activities. In other words they were a sort
of 'Poetic'.

Obviously, this is also true of Appia, Craig and
Fuchs, but especially so of Copeau and other
contemporaries, particularly for the directors of
avant-garde Russian theatre, this having gone

through a very enthusiastic and fruitful period in the
years just before and immediately after the Soviet
Revolution.

The most renowned names in this school are those
of Meyerhold, Evreinov, Tairov and Vakhtangov,
whose roots link them closely in both theory and
practice with the activities of the Symbolists in the
West. The guiding principles in their work are the
notions of convention, style and theatre. The father
of the French Naturalist school, Zola, had held that
it was the breaking free from convention that marked
out the different stages in the growth of theatre.
Gordon Craig had replied that conventions are
indispensable for theatre: it is by a convention that
one allows one event to be translated in terms of
another and one specific period of time to be contained in a shorter one. Craig believed theatre must

be clearly and definitely a matter of convention, like Japanese theatre in which to carry one's hand to one's eyes has the conventional meaning of weeping.

For Vsevolod Meyerhold (1874–c 1940) concern for conventions is not so much an ingredient in new theatre, as the feature that serves to distinguish it as his theatre. The theatre of conventions means for him one that frees the actor of a clutter of scenery and places at his disposal a three-dimensional space; it bases the actors' speech and movements on rhythm and creates a stage-setting by slight touches the audience is asked to complete. Furthermore, the theatre of conventions concentrates on effective, sculptural groupings and does not strive for bewildering variety, but is satisfied with the essential minimum of movement, since the actual impression of movement is created much more by the arrangement of lines and colours.

Before the Revolution Meyerhold's productions certainly had these features. In the staging of Ibsen's play, *Hedda Gabler* (1906) the moments of silence and of immobility were very many indeed; the stage the actors had available was quite narrow and each was obliged to lend a certain statuesque quality to the character he represented—Brak, the judge, 'imitated the movements of a faun on a pedestal', and Hedda was enthroned like a queen on an enormous armchair covered with white furs. Throughout the whole duration of the very long scene in which Hedda meets Lövborg, her one-time lover, the characters did not even once change their posture or the direction of their gaze—they confronted each other from a distance, each at one end of the stage, and recited their lines in a tone that was cold and subdued.

A word in passing about the curious fate of Henrik Ibsen, the first and foremost Scandinavian dramatist, very popular throughout Europe at the end of the 19th century and a bone of contention between schools that were opposed in their principles. Antoine interpreted him in terms of the most complete Naturalism. His Italian disciple, Ermete Zacconi, used Ibsen as a testing-ground to display in mime his own knowledge of pathological medicine. On the other hand, Lugné-Poë and Meyerhold read into his plays a whole series of 'correspondences', symbols pointing to higher, absolute realities. A curious fate, though only apparently so, since after attempting a romantic reconstruction in a far-away world of the themes of the Nordic saga, Ibsen subsequently turned to folk-lore, and even those characters in his more mature works which seem to be taken directly from the contemporary scene preserve their profound ambiguity, which makes it possible to interpret them either as moral parables or, alternatively, precisely as metaphysical symbols. This ambiguity is even clearer in Strindberg, not just because of the express references to oriental theosophy to be found in such plays as *The Dream Play*, but also because it is possible without more ado to elevate the characters of *The Father* and *Miss Julie* into personified symbols of attitudes or of spiritual, eternal powers.

In what has been called the theatre of immobility *Hedda Gabler* was perhaps Meyerhold's greatest success and it would be fascinating to be able to be sure of the precise difference between such a production and Stanislavsky's staging of *A Month in the Country*, in which the actors were also motionless throughout a long interior dialogue that was concealed rather than expressed by the remarks they actually made. Meyerhold's efforts in this direction began, however, the previous year, 1905, when he produced Gerhart Hauptmann's *Schluck und Jau* in the Moscow Theatre Studio, opened by Stanislavsky to advance the work on his own system, though in practice it produced plays along quite different lines. Hauptmann is another playwright who can be defined as a Naturalist only in a very general sense. In this production of his play the striving for pictorial and rhythmical effects was laboured and in consequence superficial. Suffice it to recall the scene of two society ladies sitting on tall, box-shaped baskets and both embroidering the same long ribbon to a set rhythm as if they were a single person. Here the use of conventions passes over into another characteristic, that of style—two notions which Meyerhold sees as indissolubly linked. 'To bring out the style of a work or an event means to render explicit . . . by every means that serves to express it, the conjunction of a particular occurrence with the

age to which it belongs.' This conjunction is also an interpretation, a synthesis from a determinate standpoint: in staging Molière's *Don Juan*, Meyerhold summed up the 17th century as an age of luxury and ostentation.

It is immediately obvious how easily the use of symbols could be integrated into theatre of this sort and Meyerhold provided the demonstration in Strindberg's *There are Crimes and Crimes*, where he used chiefly colour for symbolic purposes. Yellow, which symbolises the sinfulness of Maurice and Henriette, first appears against the overall black of the setting when Maurice picks up a tie and gloves of this colour which have been given him as a present.

At the end the whole set is flooded with brilliant yellow.

Alexander Tairov (1885–1950) was quite clearly breaking through an already open door when he reaffirmed the concepts of symbolism and style at the theoretical level. However, the style he achieved in his productions in the Kamerny Theatre was notably different in structure from that of his rival. His enthusiasm for bodies in movement inclined him to attach considerable importance to the lay-out of the surface area of the stage, which, like Appia, he wanted to be in a position to offer resistance to such movement. Accordingly, he had it planned on different levels, interconnected by stairways and ramps. His own taste and that of his scene-designers, Alexander Vesnin and Alexandra Exter, came close to Cubism and caused him to regard the stage as a distant, crystalline world situated outside time. In this atmosphere reminiscent of pre-Homeric Greece he set plays as varied as Annensky's *Famira-Kifared* ('Famira the Harpist') and Racine's *Phèdre*. In point of fact, Tairov claimed that productions of the classics must take their topical relevance into account, must bring to light in them those features which had not lost their power to stimulate the emotions of a present-day audience. In theory then, he came close to the modern conception of interpretation. However, in his theatrical practice this modernity was principally a quality of his use of structure; it consisted in finding how a play could be fitted into a vision he already had waiting for it in his mind. However freely one may read Racine's masterpiece, it can never be appropriately referred to a setting of Asiatic barbarism. For the audience always realises it is in the auditorium of a theatre, faced by a theatrical production, and the actor tries to bring home this situation by the artificiality of his gestures. Hence this whole conception of theatre is a logical consequence of the insistence upon convention and style, and these in turn derive from polemical opposition to Naturalism and Psychologism. Thus the onlooker is invited to use his own creativity to complete the light touches of the production and ample scope is left for his imagination, which is no longer suffocated by a detailed and realistic composition. In this sense, theatre, style and conventions bring freedom from illusions. The avant-garde Russian theatre is, however, theatre-conscious in another sense; its inspiring motivation is often theatre itself, its history, traditions and modes of speech.

Nikolai Evreinov (1879–1953) was the most thorough theoretician of the concept of theatre, speaking of it as a pre-aesthetic fact to which one

N Ulyanov, Sketch for Meyerhold's 1905 production of Hauptmann's *Schluck und Jau* in the Moscow Art Theatre. Moscow,
Bakhrushin Theatre Museum

must look for the source of all the arts. He believed
it was necessary to steep oneself in the origins of
stagecraft, to derive inspiration from the ages of
real theatre, to obliterate from one's memory the
exorbitantly anti-theatrical 19th century. In this way
one would build up a splendid array of stage pro-
cedures and routines whose effectiveness could be
tested out and which would form the basis of a new
art of theatre. To this end Evreinov founded the
Antique Theatre to revive not the life, but the theatre
of days gone by. He arranged two cycles of productions in it (1907–08 and 1911–12) devoted to
medieval theatre and to Spanish theatre of the
Golden Age, striving to re-enact the theatre of those
days with scholarly accuracy, but above all as a
labour of love.

Evreinov also used theatre to hold a satirical
discussion about its own contemporary condition.
He staged numerous productions of this sort in the
Cabaret of the Curved Mirror, including *Vampuka,
the African Bride*, a skit on opera and the customary
way of performing it, and four presentations of the
first act of Gogol's *Inspector General*, one as Stanislavsky would have done it, another imitating the
celebrated German director Max Reinhardt of whom
one could say almost anything except that he had
any definite style, a third was Gordon Craig's vision
of another world in the midst of screens towering up
steeply heavenwards and the fourth one was a
traditional production. Undoubtedly, however, *The
Fourth Wall* was the most agreeable piece in the
series, a biting satire on Naturalist theatre. A
director was shown trying to stage Gounod's operatic version of Goethe's *Faust, Part I* as realistically as
possible—to this end he omits Faust's rejuvenation,
excludes Mephistopheles as a character, cuts out
Gounod's music, has his actors speak German
because the action is set in that country and even
finds it necessary to erect a fourth wall between the
actors and their audience, since only a stage convention quite unworthy of *Faust* had caused it ever
to be pulled down. The audience could see the
actors' shadows through a window, but could not
hear what they were saying.

Finally Evreinov worked out the theory of a
drama-form for the stage called 'monodrama' and
produced an actual example. All the characters were
shown through the eyes of the protagonist, so that if
he was in love, the girl would be portrayed as an
angel, and in opposing their love her father would be
seen as a real monster. It was a curious anticipation
of a typical device used in films, though here seeing
things through the eyes of one of the characters
becomes a physical reality—the camera replaces

him and shows us what he actually sees—while in
monodrama the leading character seems to be surrounded by his own fantasies.

The idea of pure theatre, in the sense suggested by
Evreinov's experiments, lies behind one of the most
important productions of the Russian avant-garde
when Eugene Vakhtangov (1883–1922) staged Carlo
Gozzi's *Princess Turandot* in the Third Studio of the
Moscow Art Theatre. In theory this was not so much
to have shown Gozzi's fable, as the *commedia
dell'arte* players who had performed it in the 18th
century, and from this standpoint there was an
immediate link with Evreinov's work. However, in
practice there was much more to it. The theatre was
thought of as a celebration, an evening passed
happily among friends: the actor of today may be
the audience of tomorrow, when the craftsman and
the factory worker show him, in turn, what they
have produced. Accordingly, the actors welcomed
their audience individually, showed them to their
seats as they arrived, stayed and chatted with them
for a while. The actors wore tails, and the actresses
long evening-gowns; they were dressed for a party,
but in the fashion of today. The show was heralded

by four masked-characters from the *commedia dell'arte*: Truffaldino, Pantaloon, Brighella and Tartaglia. As the curtain rose the actors moved towards the platform by way of the steep ramp set into the stage, on which were heaped a vast quantity of properties which were to be used to make the costumes. One towel became a white beard, another a turban, a table-cloth served as a cloak. There were also exotic silk trousers and other parts of real costumes, but the modern evening dress was always showing underneath. Thus, the actors did not pretend to be the *commedia dell'arte* players, at least not beyond the limits in which these could be regarded as symbolising the art of theatre; they remained themselves as actors, plying their trade with pleasure, courtesy and refinement. The rhythmical and frequently acrobatic virtuoso skill put into the performance carried the same message: our work is complete and perfect, because such is our duty to our audience. The spectators were shown all the secrets of the stage. A group of girl-clowns, the stage-servants of oriental theatre, kept coming on carrying properties or altering the appearance of the stage by means of hangings and other features.

The curtain was closed only between the fourth and fifth acts, while the clowns performed a pantomime recapitulating what had happened and what was still to come. However, their ending was not the real ending of the comedy, but a sad one: this was the only trick played on the audience to be able to give them a pleasant surprise.

Vakhtangov's *Princess Turandot* was produced in 1922, when the Revolution had succeeded and the Soviet state was an incontrovertible fact. The leading figures in avant-garde theatre had supported it, chief amongst them Vsevolod Meyerhold, who shortly became director of a theatre named after him as well as of the Section of the Cultural Commission in charge of theatrical affairs.

Meyerhold rejected forthwith the aestheticist, symbolist, static theatre of his previous style, but held on to his fundamental principles: opposition to Naturalism and Psychologism (not unreasonably, he now defined these as typical forms of bourgeois culture), pure theatre and the use of conventions. These principles, however, had to be used to create a new sort of theatre in keeping with the new themes that had emerged in the Revolution of the Proletar-

iat. The enchanted rhythm of his earlier productions and their symbolic conjunctions of lines and colours could no longer suffice. The need was for something to express enthusiasm in working to build up the new society of the proletariat and the joy of living in a world that had been liberated from class domination. To meet this requirement the new formula was Constructivism and Bio-mechanics. Scenery had no longer to be the setting in which the actor moved, but the machine he used for his work—which was to carry Appia's thesis to extremes. 'The place of descriptive scenery was taken by the machine and this allowed stage movements to be represented with an abundance and variety hitherto unknown. . . . Every single part of the machine was set in operation and any purely decorative features were eliminated. . . . The stage was transformed into a framework to be given its shape by means of objects'; a structure comprising poles, slides, stilts, huge wheels and ladders, which actors skilled in Bio-mechanics and advanced acrobatics made use of to play their parts in a frenzied rhythm of physical action.

The major achievements of Meyerhold in an uninterrupted series of productions inspired by Constructivism and Bio-mechanics were the performances of Ostrovsky's *The Forest* and of Crommelynck's tragic farce *Le cocu magnifique* ('The Splendid Cuckold'). In the latter, Bruno's jealousy induces him to force his wife to give herself to all the men of the village, without his even then being able to furnish any proof of her infidelity. This was performed on a scaffolding made out of a ladder, a slide, platforms and revolving doors behind which revolving wheels and mill-paddles marked the increasing tension in the drama. The actors had no make-up and wore blue overalls. Their acting was at lightning speed, especially in large group scenes, but their voices were unusually sweet and melodious. The protagonist was invariably accompanied by his *alter ego* who re-enacted in mime all the anguish he was suffering. The action shifted continually from one level to another and, one might say, from one piece of equipment to the next.

However, not all of Meyerhold's productions after the Revolution were along Constructivist and Bio-mechanical lines. Many of them reveal the stature of a Meyerhold less restricted by a formula, more aware of actual content, more liberated in his imagination, in a word, richer and more mature. This is particularly true of plays whose subject is the criticism of social life in the past—Ehrenburg's *Trust D.E.*, Faiko's *The Teacher Bubus*, and Erdmann's *The Mandate*.

In 1926 Meyerhold staged Gogol's *Inspector General*. If in Gogol's work the portrait of the corruption in the society and the bureaucracy of the old régime was already savage, in Meyerhold's production it became hypnotically hallucinating. The arrival of the mysterious inspector is transferred from the provincial town in which Gogol had set it, to St Petersburg, and the action then unfolds in fifteen pictures in which are inserted many lines taken from Gogol's other works, especially from *Dead Souls*, as if to offer a synthesis of all the author said about the decadence of Russia in the past. In front of a semicircular structure, comprising fifteen doors, was placed a small platform, 10 feet by 16 feet, which was covered with different furnishings for each picture, to give the impression of moving from one room to the next in the palace where the drama takes place. The whole stage was used only here and there; when, for instance, the bureaucrats offer money to Khlestakov, they pop out of the doors at the back of the stage like so many robots from a cuckoo-clock, and hold out to the fake inspector rolls of banknotes, which he siezes like a greedy automaton. Such moments aside, the action, which was always tightly-knit, was concentrated on the central platform, and the restricted space obliged the actors to move with meticulous care and self-control. All the main characters were transported into an atmosphere of the grotesque bordering on the macabre, and their humanity was degraded to the level of the wild beast, or encapsulated in the mechanical gestures of a robot. Khlestakov and the mayor were accompanied all the time by their ghostly doubles, and Anna Andreyevna by a group of petty officials paying court to her and drawing the audience's attention to the persistent, unsated lusts of this nymphomaniac. Khlestakov's crudity passed all bounds without the refined society into which this little cheat had introduced himself ever seeming even to notice it—he belched, scratched, yawned, spat and, while he was drunk, danced holding a lady in a bear-hug, almost stripping her naked in his efforts to keep his balance. Khlestakov's servant, Ossip, alone in all this decadence preserved intact his healthy self-confidence as a peasant, a concession to the incoming myth of the positive hero.

However, Meyerhold's star was about to decline. As a person he was not morally beyond reproach, but he had sincerity and enthusiasm. As an artist he came close to Reinhardt in the restless turmoil of his imagination and to Craig in his close attention to style. Thanks to Zhdanov the doctrine of Socialist Realism was affirmed in the Soviet Union and was accompanied by a renewed cult of the classics ('Let's get back to Ostrovsky!'). The ageing Stanislavsky was chosen to be high-priest in this theatre and represented the high-water mark of a middle-class vogue for psychological analysis. Meyerhold was obliged to go in for self-criticism to begin with, but never demeaned himself and was later imprisoned and executed.

Chapter 25

THEATRE AND POLITICAL STRIFE

In *The Inspector General* one can already speak of political theatre. Its extremely tendentious interpretation of history, which no sort of realism could ever have succeeded in producing, set out to create a fresh awareness and to indicate, by means of contrast, the ideals of a new civilisation. However, in the years that followed Meyerhold applied himself with enthusiasm to much more burning issues in the political struggle. Together with Mayakovsky he tackled topical problems within the Soviet state: the survival of the *petit bourgeois* mentality (*The Bedbug*, 1929) and the abuses of bureaucracy (*The Bath-house*, 1930). Meyerhold had already produced Mayakovsky's *Mystery-Bouffe* and accepted the author's collaboration in staging these two plays, something he did on no other occasion. There resulted two strong, hard-hitting productions in which the satire was no longer aimed at the past, but at distortions within the present situation. In *The Bath-house* the haughty bureaucrat was portrayed 'as a clumsy, dim-witted clown' at whose doors petitioners had to wait for ages and changed into puppets.

In the Soviet Union real political theatre died with Meyerhold to be replaced by the other-triumphant exaltation of her revolutionary conquests. Yet during the Revolution and in the years immediately following, political theatre in the U.S.S.R. was the subject of other, even more enthusiastic experiments. In keeping with the principle that the revolutionary proletariat was well able to work out its own culture for itself, the 'Organisation for Proletarian Culture' (*Proletkult*), under the theoretical guidance of A Bogdanov, sought to strike out along radically new lines in the arts. It was, however, soon liquidated because it had tried to be completely independent of the government and of the party-machine. Because of its social character the theatre was seen immediately as the ideal means of securing the cultural collaboration of the masses and so as an intrinsic part of the organs of government and of the party-machine. Workers' theatres sprang up almost everywhere. They were called self-activating, in the sense of not taking over the methods of the professional theatre and of working out their own instead, inspired more by demonstrations in the streets, festivals, collective singing, public debates and the 'living newspapers' already put on stage by Red Army soldiers. Such productions provided machinery for the analysis of the political issues of the day and were likewise the first skirmishes in a real cultural revolution which Meyerhold's October theatrical manifesto had certainly not been able to bring about.

It was in the context of the Proletkult that Sergei Eisenstein, subsequently a great film-director, gained his first practical experience, and evolved his idea of 'attraction' as a strong, emotional feeling imposed upon the audience, in productions for which he very successfully borrowed from popular cultural sources anything from a song to a horse-riding stunt. However, his very presence in the Proletkult already signalled the intellectuals' counter-attack, and Soviet

Scene from Brecht's *Mother Courage* in the Berliner Ensemble.
Photo: Ugo Mulas

303

V Kiselev, Characters from Mayakovsky's *Mystery-Bouffe*: the Menshevik, the Devil, the Frenchman and the Empire, 1921. Moscow, State Central Theatre Library

proletarian theatre had very soon to yield to professional expertise.

However, it was in Germany, rather than in the Soviet Union, that theatre was deliberately and systematically used as a weapon in the political conflict. The cultural as well as the social conditions for such a step were certainly not lacking. The abortive revolution of 1919 had left behind a strong proletarian movement which felt betrayed rather than defeated. Its best leaders, Karl Liebknecht and Rosa Luxemburg, had been assassinated but their spiritual presence was stronger than ever. The excessively severe economic crisis favoured social conflict; reactionary *petit bourgeois* and military movements set themselves to stir up trouble. German theatre had, in any case, been flourishing strongly since before the war. The activities of Georg Fuchs in connection with the Munich Secessionist movement have been mentioned already. Max Reinhardt (1873–1943), the great Austrian-born director who became the greatest force in the German-speaking theatre and exerted a powerful influence in other countries as well, had three theatres at his disposal in Berlin the Deutsches Theater (German Theatre), the Kammerspiele (Chamber Theatre) and the Grosses Schauspielhaus (Great Playhouse). There and in the theatres he controlled at various times in such places as Vienna and Salzburg he was able to give free rein to his extremely lively and eclectic imagination, which provided him with ever new solutions to production problems and enabled him to look at the spatial relationship between stage and auditorium in a fresh light. In 1909–10 he had transformed the vast Olympia Hall in London into a Gothic cathedral to accommodate both actors and spectators (in *The Miracle*) and he had produced Sophocles' *Oedipus Rex* in a circus, using the arena like the orchestra in antiquity and setting up as scenery on a monumental scale columns and ranges of steps, while using lights to organise the space. Reinhardt, moreover, had also been a disciple of Otto Brahm who had produced Gerhart Hauptmann's *Die Weber* ('The Weavers'; 1892) and had since the end of the 19th century brought the very lowest classes onto the stage in a series of productions associated with the Naturalist ideas of Zola and Antoine, thus confronting his audience with urgent social problems.

A more obviously political line of thought had been introduced into the theatre of the Expressionist Movement. This was possibly the only one of all the avant-garde movements to state clearly not only its aesthetic ideals, but also its moral stance which aimed at the free expression of the human personality. It was in the main the second generation in the movement, the 'war-time Expressionists', who imparted a more or less decided tone of propaganda to much of their artistic and especially their theatrical output, hitting out against warfare and also against the capitalist suppression of the personality. If their efforts were later reduced to sentimental humanitarian appeals instead of practical suggestions for the struggle, this was due to the mystical element, which was always to be found even in the most politically aware of the Expressionist writers, of whom in addition to Wedekind and Hasenclever, we can mention particularly, Fritz von Unruh, Georg Kaiser, Reinhard Göring and, above all, Ernst Toller.

In *Die Wandlung* ('Transmutation'; 1919), one of Toller's early plays, warfare and social structures were made the subject of the accusations voiced by the Veteran. This was produced at the Tribüne under the direction of Karl Heinz Martin, who provided a dense, close-knit setting, with a minimum of ineffectual gestures and the scenery the barest hint of a suggestion—the bars of a window, a whitewashed wall, a fire. A few years later, in 1927, his maturest and most committed play, *Hoppla, We Live!*, was staged by Erwin Piscator. In this the Expressionist myth of man's basic goodness is replaced by pessimistic depression, soon to be fully justified by the suicide of the German social-democracy and the rise of Hitler.

It is usual to pick out Piscator as the first to provide political theatre with a philosophy and a form of its own. First of all, he maintains that the word 'art' is to be outlawed from the programme of the political theatre since, especially in recent years, theoreticians and directors of bourgeois theatre have rinsed out their mouths with it quite a lot. Piscator did not intend to play the artist, but the politician, that is 'conscientiously to acknowledge the need for the class-struggle and to broadcast the idea of it'. This does not mean one can afford to ignore questions of theatrical form, since to produce theatre in the raw would be poor workmanship and a betrayal of one's own revolutionary mission. However, it does mean that one must establish a new relationship with one's public, based on one's educational aims at the rational level—not stirring up aesthetic or sentimental feelings, but triggering off the working-class spectator's dynamic desire to know. Bourgeois theatre has thrived for centuries on the false assumption that spectators have no intrinsic rôle in production, when in fact they have to become its innermost soul. Piscator goes so far as to claim, though in a self-contradictory way, that proletarian

theatre will manage without professional actors, because the diffusion and further appreciation of the Communist ideal cannot be the task of one individual profession, but is the aspiration of the whole collectivity. However, he does not develop this fundamental point. Instead he works out in theory and practice a new model for theatrical productions, adapted to political and social propaganda and analysis, a model quite foreign to any interest in art as such: he never pauses even for a moment to ask what is theatre, what elements it comprises and what determines its nature.

Piscator is also opposed to Naturalism, which in his opinion cannot express the demands of the masses. From the formal standpoint the new idea of theatre is based on the latest advances in stage-technique: electric lights, rotating scenery and the like. Political theatre productions must not merely be able to portray individual events, but to analyse their social and economic implications and place particular facts in their historical context. Thus the problem became that of enlarging the dramatic picture to epic proportions by introducing into it narrative and descriptive features. To this end Piscator proposed the organisation of the action on stage in several dimensions of communication and the introduction into the production of explanatory matter, posters, slides and sequences on film. A dialectical or causal link brought together these different elements, so that the seemingly private 'event' being enacted on the stage could be understood as the effect of some apparently remote cause —historical events projected on film, or documented by slides and written material. Piscator's ultimate aim was to bring together the entire history of the globe in a vast network of connections and relationships and he showed this, almost in a parable, in the most ambitious of all his productions, *Rasputin*, staged in November 1927. The scenery comprised a huge canvas hemisphere representing the world, and the segments of which it was composed could open quickly to allow one or other section of the stage to be seen as the scenes of the play were enacted there. Films were also projected onto the hemisphere, the curvature of which distorted the view, and these chronicled the great military and political events that had in any way been connected with Rasputin's career at the Romanov court, so that the fate of this monk, healer and minister was turned into a survey of the destiny of Europe. The film played three rôles. It was educational, because it communicated objective facts, enlarged the scope of the subject-matter in space and time in order to show how the events portrayed on stage depended on others at a distance. It was dramatic, because it was a substitute for acting scenes whose presentation on stage would have been artificial and hardly convincing. It was interpretative, because it addressed the audience directly to offer criticism, make accusations, or explain what was happening—in this latter case, the film was not projected onto the hemisphere, but over to the side, as a sort of time-chart of events.

Not all of Piscator's productions had the spectacular and elaborate features or the baroque grandeur of *Rasputin* (the idea of portraying the world in its entirety was certainly baroque), however, the key idea was the same in all of them. In Toller's *Hoppla, We Live!*, as Thomas awakes from the long-standing lethargy of his madness and discovers his comrades-in-arms from the days of the revolutionary struggle all encapsulated in the social system, this is related dramatically to that war and revolution, as the

305

principal events in them are projected on film. The stage-set for *Konjunktur* (1928), a large oil-rig, was built up before the audience's very eyes, and the construction of it marked out the different stages in the dramatic search for oil, while the film illustrated the interests of the great imperialist financiers. What effective political meaning could have attached to such productions is hard to say: the audience must have felt inevitably crushed by events greater than themselves and may have been conditioned to accept an unyielding determinism, despite any references that were made to the value of a revolutionary spirit of initiative. However, their informational value was undoubtedly considerable ('unleashing the working-class audience's desire to know'), because Piscator was a genius in arranging his enormous amount of material very clearly and so driving his point home.

Piscator's writings, though only here and there, contain many of the ideas that are central to Bertolt Brecht's theatrical ideals and practice, such as those of 'epic theatre' and 'alienated performance'. To discuss who first had these ideas would be absurd. Between 1925 and 1929 Piscator and Brecht worked

Reigbert, Sketch for the 1919 Kiel production of Hasenclever's *The Son*. Munich, Theatermuseum

Reigbert, Sketch for Brecht's *Drums in the Night*. Munich, Theatermuseum

Two scenes from Erich Engel's 1928 production of Brecht's *Threepenny Opera* in the Theater am Schiffbauerdamm: Macheath in prison with both his fiancées; and Macheath's hanging. Munich, Bilderdienst Süddeutscher Verlag

as neighbours and on the basis of a shared ideology. What is necessary is to emphasise the importance of these ideas for the construction of politically meaningful theatre.

Brecht's career was longer and more intricate than that of Piscator, who fled to America with the advent of Nazism and being no longer able to produce plays eventually opened a school there, Judith Malina, the promoter of The Living Theatre, being one of the pupils. Brecht was born in Augsburg in February 1898, was first a theatre critic and briefly a literary adviser to the Munich *Kammerspiele*, but he soon went to Berlin where he established himself as a promising young playwright, a keen polemicist for the New Drama (his own) and the author of a smash hit, *The Threepenny Opera* (1928). When Hitler came to power he fled first to Scandinavia and then to America, where he worked—not very successfully—in Hollywood. Having managed to get around the witch-hunting Un-American Activities Committee, he eventually returned to Europe. After a short stay in Switzerland, he settled down in East Berlin where he helped to found a powerful new theatre company, the Berliner Ensemble, in

Scene from Brecht's *Mother Courage* in the Berliner Ensemble. Photo: Ugo Mulas

1949. Poet and novelist, as well as playwright and director, he died in 1956, and was among the chief personalities in contemporary theatre.

His dramatic output extends from *Baal*, which he wrote in 1918, up to 1953 and centres, from the ideological if not the theatrical point of view, around the years 1928–33 when he produced a series of what he called didactic pieces (*Lehrstücke*): *The Yea-sayer and the Nay-sayer*, *The Exception and the Rule*, *The Horatii and the Curiatii* and *The Measure Taken* —short plays in which one particular moral or political question was discussed and usually worked out by a sort of court-case.

Of course there are pieces which are not concerned with the rehabilitation of the dramatic character but have a rather more complex, well-constructed plot, and tend to be richer and more vibrant than the didactic pieces. However, it is in these latter that Brecht provides the clearest examples of what he meant by political theatre as an instrument of dialectical understanding and for Marxist-Leninist analysis. The didactic pieces are not so much for the audience as for the actors who, in confronting actively and directly the existing problem, can succeed in grasping its real terms and so can point to possible solutions which are not necessarily the author's own.

The didactic pieces also clarify the basic notion of Brecht's approach to theatre: 'alienation'. This is especially true of *The Measure Taken*. Four Communist activists take it in turns to play the part of their dead comrade and to explain why they had to murder him. To act in an alienated (or distanced) way means that the actor avoids total, uncritical identification with the character he is portraying; by standing away from him he can in a sense be said to be judging him. Such acting is to some extent abstract, or at any rate cool rather than highly emotional. It does not truly present everything that was or might have been the achievement of the person in question, but only those deeds thought essential for an understanding of why he must have acted in one particular way, or necessary for an analysis of the problem on the table. The stage-setting, too, will not give a reliable picture of the specific surroundings, but will only show its characteristic or relevant features. The ideas and practical contributions of Casper Neher were decisive in the planning and detailed execution of Brecht's own scene-settings, which instead of complete scenes comprised various stage-properties, but yet, as far as possible, had to be real, so that one could sense in them the density of human effort that had fashioned them and then worn them out by constant use. Particularly after he had returned to Europe and had helped to found the Berliner Ensemble, as Brecht developed his leanings towards superb craftsmanship in production, this preference for the real property which, like the whole performance, was the work of a skilled craftsman, proved to be the hallmark of authenticity marking out his own stage practice.

To the alienation of the actors, who remain distinct from the characters they play, there corresponds the alienation of the audience, who are always fully aware that they are in the theatre not to participate in a real happening without being noticed and almost by accident, but to witness the re-enactment of a piece worked out in a laboratory. Their pleasure in so doing is that most typical of modern man, living in a scientific age; it is delight in knowledge. It was only in 1948, after his work with didactic pieces was long over and done with, that Brecht re-introduced this idea of pleasure (*Spass*) into his *Short Organon for the Theatre* (his breviary of theatrical aesthetics). The theatre-goer's (partial) detachment from the characters of the stage action, which keeps part of his mind free for critical thought instead of being swamped by unreflecting emotion, is reinforced by other ingredients in the production in conflict with one another: the singing clashes with the speech, the scenery with the use of mime, etc. Brecht's epic style of production consists entirely of dialectical contradictions with regard to which the audience is challenged to take up a position.

The idea of epic is closely linked with that of alienation: the narrative mode is one designed to put the spectator at one remove from the action. Brecht sees a clash between epic and dramatic theatre. The scenes in epic theatre are not tied together in the close-meshed weave of the well-made play but they are separate as dialectical elements. Placards, subtitles or other means are used to tell the audience the content of each scene, so that there is no build up of tension about how it will end, but attention is focussed on the mechanism, on how one thing leads to another, on the sort of causality at work, on the intermeshing of circumstances.

For Brecht, as for Piscator, political theatre is a tool in the understanding of social mechanisms. This mechanism, however, is not understood by showing the causes and their effects, or by juxtaposing public and private events, but rather by studying the repercussions of the overall organisation in some particular case. There is no need to portray the great manufacturers of arms in order to analyse war as a source of profit. It is enough to take the poor sutler, Mother Courage, since, if she is to survive in her miserable business, she must sacrifice all her sons to Moloch. Nevertheless Brecht does not, any more than Piscator, develop the theme that could have been a really solid basis for political theatre, taking this to mean not just theatre about political subjects, but theatre that is political activity. It is only for a fleeting moment that he realises reality is understood by living it, not by looking on, so that only the actor (obviously in a very general sense) can grasp completely the mechanisms in the event being analysed. In our century theatre as something to watch is very definitely not enough to communicate any such analysis. Piscator's efforts to take theatre beyond itself prove this.

308

Chapter 26

The Living Theatre, New York, produce *Frankenstein*, seen here in close-up detail. The piece was performed in the Teatro La Perla for the 1965 Venice XXIV International Festival of Drama. The photo is the copyright of the Venice Museo della Biennale

THE DISINTEGRATION OF THEATRICAL SPACE

In his small Symbolist Théâtre de l' Œuvre, on 10 December 1896, Lugné-Poë had produced Alfred Jarry's *Ubu roi*, a strained, compelling play of a grotesque sort, inspired by Shakespeare's *Macbeth*. The production had taken its cue from the poverty of the Elizabethan theatre and had had to be extremely unpretentious. The actors were supposed to resemble puppets and their movements were meant to be abrupt and mechanical. The ways in which everything was described in mime gave a strong impression of unreality to the performance. One actor played the door, as an actor acts as wall in *A Midsummer Night's Dream*. A screen symbolised the hill that a group of soldiers had to march down. The costumes were childish and bizarre. Mère Ubu, a Lady Macbeth of no account, was dressed as a serving-girl; Bougrelas as a baby with a bonnet and petticoat; actors on hobby-horses were used to represent cavalry. The production was meant to break up in confusion, which had been provided for with mathematical precision. However, when Ubu in a steel-grey gown and wearing a bowler-hat moved forward from the back of the stage towards the audience, stretched out his arm, and shouted his first line, '*Merdre!*' the auditorium was in uproar and the performance became a battle led by the leading-actor, Firmin Gémier, who later founded a French popular theatre (*Théâtre ambulant*). This production contained many of the chief features of the second avant-garde: violent aggression against the audience, absurdity, sketchy symbolism, the grotesque carried to the extremes of tragedy, a breakdown in the use of language with too many neologisms and meaningless expressions, cruelty and the restriction of scenery to a few token features.

Jarry and Lugné-Poë's performance was a clear anticipation of the corrosive nihilism of the Dadaists. In the course of soirées rather than productions, in 1920, the authors and their friends, people like Tristan Tzara, Philippe Soupault, Georges Ribemont-Dessaignes, played the leading rôles, did their utmost to make language and logic break down, went so far as to make the performance as such disintegrate and offered a direct challenge to their audience, something the Italian Futurists also did, though with rather less perspicacity.

To start off with, Antonin Artaud, who in 1926 founded a theatre named after Jarry, was not far from the Dadaist position (he actually joined and worked for the Surrealist Movement). He himself was born in Marseilles in 1896 and died in a mental-hospital in 1948. Despite his many attempts to bring theatrical ventures to life, he never succeeded in producing anything sufficiently complete and solid to provoke any appreciable reaction, not even as a response to a direct challenge. Nor did his own staging of his only play, *The Cenci*, based on a 16th century theme earlier treated by Shelley and produced by Paul Fort at the Théâtre d'Art (the story of old Count Cenci's cold, incestuous passion for his daughter, Beatrice), attract much favourable attention. Nevertheless, it is impossible to exaggerate the

O Schlemmer, *Das triadische Ballet*. Zürich, Kunstgewerbe-museum. This ballet, created in 1912, was performed at the Bauhaus in 1923. It consists of three parts that form a structure of stylised dances which develop from the comic to the serious. First there is a gay burlesque against a background of lemon yellow. Next, in a pink setting, something ceremonious and solemn. The third part is a mystical fantasy set in black. Schlemmer intended his dancers' bodies to represent the geometrical laws of space, and transformed their human shape into cuboid forms. They were also to represent the functional laws of the body and its movement, to be symbols of metaphysically expressive forms

influence of Artaud on the development ot contemporary theatre. This, however, is due solely to his theoretical writings, 'discovered' by men of the theatre after the publication of his complete works, which began in 1955 for mainly literary reasons; Artaud wrote poems and novels, as well as essays.

Theatre for Artaud is a magical operation, culture that is committed and actively involved. Its function is to lance our collective abscesses, to bring to the surface all the rot, all the filth into which individuals and societies have settled down. Hence, it is sombre and bloody. It is also cruel because it brings out the hidden drama and makes us even physically aware of the way we are the slaves of metaphysically necessary laws, so that out bodily and spiritual lives are constantly at risk.

Artaud's converts of the 'Sixties enthusiastically accepted and developed these general remarks, even though they were out of date, and intrinsically related to the Paris cultural scene of the 'Thirties, which was dominated by André Breton's Surrealist Movement. Peter Brook and Charles Marowitz in England stand out among Artaud's converts for the seriousness of their efforts to understand him. In 1964 they organised a series of productions under the very title of Theatre of Cruelty, which was a sort of Artaudian rally: 'Artaud for Artaud's sake'. However, Artaud's most fruitful suggestions related to stage-craft, though he had never himself played the lead. Theatre for him is not a representation, but a reality, although in a world apart. Hence, the value of its constituents resides not in what they signify, but in what they are. Artaud's imagination was fired with the possibility of a theatre he had never seen but could not forget. In it, characters enlarged to the proportions of giant puppets moved in a continually changing atmosphere of lights, pictures, sounds, movements and noises. It would be wrong to mention a stage: for this performance the audience 'will sit in the middle on swivel-chairs. The individual scenes will be acted with a white-washed wall as background. . . . Galleries above will allow the actors to pursue each other around different parts of the auditorium.' As in primitive theatre 'there will once again be direct communication between members of the audience, and between individual spectators and actors, so that the audience reaches the thick of the action and becomes fully involved.'

The magic word had been spoken: involvement. The audience is no longer outside but inside what is going on. The actors act and speak in the midst of their audience and a direct, physical relationship is set up between them both. The performance is no longer a distant vision. Eventually, theatre is no longer performance, if this is taken to mean something to be looked at, something spectacular—the intangible, carefully framed, finished work of art that was so perfectly represented by Italian-style theatre in which the proscenium arch was the frame, the threshold not to be crossed. Such a concept was no longer tenable. The new relationship which had been created demanded a different setting and there was intense research in this direction during the years in which Artaud was working out his vision of the new theatre. Almost always, however, these theories remained unrealised.

We have already mentioned such productions as Max Reinhardt's *The Miracle*. Reinhardt himself made use of such theatres as the Grosses Schauspielhaus in Berlin, built in 1919 by Hans Poelzig, which carried the seeds of a new approach: the stage was enclosed by a much elongated, rectangular frame, but it was also connected by steps to a platform in the stalls which was a sort of extension of the stage. Walter Gropius was in charge of the great Bauhaus complex for architecture and the applied arts, where Oskar Schlemmer was trying to determine the laws for the movement in space of puppets involved in a performance, or of actors whose bodies were so 'made-up' as to have become 'abstractions'. In 1927 Gropius worked out for Piscator a project for a 'total theatre'. In this the stage could either be set in the Italian fashion at the end of the great, elliptical amphitheatre or, by removing some of the seats, it could be a circular platform projecting out into the auditorium like the orchestra in a Greek theatre, so that the audience sat two-thirds of the way round it. Alternatively, a large platform containing the front rows of seats and the small platform already mentioned as replacing the Italian-style stage could be all swung round through 180 degrees to bring it, circus-fashion, into the centre of the building.

Meyerhold had also felt hampered by the old layout and M Barckin and S Vakhtangov, the architects, had drawn up for him the project of a small, elliptical theatre similar to that of Gropius, with the audience arranged on rows of steps running two-thirds of the way round the perimeter, leaving plenty of free space for a sort of orchestra, containing two circular platforms additional to two further platforms set in against the segment of wall opposite the auditorium.

In America, Norman Bel Geddes, architect, scene-designer and director, planned in 1928 a circular stage for the Repertory Theatre. From as far back as 1919 in France Copeau and Jouvet had arranged the auditorium of the Vieux Colombier in such a way that the stage sloped down towards the stalls, and now Edouard Autant and Louise Lara in their small theatre, Art et Action, took over the ideas worked out by a Pole, Szymon Syrkus. He had created a sort of simultaneous theatre in a village near Warsaw by arranging a hall with different stage-platforms in different places. The positioning of the stages, as well as of the actors, was variable and the action took place simultaneously on two or more such stages.

This new lay-out of the theatre building certainly offered the possibility of locating the performance in a different way, but if we consider it closely, the actors are still isolated from the audience; whether the action is set in the centre, or high up, or to one side of the theatre, it always has a place of its own. The points of view were different now and not so rigidly fixed, but the theatrical event is still reduced to an object of contemplation.

Any more radical solution was bound to bring the actors into direct contact with their public, abolishing any boundary that made them seem isolated. Precedents were not lacking in the history of theatre, especially in the Middle Ages and the 17th century. Yet the European productions of The Living Theatre are certainly the clearest and most radical illustrations of this line of approach.

Before arriving in Europe from the United States, from which they had had to take flight for economic reasons and also because of the many insults heaped upon them, the Living Theatre had experienced in New York the conditions that are the story of many underground theatres. Julian Beck and his wife Judith Malina had begun to work in theatre in 1947, when still very young, first using their own apartment, then a small theatre in Cherry Lane, then an attic and

Three aspects of Jerzy Grotowski's production of Calderón-Słowacki's *The Constant Prince*. Photographs by Lionello Fabbri. The relationship between the action and the audience 'is half-way between the arena and the operating-theatre. . . . It can seem like watching blood-sports . . . or a surgical operation'. In this, as in all Grotowski's productions, the main character becomes the victim in some rite of expiation, but is simultaneously a rebel: thus, he evokes a whole series of myths, from Prometheus to Christ

finally a warehouse. In this they had been able to put on quite ambitious productions, such as Jack Gelber's *The Connection*, which introduces us to a meeting of drug-addicts, and *The Theatre of Chance*. In this the order of the lines is decided by drawing lots, because of the musician John Cage's open-ended theory of art which is remotely inspired by Mallarmé. Even more important were the productions of the savagely realistic *The Brig* by Kenneth Brown, a day in a naval prison, and of Brecht's *A Man is a Man*. The protagonist, Galy Gay, transformed out of a poor porter into a savage soldier, was presented as a man who was perfectly and clearly aware of his own mistakes which he pointed out himself on stage.

The fame of The Living Theatre had spread to Europe by 1960 and earned the company an invitation to take part in the Théâtre des Nations festival in Paris in 1961. However, they did not finally leave America till 1964. The interest immediately aroused in Europe was enormous, although their productions were not, at first sight, remarkable: *Mysteries—and Smaller Pieces* was just a series of mimed exercises which sometimes turned on the audience in an aggressive way and in Genêt's *The Maids*, the chamber-maids were played by male actors. However, in 1965 at the Venice Festival they presented *Frankenstein*, very vaguely inspired by Mary Shelley's supernatural story. After remaining for a long time motionless on stage, where an experiment in levitation was in progress, the actors jumped out into the stalls, some to escape, others to capture those who were trying to; they chased each other

among the audience with ferocious cries, sometimes falling all over people. Even if the spectator did not appreciate the danger of the hunt, he at least experienced his own. Subsequently the prisoners were put to death in a variety of ways to enable Doctor Frankenstein to build his monster whose body was outlined by a great network of tubes erected on the stage.

Antigone was performed in 1967, Brecht's adaptation of Sophocles' tragedy, on the translation of which Judith Malina had been working since 1961. In a sense the relationship between the stage and the auditorium was institutionalised in terms of meaning: the stage was Thebes, where most of the action took place; the auditorium was Argos, which the Thebans wanted to conquer in war and hold in subjection. Thus the battle-scenes took place in the auditorium together with the death of Eteocles, around which the whole play revolved. Members of the audience therefore had a precise rôle: they were the Argives, the enemies, although the real enemy of everyone was Creon, the tyrant. The audience really lived through the risk of hostile action by the Thebans, who came not merely to die at their feet, but to insult them and to come to blows with them as well.

In this light, the theatre needs no setting. All that is required is an empty space which can always be arranged differently to meet the needs of the production, which may call for very close participation by the audience or may exclude this entirely.

Thinking along these lines Jerzy Grotowski was always giving a new spatial arrangement to the

Ferai and Kasporiana by Peter Seberg directed by Eugenio Barba. Photo: Ugo Mulas. In Barba's productions more weight is given to the choral action than in Grotowski's, which focus more on the characters, the great Ryszard Cieslak invariably playing the lead. However, Barba is also attracted by archetypal characters: *Ferai and Kasporiana* refers to the myth of Alcestes who, in the Greek account, chose to die in place of her husband, Admetus

Josef Svoboda's scenery for Karel Jernek's production of Alban Berg's *Wozzeck*, Act I, Scene II. Milan, Teatro alla Scala

productions he put on in the Opole Laboratory Theatre in Poland, where the audience always had a different part to play. We can wonder how much he owes to the example of Szymon Syrkus. For Marlowe's *Doctor Faustus* three tables were arranged in the auditorium, as if it were the refectory of a monastery. Faustus, already defeated and knowing he is destined for damnation, calls together his friends for a parting-meal—a sort of rebels' last supper. The audience share in this as if they had been invited along with the actors, whose acting to re-evoke the story of Faust takes place on top of the tables. In *Acropolis*, Stanislaw Wyspianski's play about the old legend of the resurrection of the dead, the action was set in a Nazi extermination camp. The actors move freely among the seats for the audience, but these cannot participate in any way, because, unlike the actors, they have not yet been initiated into the mysteries. The actors build up around them and over their heads a ridiculous structure of second-hand pipes, the civilisation of slave-labour, of the gas-chamber: '*Arbeit macht frei*' —'Work brings Freedom'). However, in an adaptation of Calderón's *The Constant Prince* the action takes place in a sort of arena, well or lions' den, closed off by four wooden walls, and the audience is firmly shut out and can see Prince Ferdinand's sacrifice only by craning their necks over the top of

the walls. There is a similar flexibility in his use of theatrical space in the best of Grotowski's disciples, Eugenio Barba, an Italian working in Denmark, who for more serious productions (*Ferai and Kasporiana*) has chosen to arrange the audience around an open space in which the action unfolds. In all such productions the dramatic action remains linear and the attention of all the members of the audience, whatever be their rôles, is concentrated simultaneously on the same event. For all of them time and place are those required by the dramatic development. This unity can also be broken. In the theatre, as in life itself, a spectator can witness or share in various events which he is related to by personal choice or mere chance, and situations are quite interchangeable. Richard Schechner organised space in such a way that when the New Orleans Group played Ionesco's *Victims of Duty* (1967) only certain scenes in the production could be followed from any particular seat. In Italy, too, in collaboration with Edoardo Sanguineti, the writer, Luca Ronconi, the director, produced in the open-air an adaptation of *Orlando Furioso* in such a way that four different things were always going on at the same time either in boxes or on wheeled contraptions cutting their way rather dangerously through the crowd. The area in which the drama unfolded was the world, the fantastic world of Ariosto, and each member of the

Scene from Luca Ronconi's production of Sanguineti's *Orlando Furioso*. Photo: Ugo Mulas audience could witness the adventures of one of the characters, but was excluded from the doings of the others, until they came his way in the course of their travels.

At all events the abolition of the boundary that separates or used to separate the actor from the audience is a prerequisite if the latter is to be involved. On the other hand, the mere proximity of the actor sharpens the sense of physical presence which many see as the distinguishing feature of theatre. It seems that the action has to impress the audience directly, physically; and so in their *Antigone* The Living Theatre actors aim blows at their spectators, the Argives, and in *Victims of Duty* they try to kiss them.

However, this sort of involvement was soon regarded as obsolete. The audience comes to expect it and so deadens the effect of the actor's aggressivity towards them, since it is, after all, only symbolic. The spectator is thus passive once more and so, therefore, is the performance. In any case, it is argued an audience can be just as much 'involved', if not more so, on a purely intellectual level, but this is precisely what happens in all the other sorts of theatre. There is then a shift in the terms of the problem. It is no longer a question of administering emotional shocks to the audience by physical action against them, but rather of stimulating them to some immediate response, some assumption of responsibility, some collaboration in the real work of producing theatre.

Grotowski could not go along with this: for him the absolutely and uniquely central character in theatre is the actor, who needs what actors in the East receive, a long, arduous apprenticeship to remove all the obstacles that stand in the way of his own revelation, of which the audience will then be the recipient. On the other hand, The Living Theatre did go along with it. What they share with Grotowski is the ideal of a theatre that is 'poor'. While up-to-date techniques make it possible to stage a variety of extraordinary 'effects', which are undoubtedly superior to those of Baroque and 19th-century theatre, they still fall far short of what cinema can do, creating incredible visions of artificial, luminous, transparent, mobile and totally transformable worlds, like those of the Czech set-designer Josef Svoboda.

Like The Living Theatre, Grotowski and Barba believe that whatever needs to be said in theatre can be expressed simply by using the human body for the purpose, in mime, gesture, voice. Theatre celebrates the human body, and frees it, so to speak, from technology. However, while Grotowski holds that bodily expression needs to be continually refined and is perfect only when each limb can respond immediately and precisely to any demand made of it, Julian Beck and his companions believe the human body, which is always sacred, is an instrument for a communication that cannot be other than mutual and is, indeed, the essential instrument of communal living. Therefore in *Paradise Now*, The Living Theatre's last production in Europe before they moved to Brasil, the public was invited by the actors to take part in a mystical project with an Eastern flavour (which admittedly did not come over at all in the production)—to live a community experience.

Such a foundation makes it possible to see a new use for theatre. On the one hand, when theatre has been stripped of all the tinsel of scenery, costumes, and make-up, it becomes an instrument that can be brought easily and swiftly into play. There is no need even for a theatre: any open space will do. Politically committed theatrical groups grasped the significance of this at once and a large number of small companies began to act in the streets and public squares, outside factories and wherever they could find an audience willing to watch them.

The Bread and Puppet Theatre is a group of young Americans led by a sculptor of German origin, Peter Schumann, and the actors prepare in their workshop enormous masks, the giant puppets mentioned by Artaud. Then, when they have something to say, they go down into the street, link up with a demonstration against the war in Vietnam or simply attract the attention of passers-by and bring into action these giant puppets of theirs, imagined on the same scale as the New York skyscrapers, presenting short symbolic or cautionary tales. The Bread and Puppet Theatre has also produced shows for enclosed spaces and even traditional theatres, such as the extraordinary *The Cry of the People for Meat*. This is a synthesis of the history of the world presented with the giant masks prepared for open-air acting and which achieve the dignity of authentic *commedia dell'arte* masks, though modern and tragic: Uncle Fatso, the Vietnamese Lady, the Great Warrior. Yet the more original contribution of the group is their going out into the streets and fusing theatre with life—an approach shared by several other American groups: the Teatro Campesino in New Mexico, which is trying to rediscover ancient forms of folk theatre, or the Berkeley Agit Prop Theatre, comprising students who intervene in particular circumstances with short sketches put together half an hour before the performance; or again Ronnie Davis's San Francisco Mime Troupe, which calls itself guerrilla theatre.

The Living Theatre. Two scenes from Sophocles' *Antigone*. Parma, private collection. (*Above*): Creon has crushed the people and their leaders; (*below*) the vultures are threatening Antigone. The mime is often a fantastic but exact translation of the words into gestures. Photo: M C Gaffier

This sort of theatre is within everybody's reach, so that the spectators are involved not at the level of physical contact, but in an immediate discussion, or perhaps in accepting responsibility for joining the actors in analysing and working out a particular problem, opening the debate as part of the theatrical performance, instead of discussing the show when it is all over. If one can still call it a show.

In contemporary theatre all the old internal relationships are short-circuited: that between a play and the performance, because even when there is a script it has become just an excuse, a peg for the rest of the performance; that between the character and the actor, because Grotowski's sort of actor, for instance, plays himself in the character and one actor often plays several characters and vice-versa; that between the director and the actors, because self-directing groups on a consensus basis are increasingly common and sometimes, as Copeau hoped and as The Living Theatre has done, the company becomes a leaderless commune; finally, that between the theatrical representation and what it portrays, because, as Artaud wanted, theatre now represents nothing but just is: it is not pretence, but just reality, an event, a happening.

For all that, theatre would still remain a performance comparable to cinema, the only difference being a practical one, that it could not be re-run like a film, but for the fact that it demands an immediate response, we cannot say from whoever watches it, but from whoever is there when it happens, and not a critical response, but a creative one. If Brecht's proposals are valid, it will no longer be the simple liberating act of the public taking their clothes off in *Paradise Now*, but creativity with a purpose, harnessed rationally to the understanding of life.

ACKNOWLEDGMENTS

Page numbers are indicated by large figures: small figures indicate the particular illustration where there is more than one on any page. They should be read from left to right and from head to foot of a page.

Archivio Mondadori: 71, 145, 198, 210, 211 $_{2/4}$, 213, 215; Giorgio Bertulli, Fano: 154 $_1$; Joachim Blaüel, Munich: 151 $_1$, 233 $_{1/6}$, 238, 242–43, 244, 306 $_2$; Aldo Boria, Villafranca Verona: 87 $_2$, 265, 269; Établissements Bulloz, Paris: 59; Chomon-Perino, Turin: 252; M Delcroix, Cambrai: 171 $_1$; Horacio De Sousa Novais, Lisbon: 78 $_3$; Derrick E Witty, Wraysbury: 81 $_2$; Heinz Finke, Constance: 86; Françoise Folliot, Paris: 184 $_2$, 185, 190, 193, 194, 195 $_1$, 256 $_1$; Lionello Fabbri, Rome: 314; 315; John R Freeman, London: 4, 146, 147 $_2$, 221, 224, 225, 226 $_1$, 248 $_2$, 249; Giacomelli, Venice: 121, 149 $_{2-3}$; Giraudon, Paris: 56 $_2$, 105, 162 $_1$; Hans Hinz, Basle: 292; Istituto di Storia dell'Arte, Pisa: 172 $_{1-2}$, 173 $_{1-2}$; Kodansha, Tokyo: 39, 56 $_1$; R Lalance, Paris: 110, 116–17, 168, 171 $_2$, 172 $_2$, 174–75, 178, 188–89, 192, 233 $_7$, 247, 255, 257, 258, 276 $_2$, 288; Federico Arborio Mella, Milan: 67 $_1$, 81 $_1$, 112, 113, 114–15, 116, 118–19, 126, 127, 128, 132, 134–35, 139, 142, 149 $_{1-4}$, 150, 151 $_2$, 152–53, 154 $_2$, 155, 160 $_1$, 161, 163, 164, 165, 170 $_3$, 208, 212, 218, 222, 226 $_2$, 227, 235, 248 $_3$, 259 $_2$, 260, 261, 262, 280, 283; Mercurio, Milan: 162 $_2$, 230, 245, 263; Mimura, Osaka: 275 $_3$; Caecilia H Moessner, Munich: 43; Ugo Mulas, Milan: 302, 307 $_3$, 316; Raffaele Nello, Lipari: 50; Agenzia Novosti, Rome: 74, 282, 284, 285, 294, 295, 299; Carlo Orlandini, Modena, 104; Fabrizio Parisio, Naples: 32, 36, 62, 64, 65, 66, 67 $_1$, 70; Giovan Battista Pineider, Florence: 106, 124, 133, 136, 144, 148, 234 $_{1/4}$; Roger Pic, Paris: 254; Folco Quilici, Rome: 12, 15, 21; Giustino Rampazzi, Turin: 102–03; Réalité, Paris: 270, 271; Fulvio Roiter, Rome: 16, 17 $_2$, 19, 20; Gerard Roucante, Aix-en-Provence: 80 $_1$; Giovanni Sandrini, Vicenza: 130; Antonio Seguini, Udine: 84; G Tomsich, Rome: 17 $_1$; Umemura, Tokyo: 275 $_{1/2}$; Van Moppés, Paris: 277; Roger Wood, London: 58; Zauho Press, Tokyo: 272–73; Joseph P Ziolo, Paris: 276 $_1$. The two photographs of The Living Theatre are taken from J Jacquot, *Les voies nouvelles de la mise en scène*, CNRS.

Illustrations not listed above have been supplied directly by the institutions mentioned in the captions.

Bibliography

The following bibliography is merely intended to be selective and gives special emphasis to relatively recent and accessible works. An exhaustive bibliography will be found in the several volumes of Kindermann's *Theatergeschichte Europas*.

GENERAL THEATRE HISTORIES AND REFERENCE WORKS

Altman, G, et al, *Theater Pictorial: A History of World Theater as Recorded in Drawings, Paintings, Engravings and Photographs*, Berkeley, 1953

Apollonio, M, *Storia del teatro italiano*, Florence, 1951–54 (2 vols)

Arpe, V, *Bildgeschichte des Theaters*, Cologne, 1962

Blanchart, P, *Histoire de la mise en scène*, Paris, 1949

Brockett, O G, *History of the Theatre*, Boston, 1968

———, *The Theatre: An Introduction*, New York, 1969 (2nd edition)

D'Amico, S, *Storia del teatro drammatico*, Milan, 1958 (4 vols)

——— (ed), *Enciclopedia dello spettacolo*, Rome, 1954–66 (9 vols and 2 supplements)

Decugis, N, & Reymond, S, *Le décor de théâtre en France du moyen âge à 1925*, Paris, 1953

Devrient, E, *Geschichte der deutschen Schauspielkunst*, Berlin, 1905 (2 vols)

Dubech, L, et al, *Histoire générale illustrée du théâtre*, Paris, 1931–34 (5 vols)

Evreinoff, N, *Histoire du théâtre russe*, Paris, 1947

Freedley, G, & Reeves, J A, *A History of the Theatre*, New York, 1968 (3rd edition)

Gascoigne, B, *World Theatre*, London, 1968

Gassner, J, & Quinn, E (eds), *The Reader's Encyclopedia of World Drama*, New York, 1969

Gregor, J, *Monumenta Scenica: Denkmäler des Theaters*, Vienna, 1924–30 (12 portfolios); also New Series, 1954 (one portfolio)

———, *Weltgeschichte des Theaters*, Zürich, 1933

———, *Geschichte des österreichischen Theaters*, Vienna, 1948

Hartnoll, P (ed), *The Oxford Companion to the Theatre*, London, 1967 (3rd edition)

Hewitt, B, *Theatre USA, 1668–1957*, New York, 1959

Hughes, G, *A History of the American Theatre, 1700–1950*, New York, 1951

Kindermann, H, *Theatergeschichte Europas*, Salzburg, 1957 70 (9 vols)

Knudsen, H, *Deutsche Theatergeschichte*, Stuttgart, 1959

MacGowan, K, & Melnitz, W, *The Living Stage: A History of World Theater*, New York, 1955

Mander, R, & Mitchenson, J, *A Picture History of the British Theatre*, London, 1957

Mantzius, K, *A History of Theatrical Art*, London, 1903–21 (6 vols)

Moussinac, L, *Le théâtre des origines à nos jours*, Paris, 1957

Nagler, A M, *Sources of Theatrical History*, New York, 1959

Nicoll, A, *Masks, Mimes and Miracles*, London, 1931

———, *The English Theatre: A Short History*, London, 1936

———, *The Development of the Theatre*, London 1966 (5th edition)

Southern, R, *The Seven Ages of the Theatre*, London, 1962

Taylor, A, *The Story of the English Stage*, Oxford, 1967

Welsford, E, *The Fool: His Social and Literary History*, London, 1935

Varneke, B V, *History of the Russian Theatre*, New York, 1971

NON-EUROPEAN THEATRE

Ahuja, R L, *The Theory of Drama in Ancient India*, Ambala, 1964

Arlington, L C, *The Chinese Drama*, Shanghai, 1930

Bowers, F, *Japanese Theatre*, New York, 1952

———, *Theatre in the East*, New York, 1969

Brandon, J R, *The Theatre of Southeast Asia*, Harvard University Press, 1967

Ernst, E, *The Kabuki Theatre*, New York, 1965

Gargi, B, *Theatre in India*, New York, 1962

———, *Folk Theatre of India*, Washington, 1966

Holas, B, *Les masques Kono: leur rôle dans la vie religieuse et politique*, Paris, 1952

Jacquot, J (ed), *Les théâtres d'Asie*, Paris, 1961

Kalvodová, D, Sís, V, & Vanis, J, *Chinese Theatre*, London, 1959

Keith, A B, *The Sanskrit Drama*, London, 1924

Macgowan, K, & Rosse, H, *Masks and Demons*, New York, 1923

O'Neill, P G, *A Guide to Nō*, Tokyo, 1953

Bieber, M, *The History of the Greek and Roman Theatre*, Prince-

Ridgeway, W, *The Dramas and Dramatic Dances of Non-European Races*, Cambridge, 1915

Scott, A C, *The Kabuki Theatre of Japan*, London, 1955

———, *The Classical Theatre of China*, New York, 1957

Shaver, R M, *Kabuki Costume*, Tokyo, 1966

Williams, F E, *Drama of Orokolo*, Oxford, 1940

Yajnik, R K, *The Indian Theatre*, New York, 1970

Yacovleff, A, & Tchou-Kia-Kieu, *The Chinese Theatre*, New York, 1922

Zung, C S L, *The Secrets of the Chinese Drama*, Hong Kong, 1937

GREEK AND ROMAN THEATRE

Allen, J T, *Greek Acting in the Fifth Century*, Berkeley, 1916

———, *The Greek Theatre of the Fifth Century before Christ*, Berkeley, 1920

———, *Stage Antiquities of the Greeks and Romans and their Influence*, London, 1927

Anti, C, & Polacco, L, *Nuove ricerche sui teatri greci arcaici*, Padua, 1969

Arnott, P D, *An Introduction to the Greek Theatre*, London, 1959

Beare, W, *The Roman Stage*, London, 1955 (2nd edition)

Bieber, M, *The History of the Greek and Roman Theatre*, Princeton, 1961 (2nd edition)

Capps, E, *Vitruvius and the Greek Stage*, Chicago, 1893

Dieterich, A, *Pulcinella: Pompejanische Wandbilder und römische Satyrspiele*, Leipzig, 1897

Dörpfeld, W, & Reische, E, *Das griechische Theater*, Athens, 1896

Dover, K J, *Aristophanic Comedy*, London, 1972

Flickinger, R, *The Greek Theater and Its Drama*, Chicago, 1936 (4th edition)

Haigh, A E, *The Attic Theatre*, Oxford, 1907 (3rd edition)

Kitto, H D F, *Greek Tragedy*, London, 1961 (3rd edition)

Mahr, A C, *The Origin of the Greek Tragic Form*, New York, 1938

Navarre, O, *La comédie des moeurs chez Aristophane*, Toulouse, 1931

Neppi Modona, A, *Gli edifici teatrali greci e romani*, Florence, 1961

Pickard-Cambridge, A W, *The Theatre of Dionysus in Athens*, Oxford, 1946

———, *The Dramatic Festivals of Athens*, Oxford, 1968 (2nd edition)

Pohlenz, M, *Die griechische Tragödie*, Göttingen, 1954 (2nd edition; 2 vols)

Séchan, L, *Études sur la tragédie grecque dans ses rapports avec la céramique*, Paris, 1926

Sittl, C, *Die Gebärden der Griechen und Römer*, Leipzig, 1890

Untersteiner, M, *Le origine della tragedia e del tragico*, Turin, 1955

Webster, T B L, *Greek Theatre Production*, London, 1970 (2nd edition)

MEDIEVAL THEATRE

Alt, A H, *Theater und Kirche in ihrem gegenseitigen Verhältnis historisch dargestellt*, Berlin, 1846

Chambers, E K, *The Mediaeval Stage*, Oxford, 1903 (2 vols)

Cohen, G, *Le théâtre en France au moyen âge*, Paris, 1928

———, *Histoire de la mise en scène dans le théâtre religieux français du moyen âge*, Paris, 1951

Cottas, V, *Le théâtre à Byzance*, Paris, 1931

Crawford, J P W, *Spanish Drama before Lope de Vega*, Philadelphia, 1937 (2nd edition)

D'Ancona, A, *Origini del teatro italiano*, Turin, 1891 (2nd edition; 2 vols)

Farol, E, *Les jongleurs en France au moyen âge*, Paris, 1910

Froning, R, *Das Drama des Mittelalters*, Stuttgart, 1890–91 (3 vols)

Grace, F, *The Mediaeval French Drama*, Oxford, 1954

Hardison, O B, *Christian Rite and Christian Drama in the Middle Ages: Essays in the the Origin and Early History of Modern Drama*, Baltimore, 1965

Hunningher, B, *The Origin of the Theater*, New York, 1961

Petit de Julleville, L, *Les mystères*, Paris, 1880

———, *Les comédiens en France au moyen âge*, Paris, 1885

———, *Répertoire du théâtre comique en France au moyen âge*, Paris, 1886

Reich, H, *Der Mimus*, Berlin, 1903

Septet, M, *Les prophètes du Christ: étude sur les origines du théâtre au moyen âge*, Paris, 1878

Southern, R, *The Medieval Theatre in the Round*, London, 1957

Toschi, P, *Dal dramma liturgico alla rappresentazione sacra*, Florence 1946

———, *Le origini del teatro italiano*, Turin, 1955

Young, K, *The Drama of the Medieval Church*, Oxford, 1933 (2 vols)

RENAISSANCE AND BAROQUE THEATRE

Adams, J C, *The Globe Playhouse*, New York, 1961 (2nd edition)

Baur-Heinhold, M, *Theater des Barock*, Munich, 1966

Bentley, G E, *The Jacobean and Caroline Stage*, Oxford, 1941–68 (7 vols)

——— (ed), *The Seventeenth Century Stage*, Chicago, 1968

Bjurström, P, *Giacomo Torelli and Baroque Stage Design*, Stockholm, 1962

Campbell, L B, *Scenes and Machines on the English Stage during the Renaissance*, Cambridge, 1923

Chambers, E K, *The Elizabethan Stage*, Oxford, 1923 (4 vols)

Creizenach, W, *Geschichte des neueren Dramas*, Halle, 1893–1916 (5 vols)

Deierkauf-Holsboer, S W, *Le Théâtre du Marais*, Paris, 1954 (2 vols)

———, *L'histoire de la mise en scène dans le théâtre français à Paris de 1600 à 1672*, Paris, 1960

———, *Le Théâtre de l'Hôtel de Bourgogne*, Paris, 1968–70 (2 vols)

Duchartre, P, *The Italian Comedy*, London, 1929 (reprinted New York, 1966)

———, *La commedia dell'arte et ses enfants*, Paris, 1955

Harbage, A, *Shakespeare's Audience*, New York, 1941

———, *Cavalier Drama*, London, 1936

Hewitt, B (ed), *The Renaissance Stage: Documents of Serlio, Sabbatini, and Furttenbach*, University of Miami Press, 1958

Hodges, C W, *The Globe Restored*, London, 1953

Hotson, L, *Shakespeare's Wooden O*, New York, 1960

Jacquot, J (ed), *Le lieu théâtral à la Renaissance*, Paris, 1963

Joseph, B, *Elizabethan Acting*, Oxford, 1951

Kennard, J, *The Italian Theatre*, New York, 1932 (2 vols)

Kernodle, G, *From Art to Theatre*, Chicago, 1943

Lancaster, H C, *Le Mémoire de Mahelot*, Paris, 1920

———, *A History of French Dramatic Literature in the Seventeenth Century*, Baltimore, 1929–42 (9 vols)

Lawrence, W J, *The Physical Conditions of the Elizabethan Playhouse*, Harvard University Press, 1927

Lawrenson, T E, *The French Stage in the XVIIth Century*, Manchester, 1957

Lea, K M, *Italian Popular Comedy*, Oxford, 1934

Lyonnet, H, *Les 'Premières' de Molière*, Paris, 1921

———, *Les 'Premières' de P Corneille*, Paris, 1923

———, *Les 'Premières' de Jean Racine*, Paris, 1924

Mastropaqua, F, & Molinari, C, *Ruzante e Arlecchino*, Parma, 1970

Mic, C, *La commedia dell'arte*, Paris, 1927

Molinari, C, *Spettacoli fiorentini del quattrocento*, Venice, 1961

———, *Le nozze degli dei*, Rome, 1968

Mongrédien, G, *Les grands comédiens du XVIIe siècle*, Paris, 1927

Nagler, A M, *Shakespeare's Stage*, Yale University Press, 1958

Nicoll, A, *Stuart Masques and the Renaissance Stage*, London, 1937

———, *The World of Harlequin*, Cambridge, 1963

Pandolfi, V, *La commedia dell'arte*, Florence, 1957–60 (5 vols)

———, *Il teatro del rinascimento e la commedia dell'arte*, Rome, 1969

Rennert, H A, *The Spanish Stage in the Time of Lope de Vega*, New York, 1909 (reprinted 1963)

Rigal, E, *Le théâtre français avant la période classique*, Paris, 1901

Shergold, N D, *A History of the Spanish Stage from Medieval Times until the End of the Seventeenth Century*, Oxford, 1967

Smith, W, *The Commedia dell'arte*, New York, 1912

Welsford, E, *The Court Masque*, Cambridge, 1921

Wickham, G, *Early English Stages, 1300–1660*, London, 1959–72 (3 vols)

Wiley, W L, *The Early Public Theatre in France*, Harvard University Press, 1960

Zucker, P, *Die Theaterdekoration des Barock*, Berlin, 1925

RESTORATION AND EIGHTEENTH CENTURY THEATRE

Alasseur, C, *La Comédie Française au 18e siècle: étude économique*, Paris, 1967

Beijer, A, *Court Theatres of Drottningholm and Gripsholm*, Malmö, 1933

Boswell, E, *The Restoration Court Stage, 1660–1702*, Harvard University Press, 1932

Bruford, W H, *Theatre, Drama, and Audience in Goethe's Germany*, London, 1957

Gaiffe, F, *Le drame en France au XVIIIe siècle*, Paris, 1910

Hogan, C B, *Shakespeare in the Theatre: A Record of Performances in London, 1701–50*, Oxford, 1952

Hotson, L, *The Commonwealth and Restoration Stage*, Harvard University Press, 1928

Joseph, B, *The Tragic Actor*, London, 1959

Kindermann, H, *Theatergeschichte der Goethezeit*, Vienna, 1948

Knudsen, H, *Goethes Welt des Theaters*, Berlin, 1949

Lancaster, H C, *Sunset: A History of the Parisian Drama in the Last Years of Louis XIV, 1701–15*, Baltimore, 1945

———, *French Tragedy in the Times of Louis XV and Voltaire, 1715–74*, Baltimore, 1950 (2 vols)

———, *French Tragedy in the Reign of Louis XVI and the Early Years of the French Revolution, 1774–92*, Baltimore, 1953

Mélèse, P, *Le théâtre et le public à Paris sous Louis XIV, 1659–1715*, Geneva, 1934

Lynch, J J, *Box, Pit and Gallery: Stage and Society in Johnson's London*, University of California Press, 1953

Odell, G C D, *Shakespeare from Betterton to Irving*, London, 1921 (2 vols; reprinted 1963)

Oliver, J-J, *Henri-Louis Lekain de la Comédie Française*, Paris, 1907
——, *Voltaire et les comédiens interprètes de son théâtre*, Paris, 1900
Oman, C, *David Garrick*, London, 1958
Pietsch-Ebert, L, *Die Gestalt des Schauspielers auf der deutschen Bühne des XVII. und XVIII. Jahrhunderts*, Berlin, 1942
Rommel, O, *Die Alt-Wiener Volkskomödie*, Vienna, 1952
Scholz, J (ed), *Baroque and Romantic Stage Design*, New York, 1962
Smith, D F, *Shakespeare in the Eighteenth Century*, London, 1928
Southern, R, *The Georgian Playhouse*, London, 1948
——, *Changeable Scenery: Its Origin and Development in the British Theatre*, London, 1952
Summers, M, *The Restoration Theatre*, London, 1934
Van Lennep, W, et al (eds), *The London Stage, 1600–1800*, Southern Illinois University Press, from 1960 (several volumes; as yet incomplete)
Young, B E, & G P (eds), *Le Registre de La Grange, 1659–1685*, Geneva, 1947 (2 vols)

NINETEENTH CENTURY THEATRE

Allévy, M A, *La mise en scène en France dans la première moitié du 19e siècle*, Paris, 1938
Antoine, A, '*Mes souvenirs*' *sur le Théâtre-Libre*, Paris, 1921
Baldick, R, *La vie de Frédérick Lemaître, le lion du Boulevard*, Paris, 1961
Beaulieu, R, *Les théâtres du Boulevard du Crime*, Paris, 1905
Bissel, C H, *Les conventions du théâtre bourgeois contemporain en France, 1887–1914*, Paris, 1930
Booth, M R, *English Melodrama*, London, 1965
Brereton, A, *The Life of Henry Irving*, London, 1905 (2 vols)
Descotes, M, *Le drame romantique et ses grands créateurs*, Paris, 1955
Disher, W, *Blood and Thunder: Mid-Victorian Melodrama and its Origins*, London, 1949
Fletcher, R, *English Romantic Drama, 1795–1843*, New York, 1966
Halliday, F E, *The Cult of Shakespeare*, New York, 1957
Lewes, G H, *On Actors and the Art of Acting*, London, 1875
Loewy, S, *Deutsche Theaterkunst von Goethe bis Reinhardt*, Vienna, 1923
Mayer, D, *Harlequin in His Element: The English Pantomime 1806–1880*, Harvard University Press, 1969
Moody, R, *America Takes the Stage: Romanticism in American Drama and Theatre, 1750–1900*, Indiana University Press, 1955
Petersen, J, *Schiller und die Bühne*, Berlin, 1904
Richards, K, & Thompson, P W (eds), *Essays on Nineteenth Century British Theatre*, London, 1971
Rowell, G, *The Victorian Theatre*, London, 1956
Southern, R, *The Victorian Theatre*, Newton Abbot, 1970
Stahl, E L, *Shakespeare und das deutsche Theater*, Stuttgart, 1947
Trewin, J C (ed), *The Diaries of William Charles Macready*, Southern Illinois University Press, 1970
Watson, E B, *Sheridan to Robertson: A Study of the Nineteenth Century London Stage*, Harvard University Press, 1926
Waxman, S M, *Antoine and the Théâtre-Libre*, Harvard University Press, 1926

TWENTIETH CENTURY THEATRE

Anderson, M, et al, *Crowell's Handbook of Contemporary Drama*, New York, 1971
Appia, A, *The Work of Living Art/Man is the Measure of All Things*, University of Miami Press, 1966
Artaud, A, *The Theatre and Its Double*, New York, 1958
Bablet, D, *Esthétique générale du décor de théâtre de 1870 à 1914*, Paris, 1965

——, *Edward Gordon Craig: The Story of his Life*, London, 1968
Béhar, H, *Études sur le théâtre dada et surréaliste*, Paris, 1967
Biner, P, *The Living Theatre*, Lausanne, 1968
Braun, E, *Meyerhold on Theatre*, London, 1969
Brecht, B, et al (eds), *Theaterarbeit*, Dresden, 1952
Brockett, O G, & Findlay, R R, *Century of Innovation: A History of European and American Theatre and Drama since 1870*, Englewood Cliffs, 1973
Clurman, H, *The Fervent Years: The Story of the Group Theatre in the Thirties*, New York, 1957
Craig, E G, *On the Art of the Theatre*, London, 1905 (republished 1968)
Croyden, M, *Lunatics, Lovers & Poets*, New York, 1972
Dickinson, T H (ed), *The Theater in a Changing Europe*, New York, 1937
Esslin, M, *Brecht: A Choice of Evils*, London, 1971 (new edition)
Ewen, F, *Bertolt Brecht: His Life, his Art and his Times*, London, 1970
Fischel, O, *Das moderne Bühnenbild*, Berlin, 1923
Gorchakov, N, *The Theatre in Soviet Russia*, New York, 1957
Gorelik, M, *New Theatres for Old*, London, 1947
Gregor, J, & Fülöp-Miller, R, *The Russian Theatre*, Philadelphia, 1930
Grotowski, J, *Towards a Poor Theatre*, London, 1969
Hainaux, R (ed), *Stage Design throughout the World since 1935*, London, 1957
—— (ed), *Stage Design throughout the World since 1950*, London, 1964
—— (ed), *Stage Design throughout the World since 1960*, London, 1973
Henderson, J A, *The First Avant-garde, 1887–1894*, London, 1971
Herald, H, *Max Reinhardt: Bildnis eines Theatermannes*, Hamburg, 1953
Jacquot, J (ed), *Le théâtre moderne*, Paris, 1965 (2 vols)
—— & Bablet, D (eds), *Le lieu théâtral dans la sociétt moderne*, Paris, 1963
—— & Bablet, D (eds), *Les voies de la création théâtrale*, Paris, 1970
—— & Bablet, D (eds), *Le lieu théâtral dans la société moderne*, péen, Paris, 1971
Kirby, M, *Happenings*, New York, 1965
——, *Futurist Performance*, New York, 1971
Marowitz, C, & Trussler, S, *Theatre at Work*, London, 1967
Marshall, N, *The Other Theatre*, London, 1947
Miller, A I, *The Independent Theatre in Europe, 1887 to the Present*, New York, 1931
Moussinac, L, *The New Movement in the Theatre*, London, 1931
Nemirovitch-Dantchenko, V, *My Life in the Russian Theatre*, London, 1937
Osborne, J, *The Naturalist Drama in Germany*, Manchester, 1971
Pearson, H, *The Last Actor-Managers*, London, 1956
Piscator, E, *Das Politische Theater*, Berlin, 1929
Robichez, J, *Le symbolisme au théâtre: Lugné-Poë et les débuts de l'Oeuvre*, Paris, 1957
Sayler, O M (ed), *Max Reinhardt and His Theatre*, New York, 1924
Slonim, M, *Russian Theatre from the Empire to the Soviets*, Cleveland, 1961
Stanislavsky, K, *My Life in Art*, Moscow, 1958
Tairov, A, *Das entfesselte Theater*, Potsdam, 1927
Temkine, R, *Grotowski*, Lausanne, 1968
Veinstein, A, *Du Théâtre Libre au Théâtre Louis Jouvet*, Paris, 1955
Willett, J, *The Theatre of Bertolt Brecht*, London, 1967 (3rd edition)